THE
FATALIST

CAMPBELL McCONACHIE

hachette
AUSTRALIA

hachette
AUSTRALIA

Published in Australia and New Zealand in 2017
by Hachette Australia
(an imprint of Hachette Australia Pty Limited)
Level 17, 207 Kent Street, Sydney NSW 2000
www.hachette.com.au

10 9 8 7 6 5 4 3 2 1

National Library of Australia
Cataloguing-in-Publication data

McConachie, Campbell, author.
The fatalist/Campbell McConachie.

978 0 7336 3679 0 (paperback)

Rose, Lindsey Robert. 1955–
Serial murderers – Australia – Biography.
Serial murders – Australia – History.
Murder – investigation – Australia.

Cover design by Grace West
Cover photographs courtesy of Newspix and Stocksy
Text design by Bookhouse, Sydney
Typeset in 12/16.3pt Minion Pro by Bookhouse, Sydney
Printed and bound in Australia by McPherson's Printing Group

AUTHOR'S NOTE

This story is informed by documents on the public record, interviews conducted by me and the work of other writers.

Much of what is written of Lindsey Rose's direct experience is based on what he told me and often was impossible to verify independently. Where there were contradictory accounts I have depicted what seems most likely (other than a few cases where the conflict is shown).

While I believe all of the events described took place, many of the episodes contain creative reimagining of those events. Enough has been written elsewhere on the 'greater truth' sought by such an approach – and the pitfalls. Any resulting error most likely falls from me rather than my sources.

The names and circumstances of many people have been changed as a courtesy or for 'legal reasons'. For similar reasons (but also for narrative economy) some 'characters' are amalgams of different people, some of whose identities were never known to me.

I did not interview any friend or relative of the people murdered by Lindsey Rose. I was advised that most people in this terrible position prefer not to be reminded of such painful memories. For any hurt this book may cause you, I am sorry.

CMcC

Penny didn't get it.

She'd come to visit and she hadn't heard him – didn't want to hear the answer – and now she was gone. He removed his glasses and his prison cell became a sunken cabin.

That wasn't how it was supposed to go.

She'd been fifteen when she began writing to him in prison – a few months before that pointless farce of a trial. Her letters contained the minutiae of teenage life: her school, her mother and stepfather – a relatively normal life (no-one else knew the truth of her father) – and he'd offered fatherly advice if the opportunity came.

In recent years her letters had kept to the script but sometimes she'd drop hints and then he knew the question was still there, woven into the fibres of every page: *Why do I have a father who murdered five people?*

When you're older, Penny, when you're older I'll try and explain it to you.

She was older now, nineteen. *Soon*, he'd written recently, *soon I'll tell you how I turned to The Dark Side. I am your father.*

She had replied immediately. How could he be so insensitive, making Darth Vader jokes about taking other people's lives? And soon after that, Penny's maternal grandfather had died and Penny was in New South Wales for the funeral so she'd come to visit her dad. Her first visit as an adult and it had been a bust.

He stood as she was led in. The reticent teenager of her last visit was gone. In her place the smart blouse and skirt of the budding lawyer that she was and a determined gait coming at him. As she drew close he saw the blue flint in her eyes, his own, and her mother's clenched jaw. He was hoping to find a way to bridge the bottomless ravine that was their relationship, but he could see resolve built into the tension of her shoulders. For now he'd let her set the agenda.

The hug was business-like and they sat.

'You killed people. How could you . . . Why would you do that?'

He'd imagined writing her a series of letters so she'd have an understanding of his life and what had brought him to criminality. He'd explain how he'd been bullied and stood over all his life, tried to do the right thing for so long. But he'd never got around to sending those letters and there, in the room with him, she'd wanted to know. So he began with the story, just the start, of himself as a young boy and his mother, Glenda.

His mother, the despot, had died only a few months before. After all the booze and the pills and then the strokes and the surgery, it was a miracle the brain aneurism had waited so long to claim her. The prison psych had come in and told him she was dead and waited for a reaction which never came. He felt nothing – not even a glimmer of satisfaction at the death of this woman he'd learned to hate with a vengeance. Now that she was gone he had no reservations about speaking of her disposition and from there he planned to explain to Penny why he later came to despise all bullies for exercising power over others. But he never made it that far.

'How can you sit there and make excuses for yourself?' Penny said.

He could've explained it to her, why describing the origins of his criminality was different to making excuses for it. But if she didn't want to hear it, why should he have to bend over backwards?

'Well, if you don't want to know, don't ask,' he said.

Her face turned to granite and he shrugged his shoulders at her silence. He knew it was his stubborn streak, but the moment he'd uttered those words the decision had been set in stone and he couldn't go back now.

'So, how's your mother?' he asked. 'Still crazy?'

She shook her head at him, incredulous, and changed the subject. Then it was small talk; news about the rest of the family, university – she was passing law with flying colours – and he made all the right noises.

And now he could almost pretend that this girl – his – this woman, was part of his life and even that she was pleased to be in his company. She told him more about her life, another world, and their surroundings fell away. He saw the strength in her – she'd be okay.

At the end of the hour they stood and she hugged him briefly, a kiss on the cheek and a final sizing up, and when she turned to go Long Bay snapped back into focus like a flashbulb and enveloped him.

Now he sat wiping his spectacles in his blurry cell and put her from his mind, turned on the television for the background noise.

PART 1

When people look at the dangerous violent criminal at the
beginning of his development process rather than at the very
end of it they will see, perhaps unexpectedly, that the
dangerous violent criminal began as a relatively benign
human being for whom they would probably have more
sympathy than antipathy.

LONNIE ATHENS,
THE CREATION OF DANGEROUS VIOLENT CRIMINALS[1]

The rabbit never had a name.

The boy's mum was at the pub and his gran was having a lie down and when he was alone with Maxie like this, the backyard was their dominion. It was Maxie's idea to take the rabbit out of its cage to play with. They chased the white floppy rabbit around the yard. It was slow, fat from being cage-bound, but still fast enough to elude the boys' grasping hands. When it hopped between the smaller boy's feet he stifled the shriek, not wanting to wake Gran.

Two small boys with identical eyes, pale like the rabbit's. Though Maxie's hair was dark and the small boy's red, both had squarish heads framed by curls and with the similar set of their mouths they could be mistaken for brothers. But Maxie was the other boy's uncle, barely two years older.

Midafternoon, late summer, the sun still had bite and across the patchy lawn they darted, in and out of the shade of the old paperbark, mid-peel, its pink trunk adorned with fibrous streamers. Maxie held the rabbit and then the smaller boy saw him drop it on the end of a log that fronted a flower bed. It might have been an accident but the second time was deliberate and Maxie laughed and the boy, three years old, wanted to play too. He hugged the rabbit to his chest and its legs kicked feebly into his thigh. The white fur was comforting in its softness and he beamed at Maxie and took his turn to drop the rabbit on the log.

After a while the rabbit hair began to itch their arms and necks, which were sticky with sweat and grime, and then Maxie saw that the rabbit wasn't moving anymore and they laid it down in the backyard and left it on the grass and went inside.

2

When I first drank beer with Lindsey he'd already killed three people. Oh, we had no idea.

He'd walk into the front bar of the Burwood Hotel and he'd scan the room. To the eyes he met and knew he'd nod a hello, or perhaps he'd bellow it if it was late-night noisy, and if I'd looked up from the form guide or the pool table I'd look away and hope it was me he came to talk to. He was ebullient and he would give you his full attention. It was 1988 and, it turned out, we barely knew him at all.

The stagecoach began running from Sydney to Parramatta in 1814 and – if it survived the muddy track and the prolific bushrangers – it would stop and change horses at Burwood, about halfway. When I moved to Burwood in 1988 the muddy track had long since been transformed into Parramatta Road and those bushrangers . . . well, they'd long died out, of course, but their presence echoed through the decades, living on in subsequent generations of desperate, broken men.

Burwood was a staging area for me too: a twenty-minute train ride to my city office job and a bit longer the other way to Macquarie University, where I studied three nights a week. I suppose Burwood must have been a fairly sleepy suburb overall, but my ant-trails only took me along two busy streets – Burwood Road (the train station and the Burwood Hotel) and Belmore Street (past the shopping centre car park to our block of flats) – so it was always a bustling hive of activity to me.

The Burwood Hotel had a saloon bar with two pool tables and a linoleum floor and a lounge bar at the back. We drank in the saloon bar, the 'front bar'. At the end of every night the barmaid, Jean, would call last drinks and we'd get in another round and stay put until she was screaming at us to *Fuck off and go home the lot of youse* because, unlike us, she had somewhere better to be. They may have actually hosed down the floor after we left each night, though I couldn't say for sure.

I was there with my flatmates Eric and Steve most nights. If you've ever done it, you'll know – spend twenty hours a week in your suburban hotel and you soon get to know the other regulars, the 'locals'. There were maybe twenty hard-core locals at the Burwood Hotel. I didn't know their last names, their phone numbers; we didn't send each other Christmas cards. But I'd got to know some of them well enough that after work I'd cross Burwood Road from the train station and walk straight in and there'd always be someone I knew to have a chat with, or a game of pool. And often that someone was Lindsey.

His attendance pattern was patchy – a few times a week for long periods then we wouldn't see him for months. He had no issue telling us about the brothel he was involved in out west in Campbelltown. The girls were all looked after properly and the local cops got their cut and it was spread around so all the wheels were oiled. Occasionally a green copper would come in and start hassling them and Lindsey would just make a phone call and the problem would go away. I'd heard of prostitution being sanctioned by the cops but it was still an eye-opener to meet someone who would tell you all about it.

Lindsey was good for a chat and a laugh and I remember having drunken one-to-one conversations with him late at night around the pool tables about matters of great philosophical weight – matters so weighty that I remember not a single detail.

And he tended to be the ringleader for extracurricular activities including a series of 'Burwood Boys' Nights Out'. I only attended one: a night on the Sydney Showboat. Seventeen of us sat at a long table watching the leggy burlesque show and the boys were getting a bit rowdy but watching each other like schoolkids to see how far we were going to push it (which wasn't very far).

Another night, a few of us ended up back at Lindsey's place and Chinese Phil cooked us squid, melt-in-your-mouth, the best I have tasted to this day. And then months would go by before we saw Lindsey again.

As soon as I'd moved in with Eric and Steve I'd joined the fortnightly low-stakes poker game that they'd been playing for years with these older blokes. Chinese Phil eventually became a regular player and one night Lindsey tagged along with Phil. By then I was living in Summer Hill with my girlfriend and more than a dozen of us crammed into our two-bedroom, rented semi. Lindsey rolled up blind drunk with a few grand stuffed down his sock – from a Trifecta win that day, he said – and became the life and rowdy soul of the party. As far as I recall, that poker game was the last time I saw Lindsey as a free man. That was 1994. He'd killed another two by then. Still we knew none of it.

Three years later the late-night TV news showed a police mug shot. The face looked familiar. According to the report, one Lindsey Robert Rose was a person of interest in relation to the murder of two prostitutes at a brothel in the Sydney suburb of Gladesville on Valentine's Day in 1994. I looked at the face and I heard them say Lindsey Rose and I thought of the Lindsey from the Burwood whose last name I hadn't known and then I remembered that I'd heard, a few times, people call him Rosie. Even though I'd recognised his face in the mug shot I needed this last clue – Rose, Rosie – to defeat my disbelief. It was him.

I called out to my girlfriend – she'd met him at the poker game – and all she could say was 'Fucking hell.' My mind was racing because I'd known him well enough, enjoyed his company, and even though he'd run a brothel nothing like this had even crossed my mind. When Steve heard the news he reacted with a kind of bemused exasperation: 'Oh mate, what did he think he was doing?' Eric couldn't believe it, wouldn't believe it – to this day he thinks Lindsey must be taking the fall for someone else.

Two weeks later my insides were still churning.

Perhaps it shouldn't have been such a surprise. One day I'd found a bullet on the floor beside the pool table at the Burwood. I trousered it, kept it for a few months for no good reason and eventually threw it out with the rubbish. And here was a man who hung about in that same hotel – a pub where you could find a bullet on the floor – and he ran a business of dubious legality, claimed to have paid off corrupt police and knew how to handle himself. But young (nineteen when I met him), naïve and self-absorbed as I was, still no alarm bells had rung.

I'd never seen him lose his temper, let alone get into a fight, but twice I'd seen him avoid fights by menace. Both times the same thing: some drunk guy arguing about the game of pool, whose coin was up next, and Lindsey stepped in and the guy kept arguing and Lindsey – I can picture him clearly in my mind's eye – would hunch down a little with his head pushed forward, look him right in the eye, point a finger in his face and say: 'Mate, I'm telling you, I am not the guy you want to fuck with. Let me do you a favour, you do not want to mess with me.' And he said it with such vehemence that the other guy would back away. After seeing his face on the TV news I thought back to those moments, and the subtext of his threats, and immediately knew that he'd done these things that the police on TV *alleged* that he had.

Two women lost their lives to Lindsey Rose at Gladesville in 1994 and three other people before that. The walls of their families' lives came crashing down and so did those of Lindsey's ex-wife and teenage daughter when police told them some of the history of this man – former lover, loving father – the history of a stranger.

My life carried on as before, but occasionally I'd think about Lindsey and every time it did my head in all over again. Eventually I went to the State Library and read the newspaper articles. The women at Gladesville had both been shot, though one also had her throat cut. In 1984 it was a man and a woman – the man with connections to the Calabrian mafia – both shot. And in 1987 he stabbed a woman to death during a break-in. He was sometimes labelled a former ambulance officer and other times a hitman.

A few phone calls revealed that a copy of the judgment from his trial could be obtained from the relevant court house in the city. When I arrived to collect it I stood at the window; the registrar was out but had left the whole court file for me. The adjacent window was used for receiving bail applications and the man next to me looked uncomfortable in the suit which didn't hide all of his tattoos. The clerk let me in the side door, into the office, to take a photocopy of the judgment. I was left on my own and I had this fat file with more than two hundred pages and the judgment was only thirty. The other pages were copies of documents produced at trial and I looked over my shoulder and didn't ask in case the answer was no and kept on copying. I escaped with the first hundred pages and I felt like a super-sleuth. Those pages contained detailed accounts of three murders. Years later Lindsey signed an authority form and I was given legitimate access to the whole file and I copied the rest.

But after that initial foray I took those ill-gotten pages home and read for the first time a forensic examiner's report of injuries sustained by a murder victim. The reality, the horror, of the violent extinguishment of a human life by another struck me in a way that television murder mysteries do not. As I turned those pages I imagined a ruinous despair haunting the victims' loved ones for the rest of their lives.

And then I thought back to the Lindsey Rose I'd last drunk with ten years earlier – a relaxed, confident, sociable individual by all outward appearances. How could I reconcile the man I knew with this so-called hitman who had willingly killed five people?

His inner life, his dark side, was hidden from me and I wasn't the only one. I've since spoken to a number of people who knew Lindsey well and that includes his ex-wife, Lydia, who once wrote to me that Lindsey's choices remained a mystery to her. She had married a different bloke to the one who presented himself as a killer.

But, back in 2004, the visit to the court house had only intensified my curiosity and I wrote to Lindsey, asked if I could visit him in prison.

3

Ron Lehman was a postman when he married Glenda O'Malley in 1953. The marriage didn't last long and in 1955 when their son, Lindsey Lehman, was born, Glenda was eighteen years old and single. So they lived with Glenda's family: Glenda's mother, Ethel; stepfather, Jack; and six younger siblings – Morris, Walter, Stanley, Maxie, Stella and Marjorie – ranging from age two (Maxie) to late teens. Maxie also had a twin brother, Neville, who was 'feeble-minded' and lived at the North Ryde Psychiatric Centre. Lindsey's grandfather Jack had been a Rat of Tobruk and he still suffered from what Ethel called shell shock.

This extended family of ten lived in Colin Street, Cammeray – a five-minute drive from the Sydney Harbour Bridge – and Lindsey has only a handful of memories from his early years there.

The local ice-cream vendor would drive his old converted Riley into their street with its bell ringing. He remembers a photo of himself standing by the kerb with his nappy bagging down to his knees, grinning as the ice-cream runs from the cone and down his elbows.

He remembers playing on the road outside their house, and nearby was the dead end of Colin Street and stairs running down to the street below. The first time he escaped, aged three, he ran down those stairs, took a left and then a right, downhill, the street lined with jacarandas and eucalypts, and in front of him was the Cammeray Suspension Bridge with a bush track to the side. Down he went, the track shaded and fern-lined, until he was beside the creek at the end of Tunks Park – a secret wonderland. Two hours later he wandered home, damp and smeared from fossicking at the creek bank. He received a belting, thrashed with the bamboo handle of the feather duster until the welts rose like fat worms on his legs and back and never again was he to leave the end of Colin Street.

And he remembers the pet rabbit.

•

There were few income earners in the house and because money was short they only had one cooked meal a week: a baked dinner on Sunday night. Maxie and Lindsey, the two youngest, would perch at the corner of the dining table and eat in silence for fear of being knocked off their stools.

One Saturday night, after tea, Maxie and Lindsey were still hungry, as usual. It was January, still hot in the early evening, and in another month Max would be starting school. Gran was washing up and Glenda sat in the kitchen in her party dress smoking a cigarette, jiggling her leg. The rest of the family were in the front room listening to the radio. Lindsey and Maxie were playing with a matchbox car under the kitchen table: it was a corroded Hillman Minx that Maxie had found at the playground. One of the wheels was jammed so they slid rather than rolled it across the floor, back and forth between them. Maxie never tired of repetition.

A car horn honked and Glenda took a deep breath and floated out the front door. 'Bye, boys. Lindsey, do what your gran tells you now.'

'Where you going?' asked Maxie, dully, but he was answered only by the slam of the flyscreen.

Maxie and Lindsey looked at each other under the kitchen table, Lindsey grinning conspiratorially in anticipation of what Maxie was going to do next. 'What she doing?' said Maxie.

Maxie dragged a chair to the kitchen window and climbed up. The wooden-framed window stuck at first then flew upwards in a rush. Maxie leaned out the window and looked down the driveway to catch a glimpse of his sister. Lindsey climbed up and stood on the edge of the chair on one tippy-toe, straining to see. He was too small so Maxie grabbed him around the waist and lifted him so that Lindsey's chest was leaning on the sill and he could see down the driveway.

'Mummy?' he said, but all he saw was a flash of her ginger hair through the window of a sporty yellow car, wheels spinning for a second as it pulled out and past the end of the driveway.

•

On Sunday Glenda rose late and it was hot again so the adults were sitting in the backyard, under a tree where it was cooler. Max and Lindsey had been fighting. Glenda had flown into a rage and Lindsey had been belted and they'd been banished to separate rooms for the afternoon. They were restless after being inside for so long.

The lounge room window overlooked the backyard and Lindsey stood on the back of the couch and leaned on the sill of the open window and called out. 'Look at me, Mum,' he said.

Glenda was drinking sherry and smoking and she ignored the three-year-old and carried on the conversation with her mother and her sister Marjorie. He called again and Marjorie smiled and waved but Glenda turned away.

Maxie jumped up on the couch behind him. 'Want your mummy?' he said. 'Okay.' He lifted Lindsey's thighs up higher than his hips so that he slid head-first out the window with its six-foot drop. Lindsey felt a lurch in his gut as the concrete rushed up, taking his field of vision, and into his face and into nothingness.

•

His consciousness rose from blackness, swimming up into confusion. The women were over him and Gran was telling him to wake up and he felt a vice around his head. Then someone sat him up and his brain yawed and he retched. He started to cry but fireworks exploded behind his eyes and he curled his chubby three-year-old fists over his ears and tensed into a whimper, trying to stop the pain.

Eventually Gran took him inside, gave him aspirin and applied gauze to the side of his face that had taken the impact. He spent the remaining daylight hours in his room, dozing fitfully and moaning with the pain. He missed dinner and in the evening he walked out into the living room where Mother and her brothers were sitting.

She looked up from her magazine, a jet of smoke streamed from pursed lips, and back down again. Lindsey's usual boisterous self had left him as he stood in front of her.

'What are you looking at?' she asked. 'You're such a nuisance. I can't even relax without you climbing on the furniture and getting yourself injured. Go back to your room, out of my sight,' she said.

Lindsey looked around the room, this wavering land of giants. He saw Maxie was lying on the floor at Glenda's feet with that vacant grin he sometimes got.

'Maxie,' said Lindsey, pointing to him. 'Maxie pushed me.' He had no other words and swayed left and right in frustration.

'Well, you're the one who climbed up there. Now get out!' said Glenda and lifted her glass of sherry.

He felt the blubber rise within him. He realised he was helpless before them. And he saw that the adults had turned away from him and only Maxie's empty gaze was on him. His head roared and it was like a feeling of panic and he turned and walked to his bedroom and lay down. Not fair, he thought to himself. Not fair.

> From an early age I was bullied by Uncle. He being two years older than me meant he was bigger and stronger and if something in the house got damaged during these bullying episodes, when mother got home, I would get belted pretty good with a piece of bamboo, so I got the daily double. And if Uncle had done something he would blame me and grandmother favoured her son so same result, the feather duster. It built up in me.

•

Then they moved to Long Street, Enfield. A bit more space but in a household of ten his only friends were Moppsy the decrepit cocker spaniel and Mumma Puss the cat. The uncles would always kick the cat so old Mumma Puss would go to Lindsey.

•

Two years later, aged five, he started at South Strathfield Public School, which was on the next street over, High Street.

> I remember the first day clearly. I did not have a mat and so shared a mat with a girl named Sharlene and to me she was the most beautiful girl I had ever seen. We built castles out of wooden blocks and lined up to ride the rocking horse. Our Kindergarten teacher was an old witch with grey hair and a long protruding chin.

•

In the school holidays, he rose early with his mother or he'd miss out on breakfast. Two slices of toast with jam and a small glass of milk had to last until lunchtime unless he could scavenge something else during the day.

So at 8 a.m., bellies half-full, six-year-old Lindsey and eight-year-old Uncle Maxie watched Glenda walk out the door on her way to work. From the front door they watched until her blue, two-tone Zephyr convertible disappeared around the corner and then they were off and running. They ran to the end of the block and turned right at Homebush Road on their way to Strathfield Park.

They headed for the monkey bars, as usual. The cicadas were deafening as they approached the heavily wooded outskirts of the park. When they reached the first row of gum trees, Maxie started to run. 'Ha ha, you're getting pissed on,' he said. Indeed, a fine mist of cicada urine was falling. 'Yeah, well, you drink cicada piss, ya weirdo,' Lindsey shouted back, and started to run as well, trying to keep up.

Past the trees the park opened up into a sports field. It was a weekday, near peak hour, but the sound of the Homebush Road traffic was already subsumed by the background of cicadas and warbling magpies.

They'd hoped to join in the soccer game with some older kids they'd seen the day before, but after an hour mucking around on the monkey bars the only other people they'd seen were old men and a few mums with babies and prams. Maxie was bored and started a new game – throwing rocks at Lindsey as he tried to swing across the monkey bars. Finally he clocked him above the eye and Lindsey fell to the ground. His hip was pounding, bruised from the impact. He stood, fuming, ran at Maxie and tackled him to the ground. But the wrestle was short-lived and Maxie perched on Lindsey's back and danced his knuckles across his head until he curled into a ball and Maxie tired of it.

Lindsey was puffing hard, refusing to cry, and when Maxie said 'Let's go shoot some buses' he brushed off the beating and went along. Following Maxie to the next adventure was still more appealing than going back to the stifling house.

•

Coronation Parade meets Liverpool Road at an acute angle. There in the grassy triangle, really just a glorified median strip, a World War I sandstone monument with a howitzer on top bears the names of locals who gave their lives.

'Load shell, Private,' Maxie yelled from the rear of the gun as traffic streamed by on each side.

'Shell loaded, Chief,' Lindsey barked back.

'Set fuse, Private.'

'Fuse set, Chief.'

'Okay, wait for a bus,' said Maxie, and they both stood at attention looking for targets.

'Enemy tank sighted, Sar,' said Lindsey when the next public bus came into view down The Boulevard.

'Ready . . . Aim . . . Fire!' said Maxie.

'Boom!' they both yelled and jumped with the recoil. And fell about laughing. 'Target destroyed,' said Maxie. 'Yay, die you dirty Krauts,' said Lindsey.

'Get down off there and bugger off,' an adult voice yelled. They turned to see the local police sergeant's face frowning up at them between his blue girth and his peaked cap. 'Show some bloody respect, why don't you,' he said.

Lindsey and Maxie sheepishly climbed down the back of the memorial. 'Go on, get out of it, you mongrels,' the sergeant continued and they bolted back down Liverpool Road, lungs bursting, until they were sure they were out of his reach.

•

After school, from the age of seven Lindsey would often end up at the house of either Nick or Noel (not their real names), schoolfriends. Nick's house was massive; it was the first time he'd met someone with a swimming pool in the backyard and it was in-ground. Noel's house was more modest so his place was more of a base of operations for neighbourhood skylarking. If they had money – which wasn't so often – they'd go ten-pin bowling. One afternoon they lost track of time and it was dark when they got outside and Lindsey's pump-up scooter was gone. It was his pride and joy and someone had stolen it. It was his first loss and he was devastated. When he got home his mother flogged him with the bamboo feather duster for being late and then some more for losing that beautiful scooter.

Noel and Nick both ended up in the military and Lindsey caught up with them from time to time. Later in life it turned out to be quite handy having combat-ready troops on-side.

4

Maxie hated walking Lindsey home after school and there they were, Max with three of his schoolmates, waiting at the school's back gate. They elbowed each other and sniggered. Lindsey feigned indifference, avoiding any trigger to be punched, and kept walking along High Street towards home. He was eight years old and the others were ten. He walked as quickly as he could without seeming to rush, hoping to get a gap on them. Up the road they were more likely to attack – fewer witnesses. But they stayed at his back . . . cruising. His school bag was slung over his right shoulder and when the foot clipped his heel he put his hands out and the bag came too and he barely kept from kissing the uneven concrete slabs of the footpath.

'Have a nice trip?' said one of the jackals.

Maxie guffawed the loudest, revelling in the complicity with the other boys, and chipped in: 'Yeah, how was your trip, yer little bugger?'

Lindsey considered running but knew they would catch him and then the fall, when it came, would be harder. He stood on the lawn beside the path to let them pass. The first shoved him hard and then again to make sure he fell to the ground. The second quickly pushed his face into the grass. 'Bindies!' Lindsey called out as the prickles pierced his lips and forehead. He blocked a couple of punches from the third but copped a hard slap to the back of the head. 'Four eyes,' the boy chanted (he'd been fitted with his first pair of glasses only a month before).

Maxie was last and he was the biggest and meanest of them. He couldn't get close enough, past Lindsey's thrashing arms and legs, so kicked out as hard as he could. Lindsey felt the boot-tip smash into the bone at the base of his spine and he arched his back in pain, howling. He knew they would stop the beating if he cried enough, so he exaggerated, only a little, the rolling and the groaning.

'How's your bum, dicky?' said one, but they left him alone and ambled up the road. Maxie lagged behind them, looking over his shoulder.

He stood slowly and maintained an old man's crouch. His school shirt was ripped where a button had pulled away. He cast about for the missing button and started picking bindies out of his face, wincing at the stings. His shirt had dark grass stains across one shoulder so he knew he would be up for the feather duster that evening as well. Yet there was no dread or fear in him. He was only this moment, a throbbing bone in his bum, plucking bindies from his face, looking for a small white button in the thick grass under the shade of tree branches that hung over the fence from an oblivious front yard. Later, waiting for his mother to get home, the dread would start, but for now he held back sobs as he searched and he stood outside himself and watched this pitiful boy fossicking.

Maxie was already a block away, but Lindsey kept looking until he found the button on the other side of the footpath. He started walking and when he'd crossed Telopea Avenue he could see Maxie waiting for him at the next corner. He walked up to Maxie, gingerly, limping, and checked the cross street for the others.

'They're gone, don't worry. You alright?' Maxie asked, grinning.

'What do you care, you dirty bugger,' he said.

'Come on, let's stop at Mrs Moore's. Got any money?'

He knew Maxie had been given two pennies that morning and probably still had them. Lindsey now had a craving for chocolate and wouldn't be robbed of the single penny he had himself been saving.

'You can buy your own cobbers today, Maxie.' There was a stillness in him as he said it and Maxie paused, blinking slowly.

'Whatever you say,' said Maxie. 'Bulldust.' A word uttered just to fill the space.

They walked to Mrs Moore's corner shop and bought their cobbers.

•

He was always hungry but most of all in the afternoons. Lunch was no more than two sandwiches and the cobber seemed to have done nothing but intensify the pangs. There'd been nothing in the kitchen he could get away with stealing; Gran always knew how much bread was left and there was otherwise only the uncooked vegetables for that night's soup. Soup and two slices of buttered bread was all he had to look forward to.

So he looked to the plum tree in the backyard and the upper branches looked promising, but when he reached them the fruits were greener and harder than he'd be able to stomach – he'd learned the hard way what happened if he didn't leave them for a few days more.

He stayed in the tree and admired the view. He was about fifteen feet up and from there he could see into all the neighbouring yards. Three houses up towards Cross Street he recognised a woman watering her garden. Her family were jewellers who had a shop in the city and he remembered because they were nice people and for cracker night they'd brought over spare packing cases and he'd helped to tear up those boxes and feed them into the bonfire that they had every year in their backyard.

'Hey, dummy, my sis wants ya,' said Maxie from the back step. The sing-song voice of the dobber – Maxie had told her some lie about the torn school shirt.

A good part of him stayed in the tree and watched his calm self traipse along the lawn towards the back door. Not for the first time he imagined some protector swooping into his house like Superman and taking to Maxie and then his mother with a cricket bat. But the vision dissolved in the face of his despair and he was back in his own skin and then he imagined it was himself with the bat and he was pounding it into his mother's head and he could hurt his mother like she had hurt him. He blinked his eyes as he caught himself and his body was turbulent in the thrall of his imagined revenge.

Gran, Mum and Maxie were waiting for him in the lounge room. The set of their faces was familiar. He held up a finger – *wait* – walked back out of the room and returned with the bamboo feather duster. He handed the feather duster to Mother and before a sound could rise from her open throat he turned and punched Maxie hard in the side of the head.

'I'm about to get belted for your lies. When Mum finishes hitting me I am going to punch you again. And any time I get hit because of your lies I am going to belt you again and again and right in front of Mum.'

Glenda had risen to her feet and Gran backed away with a hand to her décolletage. Silence. Maxie held his face and turned to Glenda, expecting her to unleash a tirade, but Lindsey's calm fury held the room like a magnetic field and she stood there, pinned. No-one moved and for a minute Lindsey sat in the plum tree and stood in the lounge room glowering at his mother's ogreish visage until she looked away, releasing the charge, and slumped like a marionette.

•

Lindsey told me the preceding story years after my first prison visit. He'd maintained that his transformation to criminality began in his twenties, but it seemed a bit pat and I felt like something was missing. Eventually I asked just the right question and out it came:

The letter began: 'This is the first time I have ever told anyone, ever, this: I knew I was a wrong'un early on,' then he described this turning point in his life when he'd stood up to Maxie and his mother and changed everything.

At my next visit he told me that he spoke to his mother about that day, years after it happened, and asked her why she hadn't belted him. The look in his eyes had been dangerous, she said. There were hefty ornaments in that room and if he'd gone off the deep end no-one could have stopped him – his grandfather and the older uncles were all out – and no-one would have been safe in that house.

She told him about the time she'd had a fight with her boyfriend, Morrie Pinfield, and how she'd tried to run him over with her car. She'd chased him and actually mounted the footpath to get him.

'Would you have really done it, if you could?' he asked.

'Yes,' said Glenda. The look she'd seen in Lindsey's eyes had been the same look she'd seen in her own eyes in the rear-view mirror of her Zephyr the day she tried to kill Morrie Pinfield, so then she knew that Lindsey had inherited not only her red hair, but also her filthy temper; that scorching, homicidal temper.

•

Maxie tried it on again the next day when they got home from school, but Lindsey was almost as big as his uncle now and the tide had turned. A well-timed punch to the throat and another in the ribs was enough to leave Maxie shocked and gasping. He warned Maxie that if he dobbed on him again there'd be another beating.

Later he realised the truth of Maxie. From time to time they'd all go to visit Maxie's sick twin, Uncle Neville, who lived at the North Ryde Psych Centre. There was something different about Uncle Neville but Lindsey was too young to understand and no-one told him what it was. On one visit, they were sitting at a table in the visiting room and there were kids there with outsized heads, and Maxie and Neville were sitting together and Maxie was talking to Neville even though Lindsey had long since worked out that Neville was never going to respond, gave no sign of ever noticing when anyone said a word. Maxie was chatting away in his own world, like he was playing with a doll, and the realisation fell on Lindsey like a rug: Maxie was slow. It all made sense. Why Maxie had been coddled, allowed to get away with things. The adults felt sorry for him, Lindsey supposed, for having this mental disability – or they felt guilty for some reason.

> Maxie may have been retarded, but he worked it out. If he was going to dob on me, he was going to cop it.

He never touched Lindsey again and the feather duster became the exception rather than the rule. He'd fought fire with fire – and won.

5

My police checks have been completed and I have clearance to visit. He is in the High Risk Management Unit (HRMU) in Goulburn[2] – better known as Supermax – and the Intel Officer rings me back and says that yes, Lindsey will accept my visit. In my letter I'd hinted at my curiosity about his 'situation'. Face to face I plan to ask him straight out what he thinks of a book about his life.

I am booked in to visit at 1 p.m. Saturday. On Friday I am at my office job near Sydney's Circular Quay and I go for beers at lunchtime with one of my workmates and I tell him I am already apprehensive. I have never been near any prison and here I am about to go inside Supermax.

Maud Street, Goulburn, is poorly maintained – no kerbs, no lines, crumbling bitumen – and there's some sort of abandoned industrial site around the first bend. There is no sign to say 'prison this way' so I think I've taken a wrong turn until I see the first watchtower and the sign for the visitors' parking. The car park is a patch of dirt outside the wire fence.

I pass the boom gate at the entrance and check in at the gatehouse. There are forty or so metal lockers and I wait while two other visitors empty their lockers and return keys. The desk is the size of a card table and attended by a muscled, short-haired woman in the standard light-blue Corrective Services uniform. The tattoos on her forearms are embellished with diamante studs.

She asks who I'm visiting.

'Rose.'

'He's in HRMU isn't he?'

'Yep.'

I imagine that she pauses for a second before looking back down to make some mark with a highlighter pen on the grid on her table.

'Don't think he's had a visit for a long time.'

'Oh, really? That's a shame.'

'I used to work in that unit. He always had us in stitches.'

She checks my ID and gives me a locker key. Into the locker goes my wallet and watch.

Holding my licence I walk the hundred metres along a pathway through lawn and garden beds towards Visits – a low, brick and glass building up against the high walls of the prison proper. There is a conveyor belt X-ray machine and an airlock-style security entry. I enter the first door and stand on the grey patch that will weigh me. The alarm goes off and I return to the foyer. The tiny locker key has set off the metal detector and I try again after handing the key around the airlock to the guard. Second time lucky.

I'm in a waiting room. I fill in a form and have my licence collected. The décor is bus terminal. No carpet. Lots of stainless steel. Three sets of back-to-back plastic chairs and big glass panels in front of the guards. There are two on duty, but another couple appear from time to time when a batch of visitors are led in. I've walked in with a girl, no older than nineteen, and her baby. The other visitors are a mix of women with kids and men in their thirties or forties.

One matriarch is probably late forties but looks sixty. She has that baggy turkey-neck quality right up to her eyebrows and she complains about how the prisoners get overcharged for the few goods they are allowed to purchase. The maximum deposit into a prisoner's account is one hundred dollars. When one of the young children plays up she tells him: 'Shut up or I'll kill ya meself.'

When I collect my form and say who I'm visiting I get another wary look and I can't tell if it's because I don't look like a typical visitor, or because they are naturally suspicious of visitors to Supermax. Or maybe I'm being paranoid.

She asks me to sit as she processes more visitors. A pair of older ladies arrive and the one with the short, bleached hair makes a fuss about the untimely processing of a cash deposit for her son, the prisoner. She speaks accented English through the glass, but bellows in Arabic to her companion. I have read that prisoners of Lebanese background were allocated their own yard when the prison was segregated along ethnic lines in 2001, and they seem overrepresented – in the visits room, anyway.

Everyone is asked if they have visited a correctional facility in New South Wales before and the room is small enough that we hear whatever is said.

'Yeah, been to Long Bay.'

'Silverwater and Parklea a couple of times.'

'Nuh. Been to a couple in Queensland, but.'

'Well, I went to see m'husband in Long Bay. Then we had a kid together so I went to see him again in Silverwater. Well, he was me ex-husband by then, but I took in the kid to see him. Had to do the right thing di'n I?'

The last is said with some humour, but no-one laughs. It's not that the atmosphere is desperate – everyone keeps to their own headspace and they comport themselves as they would in a doctor's waiting room. Staring blankly or talking small. No magazines, though. No-one reads anything.

The room clears and I am called. A small mounted camera takes my picture and an infra-red sensor on the counter takes my left thumbprint. They take three readings for the file then a confirmatory reading by way of check-in.

Visitors are called over a PA and buzzed through a glass door in batches.

Eventually they call me: 'Visitor for Rose.'

Unlike the other visitors, I have two hefty guards waiting behind the glass to escort me and me alone. I am buzzed through the first glass door and have my thumbprint verified again. Down a corridor there is a heavy stainless steel door and one of the guards stays with me while the other disappears around a corner to let us through from the other side. He works in HRMU and yes, he knows Lindsey.

'How's he going? I haven't seen him for a few years.'

'Oh, he's doing alright.'

'Keeping his spirits up?'

'I suppose. As much as you can in a place like this. He never causes us any trouble, so we're happy about that.'

'Yeah, I hear you've got a few troublemakers in here,' I say. I'm thinking of media reports of inmate behaviour in recent years: hunger strike (Milat), eating razor blades (Milat again), making threats against the Commissioner and an ex-girlfriend (Skaf).

He looks at me and doesn't answer. Just a half shrug. He's exhausted his reserves of conversational nicety and the door is opening now anyway. I am led through a loading dock, all concrete, and at the other end another heavy door is unlocked.

Now we're outside, walking across bitumen. We're surrounded by towering walls of steel and stone. The smooth steel must be six metres high, topped by razor wire for good measure, and to the left is an enormous locked gate. The far side is a continuous wall of stainless steel and rivets with a door stamped out as if by a giant cookie-cutter. We cross and the cookie-cutter door is unlocked.

In front of us is Supermax – and it looks like a suburban library. Single storey, with textured concrete blocks that imitate sandstone and modest lettering on the front – 'HRMU' – shaded by the edge of the sloping Colorbond roof.

We walk in, past another conveyor-belt X-ray machine (it's off), and I am asked to stand on a box so the guard can swipe me head-to-toe with a hand-held metal detector. He suddenly looks me in the eye and asks if I am carrying any contraband.

'No.'

'Steroids for Rose? I guess we'd better do a cavity search, then.'

We all grin rather than laugh out loud.

Through a fifth locked door and I'm in another foyer. Lots of glass so I can see the monitors inside the surveillance post in front of me. To the left a corridor and I can see into the two HRMU visitor rooms and through the glass I see Lindsey, in manacles, being led by two guards.

He's wearing apricot overalls, heavy canvas, high at the front and tied up at the back with a plastic key – reminiscent of both a straitjacket and a hospital smock. For a second, before he sees me, I get a startling mental flash of Hannibal Lecter: when Jodie Foster first visits him he's in a glass-fronted room wearing a prison jumpsuit.

But when he sees me, smiles and gives me a thumbs-up the image of Anthony Hopkins is dispelled. I wave back but then return to the business at hand. I'm getting my thumbprint checked for the third time.

The room is labelled 'HRMU visitor 2' and once inside we shake hands and say g'day. The guard locks us in, but I barely notice. I'd been unsure if we'd be talking through glass or if I'd feel nervous being face to face, but it's instantly like being with the old friend that I knew.

The room reminds me of a cafeteria. There's a small outdoor courtyard surrounded by smooth pastel walls and open to the sky. Inside, half a dozen round metal tables and each has five metal stools less than knee-high. Everything is bolted to the floor except for Styrofoam cups, coffee sachets and teabags.

There is one table in the courtyard and that's where we sit. He pulls the canvas at his crotch and complains about how uncomfortable the jumpsuit is. After fifteen minutes he starts to sweat in the sunshine and we go to an inside table.

He hasn't changed much. His face is more jowly than I remembered and he's missing front teeth (from the ochre tint of their residual stumps I assume he's lost them from a lack of interest in oral hygiene, but later I discover it was a bar fight in Canberra). Fingers on one hand are nicotine stained, so he gets his quota of cigarettes. He's still wearing glasses and he still looks over the top of them when he's trying to make a point.

Halfway through the visit, two of the guards unlock the door and walk in. I have asked to deposit a sum into his prison account and he has to sign a form to accept it.

'This is going to be worth a lot one day,' he says to the guard as he signs.

'Is it?'

'Nuh.'

'I thought you were talking about the pen.'

'Ha ha ha.'

In the Supermax visits room every conversation is recorded – video and audio – and in that first meeting he zips his lips a couple of times when about to mention people or actions that could incriminate others. He's perfectly comfortable with who he is and what he has done and he tells me a myriad of stories, often punctuated with his infectious, wheezing laugh, his chin drawn down into his throat. But some of his stories involve the misfortune of others – his victims – and I stop myself from joining him in laughter.

We talk for probably an hour and fifteen – impossible to know for sure as I had to leave my watch behind and no clocks are visible anywhere beyond the front gate.

He gets on well with the 'screws', he says, and they sometimes allow a few extra minutes if there is no visit to follow. He out-talks me by a ratio of ten to one – which is how I want it – and he talks almost exclusively about himself: stories from the Burwood days, his life in prison and, quite matter-of-factly, some of the details of the murders and why he'd committed them. It would take years for me to make sense of them, make sense of him.

I am surprised at how mundane it seems. We speak like old mates catching up over a beer and the talk of murder and assault should strike me as chilling or disturbing but it does no such thing. Perhaps because I've read every graphic detail, the impact wore off long ago. Or perhaps because it was such an unreal situation to be in – it was no more dramatic than discussing the plot of a Tarantino movie.

A guard taps on the glass and holds up five fingers. So I have five minutes and I try to push him for an answer to the question I'd raised early in the conversation: would he help me if I write a book about his life? He's told me he is concerned for the safety of me, my family, himself and his family, if sensitive information about certain individuals were to be published. Threats have been made. I press and he says he needs to think about it and will write me a letter.

The steel door clanks and opens and the guard calls out 'a rose by any other name' and Lindsey is on his way to the door when he remembers to ask me who else I keep up with from the Burwood days. It's the first question he's asked about me and I can only tell him about my flatmates of the time, Eric and Steve. He asks me to pass on his regards. 'Oh yeah, I always thought that Steve was a good bloke.' And for Eric (whom he called Biggles for his blue bomber jacket) I already know he has a great affection.

We shake goodbye and I need to be locked back in while they escort him away. A quick wave through the glass and then he's being handcuffed from behind. The animation that's been on his face for the whole visit is gone and his vacant stare disappears from view.

I'm left locked in the room for five minutes and I try to imagine entering a long stretch in this place. Some of the inmates here will never be released.

Back to the waiting room and my thumbprint is scanned at the same three checkpoints on the way out. Two other visitors are escorted out with me. The older of the two has white hair and looks like an older, softer version of Ivan Milat.

Then it's collecting ID and returning the locker key and I'm back outside in the dusty and baking car park.

6

Lindsey's father, Ron Lehman, visited infrequently. One year he was due to attend on Christmas Day at the house in Long Street, Enfield. Lindsey was playing with Max in the front yard when a massive metallic thump echoed down the road. They ran around the corner and when they looked up Cross Street they saw wreckage at the intersection with Mintaro. Two cars had collided and they were a mess. One of them was a white '62 Holden FB with a red flash down the side – Ron's car.

Ron was uninjured and he was recovering items from his car as it sure couldn't be driven any time soon and probably never. He'd brought some beers for Christmas lunch and some of the bottles were unbroken though they'd had a good shake and some of the tops were leaking under the pressure. Ron was lining them up on the footpath and Lindsey and Maxie watched these beer bottles frothing and when one of them popped it spewed beer froth everywhere and they laughed their heads off.

A few months later he watched from the hall as Ron came to the front door and handed a wad of banknotes to Glenda and he saw this other woman and some kids waiting in the car. Ron was a virtual stranger and it didn't even occur to Lindsey to ask who they were – he guessed his father had probably remarried and started a new family.

Ron gave him a packet of Life Savers every time he visited and a present for his birthday and at Christmas. Not much else.

The visits stopped when Lindsey was sixteen. He assumed that was when Ron stopped having to make maintenance payments.

Glenda remained unmarried through Lindsey's first eight years, though she was often out with one male friend or another. She was better when there was a bloke around, Lindsey realised: calmer, less likely to lapse into a drunken rant when there was a potential beau on the premises to impress. They'd invariably bring presents for Lindsey, but few seemed to last long and then they'd disappear.

Morrie Pinfield worked for a company that built earthmoving equipment and he'd bring these fantastic, large, scale models of earthmoving gear. Eddie Bennett owned an industrial laundry and was memorable for his 1962 Ford Fairlane – 'the tank'. It was the largest car Lindsey had ever seen.

A cop named Neville Bell lasted a bit longer. He was in 21 Division and his squad did liquor licence and gaming busts. It was a plain-clothes division, and when they went undercover they'd often want female company to avoid suspicion, so Glenda would partner up with Nev or another squad member and go out on the raids. Lindsey saw his mum picked up in marked and unmarked police cars and even once in a motorbike's side-car. He thought Neville was just the best – he'd take the magazine out of his service revolver and let Lindsey play with it.

Then she brought home a man named Bill Rose. Bill was a toolmaker from Robertshaw Controls in Burwood, where they both worked. When Lindsey found out they were to be married, he thought his life might change for the better, that this new man might be a father to him and even show him some love.

•

In 1964, Robert Menzies had been prime minister for fourteen years, Australia lost its first soldier to the Vietnam War and Lindsey's mum married Bill Rose. Lindsey was eight years old and the three of them moved into a flat in Plunkett Street, Drummoyne. It was a relief to be away from his uncles but there was only one bedroom so Lindsey's bed was in the kitchen. The toilet was a cold, rickety box outside the back door. Every few days a man would come and put a fresh block of ice in the ice box and that was their refrigeration. At least there was enough food to eat and no longer was he the youngest of ten.

Plunkett Street Public School, like all government schools, provided a small bottle of milk at play lunch and until he became friendly with other boys he would sit under a tree at lunchtime and listen to the girls playing their recorders while he ate his jam sandwich. Life was a lot calmer. Bill and Glenda both worked, so he would go to another lady's house after school. It was only a few blocks away and he'd sometimes buy a coconut at the corner shop, drink the milk on the way there and smash open the nut on the concrete footpath to get at the white meat inside. Down the hill was a little wharf off Henley Marine Drive; he'd roller-skate down there with a school friend and great adventures were had after school, fishing and skylarking off that wharf into Iron Cove Creek.

Slowly he warmed to Bill Rose, his Pa. It was his mother who was the problem. If Glenda drank too much, which was often, she'd get loud and angry and all her frustrations would boil out. One day, on his way home from school, he could hear her pounding the timber floorboards from across the street as she yelled at Pa at the top of her voice and he wondered what the neighbours must have thought, listening to that every day.

Pa was cowed into submission and no help at all. And even though the beatings had stopped, his mum was like a hawk, constantly at him and reminding him how worthless he was.

Then he got into a fight with the older boy who lived next door. This kid stuck him in the neck with a Swiss Army knife. It was really just a scratch, but to be cut like that drove him crazy and Lindsey went for him. All those years of bullying had toughened him up and this bigger kid didn't stand a chance.

It was Pa who found out first and he took the long handle to Lindsey's backside. It was the first time that Pa had laid a hand on him and while the boy being whacked was filled with bitterness and rage at this severe and unfair punishment, his observer-self felt something different: disappointment that Pa was no better than all the rest.

•

In a straight line, Drummoyne is only five kilometres from Sydney's CBD and it was medium-density living. Narrow streets, small blocks, bigger than terrace houses but not by much. Often they were reconfigured to cram two residences onto the same block and this was the case with the Roses' one-bedder on Plunkett Street. And in those spaces it was hard to have a dog but there was plenty of room for a cat and most people let their cats out at night, where they bothered the local rodents and fought and fornicated. Some nights there was little sleep to be had on account of the damn cats up all night.

An Irish couple lived nearby and Pa teamed up with the Irishman to try and earn them a good night's sleep. They made late-night sorties against the howling cats. The Irishman had fashioned a spear – a broomstick with a knife lashed to the end – but Pa didn't muck around: he was out with his .22 fitted with a home-made silencer.

Lindsey was excited listening to Pa and the Irishman planning a raid but he never knew how many cats they managed to cull. It didn't seem to make much difference to the overnight din and the next morning Pa would be there at breakfast like nothing had happened.

•

Drummoyne lasted a year then they moved a few kilometres south, over Iron Cove Creek to Leichhardt. They had a flat behind the Sydney Speed Shop on Norton Street and the owner knew Pa from the Australian Racing Drivers' Club. The shop sold car accessories, high-performance parts for race cars and associated paraphernalia.

Lindsey went to Leichhardt Public School. He hadn't made any close attachments at Plunkett Street so it wasn't so bad, moving schools again, until some of the older boys found out that he lived at the Speed Shop – then they punched his shoulder every day, demanding that he get them T-shirts. Bullies.

Leichhardt was short-lived and they moved to Ramsay Street, Haberfield – another house that had been divided up into flats and they had one of the three. He continued at Leichhardt Public School and it was a novelty to catch the bus – a double-decker – down Marion Street to the corner of Norton Street where the school was. It was threepence for the bus fare and the walk was about a mile so some days he'd walk to school and save the bus fare to buy an iceblock and some cobbers.

An Englishman in one of the other flats was a Scoutmaster and Lindsey was transfixed by the uniform and the badges. He wanted to sign up but Glenda wouldn't allow it – made some disparaging remark about goody two-shoes, but Lindsey thought she just couldn't be bothered filling out the form. He never lost the interest; it wasn't just the uniform but the sense of order that appealed to him – the contrast with his chaotic childhood.

•

Approaching his tenth birthday he woke one morning delirious and with leaden limbs. They thought it was a bad 'flu; the GP agreed and for a few days he had a high fever and sweated through the bed sheets every night. But he deteriorated further and there were more doctors and finally he was diagnosed with rheumatic fever. They showed him to his bed in the Page Chest Pavilion at the Royal Prince Alfred Hospital and told him his recovery would take a long time. After a week it seemed like a long time was up already but that was when the teacher came to give him his homework for the week to follow.

He shared a room with two men and it was hard spending most of every day in bed. His mum and his pa visited most days – Haberfield was only fifteen minutes from the RPA – and uncles and aunts on weekends. One of his room-mates was Les and he had great stories from his days as a train driver and Lindsey enjoyed his company. He was even closer to Spiro, despite his poor English, and later Lindsey thought it was amazing to have someone who began as a stranger fuss over him and take such care of him as he did.

Of course the nurses took care of the daily drudgeries of food, linen, thermometer, pills and injections, and from time to time a doctor would turn up to review his chart and peer down his throat. One afternoon Lindsey was woken roughly from sleep, raised voices, the pillow pulled from his face, and he looked up at a circle of worried faces. Spiro had started mashing the panic button when he noticed Lindsey immobile with the pillow covering his head. Lindsey explained to one of the nurses that covering his head was a habit formed in defence of his mother's nocturnal drunken rantings. Soon he came to realise that despite the crushing boredom and periods of frustration, for the first time in his life he was surrounded by people who appeared to care about his well-being and, best of all, he had some blessed relief from his mother's incessant barrage.

As his recovery progressed he used a wheelchair and took to having wheelchair races against all comers. The ward was on the sixth floor so paper aeroplane making and flight testing from the window became another favourite pastime.

When he was finally released from hospital, nine months (and his tenth birthday) had passed, but his recovery still wasn't complete and he spent three further months in bed at home with this mother. So he'd missed more than a year of school and some things, like fractions, he was just never taught. He'd been flat on his back for so long that he was weak and thin and even when he returned to school he was banned from physical exertion for weeks more – he had to build up his strength again first.

•

Then Bill and Glenda bought their own place and they moved into the brand new house way out west at Mount Pritchard. It was a new land release and the sewerage hadn't been connected. The mortgage ate up a big part of their incomes.

> I remember that we were very poor and the shit carter used to come at night to take the shit bin out.

He attended class 4A of Mount Pritchard Public School for the last twelve days of the school year and then he was back the next year for year 5 and year 6 after that. The school was rough but he could hold his own against the bullies now and eventually his mother relented and he joined the local Scout troop so he was always busy and those two years flew by.

Soon he would be starting high school and it was as good a time as any so Glenda arranged for his birth certificate to be reissued with Pa's surname and that was when he became Lindsey Rose.

7

At Long Bay he'd asked about various courses, including law and German, but was refused. He'd enrolled in adult education classes, but 'they tried to teach me about what is a verb and what is a noun and I'm way past that' so he dropped those ones. So he'd kept busy with computer courses. And for variety he'd enrolled in an art course. But then he was moved to Goulburn and lost access to the course. He was still allowed to paint, but with only a limited set of colours and he had to work out the rest himself.

> The painting, my second ever attempt, is not a painting: it is a journey. A journey of discovery. I have discovered that I can't paint for a start . . . Instead of the paintings I'm doing, I should be painting bowls of fruit to grasp the nuances of blending tone, shadows etc. It is a long journey of trial and error – in my case, heaps of error.

When he finishes the painting he asks me to take it for him. He is only allowed one canvas at a time and he has no-one else to give it to. The painting is in the naïve style, but the perspective is perfect and it appears accomplished to my untrained eye. The scene is of a busy London intersection. A double-decker red bus dominates. It bears references to Australian TV soaps: *The Sullivans* is advertised, the bus number is 96, and the destination is Ramsay Street. Other vehicles include Mr Bean's Mini, 007's Aston Martin and Dr Who's police box. I miss some of the other references and he shows me: Inspector Morse's Jag, Reg Varney from *On the Buses* and the café is from *'Allo 'Allo*. It is whimsical and it hangs now, framed, in my house.

There is also an MG in that painting, driving past the café, and he takes great pride explaining how he was able to get the dimensions exactly right, just from memory . . .

8

In 1968, Pa quit his job at Robertshaw and started a business of his own – a tool room. Glenda did the books and Lindsey sometimes helped out as well. And Pa liked to fix up cars and for the last few weeks they'd been working together, rebuilding a 1954 MG TF from the ground up – mechanicals and all. Lindsey rubbed it down between a dozen coats of Bristol racing green and by the time they were done it was fair to say he knew every inch of that MG.

On his first day at Bonnyrigg High School he ran into his old mate Harry. Harry's mother and Glenda were friends from having worked together at Driclad Plastics at Cabramatta. Later, Pa had worked as their workshop foreman. So Harry and Lindsey had got to know each other from family get-togethers and they'd got on pretty well. At school they sat together at lunchtime or when their classes overlapped.

By the end of the first week he'd spotted the bully. One of the older kids, Macarthur, was lording it up over the newcomers. Lindsey stuck up for one of the new kids and after school Macarthur was waiting outside the gate for him. Lindsey tried to defend himself and that just made the fight worse than if he'd backed off – Macarthur was far too strong. When Lindsey arrived home he was covered in cuts and bruises, his shirt was torn and his school tie had been cut. And then he copped it from his mother and that was even worse than the beating.

The following day Macarthur took a set against another one of the year 7s – a real weedy kid. So Lindsey stood up for him three days in a row and three days in a row Lindsey took a beating. On the fourth day he got the upper hand and gave Macarthur the flogging of his life: two black eyes and stitches in his cheek and eyebrow.

He was suspended for three weeks and when he returned to school the weedy kid was again covered in bruises. Lindsey got hold of an iron bar and tracked down Macarthur and in front of his mates he told him, 'No more, you will not win, you will stop bullying that kid,' and it was clear to them all what he'd be willing to do with the iron bar. It worked.

Years later, as adults, Lindsey and Harry got into a blue at the Stardust Hotel in Cabramatta with some young blokes who thought their superior numbers would make up for their lack of experience in bar fights. Lindsey and Harry made a mess of them. The cops arrived with a paddy wagon and he recognised the sergeant – it was Macarthur, the bully he'd seen off in high school.

'What happened to this lot?' he asked. 'Did you take to them with an iron bar?'

Lindsey laughed and told him exactly what had happened. Macarthur took Lindsey at his word and it was the other blokes who were taken away in the paddy wagon.

Not long after the punch-up at the Stardust it was a disagreement about a woman that ended his friendship with Harry. Lindsey had been going out with a girl named Joy. She was only the second woman he'd slept with and she was his first love.

Joy. A nice girl, she can talk underwater. In fact she would talk whilst breathing out and back in, non-stop. I had a paramedic career to pursue and was not ready for marriage. Joy wanted a husband and father for her son. It could not be me. When we split up, Harry and I were living together upstairs at his parents' house at Cabramatta West. The very next day after Joy and I split she was on with Harry. Poor old Harry was a good bloke but could not pull a chick to save his life. I told Harry that Joy was after one thing, a husband. I liked Joy but her actions were like a leech; suck on one host – when rejected jump to the next host and start sucking, or in her case, start fucking. Sorry, Joy.

Harry and I had a pact that no woman would come between us. I told them I was happy for them – I meant it – and I moved out so as not to make things uncomfortable for Harry and I did the right thing and told Harry what Joy's motives were. But Harry went cold on me for saying so and I was unhappy with him.

Eventually they got divorced after Joy had several kids.

One night, in 1994, he turned up at my place in Campbelltown. I was surprised to see him, but we sat, had coffee and chatted about old times. But Harry and I as legit mates was a thing of the past – he broke the golden rule and let a woman come between us. Out of Joy and Harry I missed Harry the most. He was my best mate. Women are a dime a dozen when you're 21 years old – or that's what you think when 21 years old. Best mates takes years.

9

A visitor to Supermax must be empty-handed. I can't take in even a scrap of paper with a list of questions. I learn to prepare my questions the night before and memorise them on the drive to Goulburn. His answers, rambling at times, are another matter. I buy a voice recorder – later replaced with a smartphone – and dictate whatever I can remember on the drive back home. Later I type up each voice recording into a trip report.

We continue exchanging letters. He is cautious:

> You don't appreciate the heavy stuff I've been involved in, some of the major figures. For your own protection I can't tell you.
>
> There is a contract on my life from the mafia – associates of the late (by my hand) Mr Edward 'Bill' Cavanagh. For this reason I have not had any contact with my family for eleven years. It would not take much for them to read your book and work out that you had contact with my family . . . you work out the rest.
>
> I would envisage the only way to tell the story accurately, without it being biased, would be to conduct extensive interviews. I assure you some of my ex-associates would rather shoot you than be interviewed by you . . .

I am open with him, with what I am trying to achieve. I'm interested in his transformation from a seemingly decent bloke with a respectable job to violent career criminal.

> I, too, have made it a mission to find out how and why inmates offend. My particular area of interest is why inmates offended and the reasons for their recidivism. But I have always been reticent re: my 'transformation' as the reasons lie deep and are personal.

I don't push against his reticence. I'll visit and write anyway. I enjoy his company, though I am still conflicted that I do, and he has little other contact with the outside world. He deserves to be here, but Supermax is a harsh place and I feel compassion on top of my qualms.

10

His time with the Scouts had ended with primary school. A highlight had been learning how many components of the standard uniform had been designed with first aid in mind (tourniquets, makeshift bandages, etc.). So he left the Scouts but took with him the rudiments of first aid and an interest in the Ambulance Service as a career. The interest only grew and through high school he undertook the Duke of Edinburgh Award and St John first aid courses – all to the same end. He also took judo classes at the local dojo. But that was for a different end: he'd decided that people were dangerous and he wanted to be able to look after himself – self-defence, that's what he told himself.

High school wasn't plain sailing. He'd become well known to Deputy Principal Blackenbury from the start. After his first few visits to the office Blackenbury asked him: 'Why do you keep getting in fights? Why be such a bully?' Lindsey asked him to think back to all the boys he'd been caught fighting with. 'Was I bigger than any of them?' he said. 'I'm only bashing up bullies who were picking on smaller kids.' Blackenbury thought about it and after that he always asked for Lindsey's version of events before doling out the punishment.

He was in year 10 now and it would be his last year of high school. Another day, another bully, another fight and Blackenbury had believed him when he said the bigger boy was the instigator but, 'Lindsey Rose, again, you've gone on with it,' he said, so it was four cuts for Lindsey and six for the larger boy.

So he arrived home with a throbbing palm from the cuts, bruised knuckles, a swollen eyebrow and the other kid's blood on his shirt.

His mother took one look at him and the scowl appeared on her face. 'What . . . ? How . . . ? Lindsey, you are a thug. Can't you go one week without getting into a fight? What is wrong with you?' she said.

'Mum, it was the other—' he began.

'I won't hear a word about it,' she said, affecting airs and graces as she sometimes did at the most preposterous moments. 'Now go and get yourself cleaned up.'

He watched her, immobile.

'Get out of my sight!' she screamed and when he didn't flinch she picked up the nearest object – a solid glass ashtray, half-full – and threw it as hard as she could. A tile broke on the kitchen wall and the ashtray, only chipped, rebounded across the bench and to the floor. It was hard to tell if she'd meant to hit him as her aim was famously terrible.

> One time she threw a knife at one of the dogs, Julie, and it stuck into her. She threw often but she'd never hit her target before so everyone was surprised when she actually got the dog.

His shoulders slumped. He recalled the day he had stood up to her and punched his Uncle Max right in front of her and she'd rarely struck him since. But her frustration at the inconvenience of a dependent child was palpable. At every opportunity she would remind him what a useless fool of a son she had.

Despite years of constant belittlement he found himself strangely surprised at this latest attack.

'One day you'll go too far, Mum, and boy you are going to regret it,' he said.

'Are you threatening me?' she said.

'What do you think?'

'You are going to cop it when your Pa gets home,' she said.

It was the first time she'd played that card. Perhaps he'd rattled her. He raised an eyebrow and turned away.

'Hmph.'

Lindsey could recognise the sound of the restored 1952 Dodge from a block away so, early evening when Pa walked in, Lindsey was already waiting in the lounge room with Mother. The scene had been playing out in his mind all afternoon.

Mother began by delivering a verdict. Lindsey was out of control and needed a firm, male hand to teach him a lesson for his insolence and violence. Pa stood nodding and turned to Lindsey, looking at him from under his eyebrows as Glenda went on. The fury rose in Lindsey as he listened to his mother and a dull ache started in his neck where it met the back of his skull. He separated himself from his anger and he watched Pa and he calmly observed his own rage and Pa started to tense up, so Lindsey got in first and shoved him hard in the chest.

'Pa, if you raise your hand to me, I will punch the shit out of you,' and he finished with a finger pointed at Pa's face.

He was nearly sixteen years old, five foot ten and stocky, but Bill Rose was a mature man, over six foot, and came at him, swinging. Lindsey got him one in the chops and then Glenda was between them, trying to break it up; she would have been hurt if they'd continued and so the punch-up was over just like that.

'Glenda, darl, there's not a lot I can do here, I'm afraid,' said Bill, wilting before the two fiery redheads.

He turned away and Lindsey and Mother were locking eyes as Bill eased himself into the next room.

'You will not try that shit on me ever again,' said Lindsey. But as he watched himself he realised that he hadn't said it out loud and, like the day in the plum tree, she saw it in his eyes – knew that part of him was missing from the room – so she heard him all the same and she let it go.

Within a day she resumed the daily torment but she didn't push so hard and sometimes she'd even back down. A few months later he finished year 10 and started an apprenticeship as a fitter and turner. He was no longer compelled to dry the dishes after dinner every night and the psychological abuse stopped cold, as if a switch had been flicked off. Sixteen years to be afforded a modicum of respect, he thought, and it was all too late.

If someone told me when I was in my thirties that childhood trauma could ruin your whole life I would have laughed it off. People needed to get over it and stop making excuses for themselves I would have said. Now I've had time to ponder my own upbringing. Years of living in constant fear, filled with hate, daily beatings, complete absence of affection; it had to make a difference. No child should go through that and I can't believe that adults could have let such a small child be treated so badly for so long. It fucked me up well and good. That's not an excuse. Not every abused kid turned out bad – but just about every crook I've ever got to know has had a shitty upbringing.

11

The next time I visit I ask what he's been up to. It sounds faintly ridiculous as I say it but he tells me about life in prison, the routine.

'A typical day starts at dawn when the Lebs start yelling Arabic to each other down the corridor . . .'

Without his glasses on he couldn't see the time, but it was barely light so it must be around 6 a.m. He tried to go back to sleep, pulled the thin blanket over his head, but the voices continued and his brain wouldn't slip back out of gear.

It was early in winter and Goulburn was cast-iron cold in the mornings. He had slept in three sets of clothes and left one set on top of the bed so he had something to put on when he got out from under the blanket. He turned on the kettle and washed his face in the sink and the cold water burned. Now he was awake.

He turned on the tiny television set and the morning news programs mostly drowned out the continued din from his neighbours. Would they ever shut up? The kettle boiled and he carefully tipped a sachet of coffee (only two more left now) into the red plastic mug and then half of the milk from a second mug in the handbasin. The bar fridge was in the day room so each afternoon at lock-up he took a small portion of milk into his cell so he could have coffee in the morning before he was released to the day room again.

The 'chuck wagon' rolled up at 8 a.m. with his breakfast in a sealed and labelled plastic bag. His daily allowance of bread (seven slices); his daily allowance of milk (600 ml); one piece of fruit (rarely in good condition – today it was a green banana); and a small box of muesli. The muesli was non-standard – a recent addition to his prison account had allowed him to purchase it from the buy-up.

Yesterday's newspapers were still in his cell and one of the crosswords hadn't been touched, which was a treat as usually they've been started and sometimes three other inmates had already had a crack. He'd realised that few of the other inmates knew about the secondary clues – like anagrams – and had decided, with conscious selfishness, to keep them in the dark.

At 8.30 a.m. he was released into the day room and he walked up and down to stretch his legs. Two cells opened into each day room but his buddy cell had been vacant for months. His last companion, Moses, had been moved to Lithgow in preparation for release.

He usually tried to mentor the young blokes who'd lost their way and Moses, Lindsey hoped, would be one of his success stories. When Moses arrived in Australia he couldn't read or write and being as big as he was – big even for a Samoan – he'd simply solved any problems he had with his fists. Lindsey had taken him through the remedial English course and taught him to read and write up to probably year 6 level – far enough that he could continue to improve himself by reading more. He'd also taken him through the small business management course offered by the Corrective Services department. Most inmates would never make it through such a course unassisted. It was one thing teaching an inmate about profit margins but it wasn't much help if he didn't know what a percentage was. So Lindsey had taught remedial maths along the way.

Moses had written to him from Lithgow saying how bored he was doing his mandatory solitary. Lindsey had written back with a gentle rocket: pick a subject, any subject, and read every book you can get from the prison library on that subject. Later in life you'll be jealous of the spare time you've got now.

Soon it would be his designated time in the exercise yard and today he would be alone to tend to the gardens. He got two hours in the yard for five days per fortnight. If it was cold and wet in the middle of winter he'd sometimes beg off, but otherwise he'd always take advantage of the reprieve from the close-in walls.

He referred to his notes. The weeding was up to date and the winter vegies should be ready for planting. The peas and beans had germinated in their grow pots and he referred to one of his gardening books to make sure he had the next steps down right. He was only allowed six books at a time and after dictionary and thesaurus he usually aimed for two gardening books and two books to read – novels or non-fiction. He'd just read a history of North Korea.

Today he would dig shallow trenches and plant the peas and beans.

The screws came at 9 a.m. – always three. A thick leather strap went around his waist and his wrists and ankles were chained to it. Two screws walked with him while the third went ahead to open the doors. His restraints were removed and the three screws surrounded him as he walked into the exercise yard. One of them had carried his transistor radio for him and he listened to music while he was planting. The yard was about ten by fifteen metres and was surrounded by a fence and then sandstone walls topped with razor wire. If there was any way to get over both, a fat lot of good it would do – you'd still be inside the main gaol with no place to go. And you're always in view of the watchtowers and men walked the walls with high-powered rifles strapped, bolt-upright, to their backs.

He started off with ten minutes of yoga to limber up. By the side of the running track is a bench set on a concrete slab with an arched steel sunshade. They called it the bus stop and it was perfect for the back stretches he needed to do to prevent stiffening.

He had no timepiece but he had a pretty good feel for the passing of time and with ten minutes left he'd planted the seedlings and given them a soaking so he took to the running track. He couldn't do much more than the ten minutes given the state of his back and the prison-issued Dunlop Volleys. He owned a new pair of proper running shoes but they were in prison storage. No personal effects are allowed into HRMU – anything beyond basic-issue must be ordered off the buy-up list – so if he wants running shoes he has to save up his $24 per week allowance to pay for them. Then hope they bring him the right size as he wouldn't put it past the Department of Corrective Services (Corruptive Services he preferred to call them) to deliberately give him a pair two sizes too small.

Long ago he concluded that the custodial staff, for whatever reason, would make something difficult for the inmates if they could, just because they could. They seemed to think he was in prison so someone could apply punishment to him – as opposed to the intent of the justice system, which was that deprivation of liberty was punishment enough.

He pondered the small mercy that he'd managed to stay at the highest privilege ranking for years – kept his nose clean and went along with the mandatory psych meetings – so was permitted to save for such a luxury as a pair of $60 runners. If he lost all privileges (as some of the others had, for contraband, or taking a run at the screws) he wouldn't be allowed to buy anything worth more than $20 and it would take him months to climb the eight steps back to the highest level.

Despite the heavy impact bouncing up through the Volleys, once he got going he felt strong, so he opened up and for the last five minutes he was beyond jogging and into a full run.

'Okay, Rosie,' said the screw and as soon as he stepped out of the sun's direct rays he felt the sweat on him turning icy. As he was re-manacled for the shuffle back to his cell he made a mental note to dry off properly and get another hot drink into him so he didn't stiffen up or catch cold.

Lunch was passed through at 11 a.m. and he ate it in the day room. Today it was ham-and-salad rolls and dried fruit with yoghurt. He ate, read, finished a crossword. For much of it he stood, out in the space.

Lock-in was 2.30 p.m. and he was back in his two-by-three-metre cell, where he'd remain for the next eighteen hours. Dinner was served shortly afterwards. Stodge, as usual: potatoes (mashed), pasta (gluey) and overboiled greens. He couldn't stomach dinner that early and put the meal straight into the microwave so he could reheat it later.

Despite all the process and being treated like a barely tamed wild animal, if he had to be locked up then the HRMU was the place to be. Other inmates called the HRMU the 'harm you' – couldn't handle the entrenched isolation – but he thought it was superior to being in the main gaol where you were far more exposed to the irrational, violent tendencies of other inmates.

•

Three years after my first visit I've been six times and we've written six letters each. Our dialogues have been wide-ranging and unfocussed: the latest prison gossip, what's wrong with the world, TV (he rates *Top*

Gear and *The West Wing*), politics and current affairs (the surfies at the Cronulla riots were just patriots) and the beginning of his life in the Ambulance Service. And snippets from the murders: the ones who had it coming and the one he didn't mean. His childhood stories, which you've just read, came later. And Donna, perhaps his most enduring friend, you haven't met yet, though he's told me much of her by now.

Three years and his position gradually softens as he gets to know me again and then he makes the commitment: he'll help me tell the story of his life. In surprise I awkwardly mumble some expression of gratitude before collecting myself.

'But what about this contract out on you?' I ask, as this has been the main stumbling block.

'Well, those sorts of things are time-bound. It was a long time ago now,' he says, avoiding my gaze.

'But I thought that's why you were in Supermax, for your own protection?'

'Maybe in part. Mostly, though, it's because I was caught with a key to my cell – a working key.'

•

The claim seems outlandish but later he gave me enough detail for it to seem feasible. And there is some support in the *Sydney Morning Herald*'s coverage of the opening of the HRMU in 2001. Apart from quoting Premier Bob Carr – 'anyone who's silly enough to say this is five-star accommodation we'll book in for a week but only when the interesting guests are here as well' – the *Herald* also reported that the HRMU's first intake constituted '. . . the worst of the worst . . . Milat, Rose and Staines are escape risks; the others have bashed prisoners or officers.'[3]

12

In 1972, straight after year 10, Lindsey was apprenticed to Comalco at Yennora and there was a TAFE component as well. Harry was in most of his TAFE classes and they looked old enough so they began to drink together after classes and then on weekends as well. Lindsey was still living in Mount Pritchard and the Stop and Rest Hotel was only a five-minute walk from home and that became their local.

When an apprentice, 16 years old, a journeyman at my work bullied me from day 1. He was twice my size and he was 21 years old. It wasn't just hazing or initiation pranks – they are part and parcel of an apprenticeship – this guy was full-on.

After a week of this I jacked up and took a swing. I missed but was told 'I will see you in the locker room after work.' I just had enough time to take my glasses off. I fought back but he beat the crap out of me. Not one guy in that locker room, tradesmen or production staff, did a thing.

Everything was quiet for a few days. I saw the bully from time to time; he was mostly busy bullying other apprentices. I spoke to some of them. He was bullying all of them, from Year 1 to Year 4.

So every time he bullied me I just started swinging. He became concerned that we'd be caught fighting and sacked. That was the rule. 'Take a swing, pack your tools.' So all the bullying took place in the locker room, out of sight of management.

This went on for weeks. Sometimes I got him a few good ones and he had cuts and bruises. But I had bruises on bruises. I told my father that the damage was from randori training at the YMCA dojo. But he knew – he knew the truth, but what could he do?

Some time later I was servicing some disc brakes on an overhead crane and saw the bully walking down the factory floor. As he walked under the crane I dropped my 15-inch shifting spanner. It missed him by inches. He looked up, saw me peering over the side of the crane. He was shocked. He knew the implications of what I had done. If the shifter had hit him in the head it would probably have killed him. That lunch time he sought me out. 'Are you fucking crazy,' he said. I told him that I had had enough. 'Don't try and duck out early, I will see you in the locker room,' he said.

After lunch I looked for him. He was in the foil mill working on thermocouples at the back of the furnaces. I walked up behind him and decked him with a piece of 3x4. A production worker found him in a pool of blood. He was taken away by ambulance.

Two weeks later he came back to work. I fronted him in the locker room and told him 'any more and I will continue this at your house,' and I told him the address and the calibre of weapon I would bring. He knew I was dead serious. He never bullied another apprentice again.

•

The work and study weren't especially taxing so he kept himself busy with other activities.

He did more St John Ambulance courses, he volunteered for Civil Defence (later renamed the SES) on weekends and the volunteer bushfire brigade and he still liked messing around with cars so he hand-picked run-down cars at the auctions and fixed them up – either to upgrade his own wheels, or to resell for profit. And he earned extra cash working part-time jobs at the Mobil service station at Canley Heights and Woodville Wreckers, where he started as a parts picker and ended up as their gearbox mechanic.

Aged nineteen he joined the Army Reserve and he served with 10 Battery, 23rd Field Regiment of the Royal Australian Artillery. At the Artillery School on Sydney Harbour's North Head he trained on 105-mm pack howitzers: portable field guns that were towed behind eight-tonne Mark III Internationals. You needed a G2 (general military vehicle licence) and a GT (gun-towing licence) to drive them around.

When he completed his apprenticeship he still wasn't old enough for the Ambulance Service – you had to be twenty-one – so he went to work in his trade. He did a couple of years with Dulhunty Engineering, based at Campbelltown. He worked on Lee Norse continuous miners and shuttle cars and he did underground maintenance at mines to the south (Coledale, near Wollongong) and the west (the Grose Valley, in the Blue Mountains). And partly because he never liked to see the man stand over the little bloke – but mostly because no-one else would do it – he became a shop steward with the AMWU.

•

There were plenty of hard-drinking men down the mines and he could hold his own but one evening, driving home with a skinful, he collected a telegraph pole. The chassis was bent, so his car was pretty much a write-off. He stripped it and sold the spare parts piecemeal until only the shell was left.

He put up a 'for sale' sign and within a week he was talking to this man. He was younger than Lindsey, short but broad, in a blue singlet that looked welded on.

'How much do you want for it?'

'Can you take it away yourself?'

'Yeah, I can borrow a car trailer and come back later.'

'Hundred bucks.'

'Okay, sounds fair.'

'Done. What are you going to do with it?'

'Rebuild it. Looks like the frame needs some work.'

''Fraid so. Have you done a few?'

He said that he'd done a couple and Lindsey asked what they were and they swapped stories about the cars they'd rebuilt. His name was Russell V. (not his real name), he drove trucks and he'd learned his mechanics at home. And, it transpired, he lived in Green Valley, just west of Mount Pritchard, and he also drank at the Stop and Rest Hotel.

That Friday night he bought Russ a beer at the Stop and Rest. They drank together and it became a habit – the first of many habits they were to share over the coming years.

•

When he turned twenty-one he applied to the Ambulance Service. He went for the interview hoping to be considered for the intake in three or four months' time. They told him that he was well qualified in every area necessary to enter the program immediately. He nodded, played it cool, smiled slowly as he shook the proffered hands. He celebrated that night at the Stop and Rest and he started his training the following Monday.

13

He completed his training, he excelled, and in no time at all he felt like an old hand.

Saturday lunchtime. We had picked up a couple of burgers each at a local takeaway and were heading back to station when we received a casualty call over the radio. Damn it, the burgers were hot and we were intending to eat them as soon as we got to the station. The call was to Kentucky Road, Riverwood, man injured. We did not want to eat cold hamburgers so we decided to eat on the way. I wonder what people thought seeing an ambulance going by, reds on, whistle going and the ambos eating hamburgers. I suppose they would not appreciate how many cold meals we ate, how many meals were half eaten or completely missed.

We polished off a burger each by Punchbowl. There was a fair bit of traffic still but we thought we were making good time. Next thing, the radio blared:

'214, don't stop just reply.'

'214 In.'

'214, further calls received on your job. Reports man fell from Kentucky Road units. Over.'

'214 roger. Out.'

I looked at my offsider, we were both thinking the same thing: the Kentucky Road units are seven storeys high.

We arrived at the scene. There were quite a few people gathered around the patient who, from reports, had jumped from the seventh floor. He had landed face down onto a concrete apron at the front of the building. To describe his injuries fully would take two pages. In summary: multiple fractures, including head and internal injuries. He was a mess.

My offsider and I were still finishing our burgers. Without anything said between us we both knew he was dead. We were standing over him, taking our last bites when I saw a bubble in the blood near his nose.

I said 'He's breathing!' and crouched down to roll him into the coma position and clear his airway. My mate said 'Don't joke,' and I said 'I'm not joking, he's alive.'

We worked on the patient for a few minutes and agreed we needed to get him to hospital quick. After inserting a Guedel airway and putting him on O_2 we loaded and transported the patient to Bankstown Hospital. As we arrived at the hospital the patient was still breathing. The doctor wanted x-rays ASAP so we took the patient around to x-ray and lifted him onto the x-ray table. As the radiologist was positioning the patient, the patient sat up, looked around, said 'shit!' and died.

'How many's that now, Lindsey?' asked Jock. They were drinking Jack Daniels at the Bankstown RSL club. Always bourbon for the suicides. For births it was cigars. Jock had been in for ten years already; he'd shown Lindsey the ropes when he started and now they were regular drinking companions when their shifts were aligned.

'Too fucking many, that's how many,' Lindsey replied. 'And how's your form with the code 4s?'

Jock just chuckled. It was a recurring topic of conversation: the inadvertent speciality. There was no picking and choosing jobs yet each officer seemed to get a disproportionate share of one type of job. If Jock got a call-out on the graveyard shift it was invariably a code 4, deceased. JJ seemed to get the code 9s, person trapped, and Bobby used to get the ODs.

And Lindsey got the suicides – though he also seemed to get a lot of the emergency births and he wondered if they somehow cancelled each other out.

'How old was this one?' asked Jock.

'Old enough to know better. Late twenties, I'd say.'

'Must be barmy,' said Jock, 'to do such a thing. Imagine it.'

'It's the young ones that do my head in. There was this fifteen-year-old girl . . . Actually lots of fifteen-year-old girls with attempted, but this one managed to get the job done. What the hell is wrong with these kids?'

Jock shook his head. It was a rhetorical question anyway. Lindsey sometimes visited failed suicides, young ones, and they told of the pressures in their lives and invariably they were the adult stresses of sex, relationship breakdowns, drugs, death and misery. He didn't know who to blame but they were growing up too fast.

Jock went for the next shout and Lindsey sat in his haze of smoke and bourbon; this late it was mostly other service personnel or solo men in the club and he contemplated the lot of the ambulance officer. You'd find someone trapped in a wreck and how were you going to save them? Assess the scene for dangers, access and diagnose the patient, provide first aid if necessary then review the physical environment. Take on board all information, which included listening to others' opinions – there was no room for egos – before designing and implementing a course of action that best resolved the technical problems of the extraction while being mindful of the condition of the patient. Executing a well-thought-out plan was exhilarating and there were plenty of opportunities – it was common to attend a dozen car accidents and a handful of heart attacks in a single shift.

Other times were demoralising. The failures didn't faze him so much – people still died, despite their efforts, but they would've died anyway – it was the verbal and physical abuse from the civilians. Usually it was drunks, when you were cleaning up after some bar fight or domestic. You'd be there trying to help someone, perhaps performing chest compressions or trying to clear an air passage, and someone, a loved one, would be wailing, getting in the way, screaming at you for taking so long or for not treating the patient correctly. After a while, being verbally abused most days and assaulted most weeks, it wore a man down.

But worse than any patient abuse was the attitude of the Ambulance Service management. What did it do to help its front-line staff? Told them to suck it up. If you told management you had a problem it was treated as a disciplinary issue – at best you'd be given a dressing down; at worst you'd be refused promotion, face suspension or be forced out of the service altogether.

'Do the lasses have all their teeth where you've just been?' asked Jock. Lindsey looked down at the empty glass in his hand and saw that Jock had placed a fresh JD and Coke in front of him.

'No, Jock,' he said, 'everything's just the same over there.'

•

He'd always had an interest in flying so he took up lessons at a flight school at Bankstown Airport. They started him off in a Piper Cherokee 140 and on the right shift he could take a lesson in the afternoon after knock-off. He was still living at Mount Pritchard with Mum and Pa and five o'clock one afternoon he got home from a flying lesson and Pa was there, still in his work clothes.

'I can't wake your mother,' he said.

'What do you mean you can't wake her?' said Lindsey and Pa led him into their bedroom.

She was curled on her right side and Lindsey pulled the curtains and thought for a second that she was gone. Her breathing was shallow and she wouldn't stir. He lifted an eyelid and the iris didn't contract so he was on the phone, ringing straight through to the ambulance control room rather than dialling triple-0.

'What's she taken, Pa?' he asked.

'She just has her medicine . . .' said Pa, so then Lindsey was rifling through the bathroom cabinet, the bedside drawer and then the kitchen and the rubbish bin. It was just the pill bottles in the bathroom. Temazepam. She'd been taking them for a few months, said Pa. The doctor said it was to calm her down and help her sleep.

Lindsey couldn't do much for her other than make sure her airway stayed clear and pack a bag and he willingly dissolved into his training, focussed solely on the mechanics of the situation. He travelled in the ambulance with her, checked her in at the hospital and made sure the attending doctor got the details right.

Once her vitals were back up he left. She was discharged the next day. It turned out she'd taken her pills, woken up, forgotten she'd taken them and taken another dose.

•

About once a month, on patient transfer duty, he'd take Frank from the Alma Road Nursing Home in Padstow to the Multiple Sclerosis Centre on Mowbray Road, Chatswood.

Frank was in his early forties and even though he'd obviously looked after himself before the MS began to cripple him, some days his muscles were too taut to get him into a wheelchair and they had to transport him on the stretcher. By the time Lindsey met him he already had a Penrose catheter fitted. The monthly trip to the MS Centre was his only time out of the nursing home.

Over time he learned that Frank had attained a high level of training in judo and jujitsu and that they'd attended some of the same high-profile competitions at the Canley Vale Bushido Judo Club. When his muscles allowed it, Lindsey lifted Frank out of the wheelchair and into the front passenger seat so he could take in some scenery. They passed various establishments on the way to Chatswood and Frank often joked about stopping in for a drink or seven.

He dropped in one evening and Frank was sitting up in bed watching TV. Lindsey told him to get his running shoes on. Frank still had the smile on his face as Lindsey pushed his wheelchair up to the sister's desk in the foyer and Lindsey convinced her to let him take Frank for a spin around the grounds.

Fifteen minutes later they pushed through the door into the Penshurst Hotel. Lindsey made the introductions. Frank played pool, drank beer, chatted and laughed and even won the hearts of some ladies. But the highlight was the darts. With Frank's condition the patrons had to clear the area when he was throwing. Everyone thought it was hilarious and the group started laying bets as to where the next dart would stick: ceiling, wall, table leg, etc. There would be a sigh of disappointment if he actually hit the dartboard.

At the end of the night they returned to the nursing home and there was a paddy wagon parked near the front door. At the front desk, the sister was complaining to the constables about irresponsibility and proper medical supervision. Meanwhile, Frank was practically falling out of his chair so Lindsey took him to his room, changed his bag and tucked him into bed.

A few of the other patients were heading towards Frank's room to hear about the night's adventures and the senior constable was waiting in the corridor. 'The sister only remembered your first name but as soon as she said it I knew it was you, Rosie, you idiot,' he said.

No laws had been broken and peace was made with the sister so eventually the constables left.

Weeks later he arrived at Alma Road, walked into Frank's room to see the bed had been stripped and the bedside cupboard was empty.

'Where's he been moved to?' he asked Frank's room-mate and the man just stared at him and then he realised that Frank was gone.

The matron apologised. They'd only found him at six o'clock that morning and Frank had been so well-liked that everyone was in shock and they'd forgotten to cancel the ambulance.

He stopped in to the back room to view Frank's body and say goodbye.

He vowed to never again let himself become attached to a nursing home patient.

•

Late 1976 Bill and Glenda sold up and moved to Queensland. Bill's tool room had been losing money for a couple of years. Bill blamed it on the Whitlam government's tax changes, which compelled small private businesses like Bill Rose's tool room to pay the same tax rate as public companies. The extra 2.5 per cent didn't sound like much, but Bill was already on a narrow margin and it tipped him into the red, or so he said. He closed down the shop, eighteen toolmakers lost their jobs and Lindsey never forgave Labor for what they'd done to his father's business and all those hard workers.

Bill had teed up a foreman job and they bought a place in Clontarf: north Brisbane, seaside. There was no talk of Lindsey coming with them. He was out and about nearly every waking moment so in recent years the family home at Mount Pritchard had offered little more than a place to lay his head at night. He moved into a boarding house in Bankstown. That was all he needed.

•

'Hey, Lindsey. I had a job around at your place today,' said Bobby. Lindsey had just returned to the station after a day of call-outs.

'What do you mean? The boarding house?'

'Yeah, yeah. A woman there, I think she was the manager. OD. Already deceased when we got there.'

'Big lady, bad perm?'

'That's her.'

'Yeah. She was my landlady. Never thought she was the full quid. I've only been there a week.'

'Jeez, Rosie, what did you say to her?' someone called out.

'He didn't say nothing. Just the sight of his face made her want to pull the pin,' said Bobby.

He laughed along with them. Oh, how they laughed. That's what the job did to them all.

•

After the demise of his landlady at the Bankstown boarding house he found a new place in Croydon Park. It was only two kilometres from Enfield so he went to see his gran. She'd moved to a smaller place on Beaumaris Street, just a few blocks from the old place on Long, after Grandpa Jack died.

He drank tea with Gran and she missed old Jack. Max and Stanley were living there too, helping look after her, and afterwards his uncles took him one block down the road to the Boulevard Hotel for beers. Max and Stanley were both working at the Dulux factory; their boss was a man named Jim Fowler and the Fowler family lived opposite the Boulevard. The O'Malleys and the Fowlers met at the Boulevard on weekends and sometimes weeknights as well, so while Lindsey had spent ten years away in Mount Pritchard, growing up, these two families had established new traditions. He began to join in and felt like a long-lost brother returned.

There was space at the end of the hotel car park where kids could play so the Fowlers would bring their daughter Donna with them. Every Anzac Day Jim Fowler would march and the families would go to the Enfield RSL Club afterwards. They'd start drinking before noon and spend the day playing two-up and getting along.

Donna was ten years old when Lindsey moved to Croydon Park. He had a soft spot for kids after all the injured ones he'd treated and he spoke with her like an adult so he became like a favourite uncle to her. When it was time for the kids to vacate the hotel Donna just had to walk through the car park to get home, but Lindsey had seen plenty of trouble in hotel car parks so he made a point of walking her to her door at night and he'd wait until the lights came on inside the house before he walked back to the pub.

14

There is a famous photo of Ivan Milat, wearing a khaki shirt and a black park ranger sort of hat and holding a shotgun across his body, staring impassively at the camera. Ivan had given Lindsey a signed copy of that photo and told him he could do whatever the hell he wanted with it. In one of my early visits Lindsey described it and offered to mail it to me. I was in Supermax being offered a photo autographed by Ivan Milat and not for the first time I was reminded of the parallel universe into which I had plunged.

'I've got no use for it and you'll probably get a good price for it.'

'Well . . .' I'd been doubting my moral compass but my gut kicked. 'I don't know if—'

'No, I'm sure you'd get a good price,' he'd said, misreading my reluctance. 'You know it's a famous photo and there aren't many, if any, signed copies around. I've always had a head for valuing things, businesses, owned hundreds of cars, trash and treasure. Trust me, there are people that collect that stuff. It'll go for a few. And don't worry about Ivan, it was no strings attached.'

'Oh, I'm sure it's worth something, that's not really—' I began.

'Ah, you're concerned about the morality of profiting from crime?'

Pretty much, I'd said, thanked him for the offer and we agreed he would hold onto the photo unless I let him know I was agreeable.

Now he tells me that the photo is no longer available.

'A few Fridays back the Special Squad came in at about 4.30 in the afternoon for a ramp. You never know they're coming, for obvious reasons . . .'

He was asked to remove all of his clothes – standard procedure. They checked him over, surgical gloves, then the drug dog went through his room. He stood outside the cell and watched them empty it – every single item, including the mattress and pillow – took them all away to be examined and X-rayed or whatever the fuck they did. Then they were on to the next cell and he heard them going down the line, ramping every one.

Most of his property was brought back two hours later. He was lying on the bunk watching TV at 9.30 p.m. when they came back in and searched everyone again. They were still at it at 11 p.m. – even rifling through seed pots in the garden. Must've been a tip off. Probably drugs.

He made a mental inventory of the property they'd taken from his cell while he put his clothes back on. Most times something wouldn't make it back. He'd been in the middle of painting #3 and they'd failed to return the palette where he'd been mixing colours; it was practically impossible to recreate the same shade of green he'd been using to paint the MASH unit tents.

It was nearly midnight when they returned his bedding and other property for the second time in ten hours. For once it looked like everything had come back in one piece. But then one of the screws told him that there was a problem with his property. He was only allowed to keep twelve photos in his cell and he had more than twenty. They stood there looking at him and he realised they wanted him to choose right then and there which photos he wanted to keep in the cell and which ones to discard. He picked up his photos, looked up at the screws and started ripping them into bits. And kept going. Every single photo, including the one Ivan had signed, destroyed.

•

'Weren't you cutting off your nose to spite your face?'

'Maybe. My thought was if they are going to make things hard for me then they could go and get fucked.'

•

He bemoans the absence of computer equipment in HRMU. For his first few years, inmates of sufficient privilege had access to computers. He used his computer time for further education, writing letters and to help fellow inmates produce court submissions.

But then one day one of the Lebs got his knickers in a twist over something and destroyed one of the printers. So the screws took away all the computer equipment and I was back to the stone age writing with a pen and paper.

His complaints about the custodial staff are more or less believable, but I come to realise that his overall attitude – the joining of the dots – is tainted by the cultural mythology of the prisoner: the screws are out to get us, the cops and the judges are all bent and our only crime is rebellion against the unfair institutions of society; a kind of Ned Kelly syndrome.

It was no different at Long Bay, he says. One of the screws they called The Mirror – whenever you asked for something, he always said he'd 'look into it'. He might as well have been looking into a mirror for all the action that resulted.

The paintbrushes are cut down so far that they were shorter than the peanut butter jar he used for rinsing and so one of the brushes was inadvertently flushed when he changed the water. It hadn't helped that he'd been waiting five months to see the optician.

The powers that be treated his failure to produce that brush like he'd orchestrated a prison break and it took a year to get a replacement. He nearly gave up painting altogether. But in the end he convinced himself that giving up would be letting them win, so he persisted. He'd been quite happy with the end result of the MASH unit painting – the perspective of the landing zone distorted by the perspex of the medivac chopper's bubble cockpit.

Saw *Avatar* last night. Great movie. It is 4.18 p.m. and am waiting for a video to come on – *Australia*. The screws put the discs in the machine but fail to press play so all that comes up on our screens in our cells is the title screen. Often that's all we get – the title screen – and the movie is never played. I have been sitting here for one and a half hours waiting for the movie to start. As soon as I switch over to watch TV I bet the movie will start which means if it's not replayed I will see only two thirds of the movie. That's normal in here. They are so incompetent. But if you ask them they'll tell you 'oh sure, we provide videos for the inmates.' Ha, what a laugh. Hey, 4.52 p.m. and the video is starting – I only had to wait two hours for this one.

15

Gary Gilmore, age thirty-six, was executed by firing squad in the US state of Utah at 8.07 a.m. on Monday, 17 January 1977. In Sydney it was 2.07 a.m. Tuesday and Lindsey was in the nurses' quarters at Auburn District Hospital. He'd finished his shift at the Quay Street control room at 11 p.m. then he'd met up with his latest fling, Wendy, and they'd gone dancing and drinking. And she was in the mood so they'd gone back to her room in the nurses' quarters and he stayed the night.

Gilmore's execution reached the front pages in Sydney. He'd been released from prison the year before after spending most of his adult life inside. Three months he lived outside, failing to adjust, before committing robberies on two consecutive nights and shooting a man dead at each. The men had done as they were ordered – their deaths were random acts of vengeance by Gary Gilmore against his own dysfunction.

There had been no judicial executions in the US for nine and a half years following a Supreme Court challenge and Gilmore became famous after refusing to appeal his death sentence – and more so after the publication of Norman Mailer's Pulitzer Prize–winning book *The Executioner's Song,* about Gilmore's life.[4]

'I ought to die for what I did,' said Gary Gilmore.

And he did.

If such a thing were to exist, Gary Gilmore's spirit, freshly sprung from Utah State Prison, might have fled across the globe seeking mischief. If it travelled fast enough it could make it in time. Across the surface of the earth – if such a corporeal constraint applied – Gilmore's spirit would only need to average Mach 2, the cruising speed of the Concorde, to get to Sydney in six hours. And if it had, it would have arrived in time to witness, or perhaps propagate, fresh horrors far exceeding the experience of even Gary Gilmore's own violent life. For six hours and five minutes after five bullets pierced Gary Gilmore's chest, a commuter train clipped a bridge in suburban Sydney.

•

They woke before 7 a.m. and Wendy got him out the back door of the nurses' quarters without being seen.

The day was clear and already warm. He wasn't back on duty until 2 p.m. so he had plenty of time to get back home to North Strathfield – he'd recently moved out of Croydon Park after a bust-up with a girlfriend. He didn't have his car so he walked around to the front entrance of the hospital and the girl behind the desk recognised him and let him use the phone. The Quay Street control room said there would be a mail car coming past from Penrith on its way to the city and it could pick him up.

He was collected in less than half an hour and introduced himself to the driver, Joe, who was from the Penrith district.

They drove north to get back to Parramatta Road. Even though this was the mail run, it was a standard ambulance and Joe kept the radio on. When they got to the intersection of St Hilliers and Parramatta Road an ambulance flew past them, whistle on, and Lindsey wondered why they hadn't heard the call on the radio. Then he remembered he was in a Mountains car and he had nothing better to do so he asked Joe if he could change the frequency.

There was more traffic on the airwaves than usual and multiple references to an incident at Granville Station. There was some sort of incident at a train station every other day – biddy down the stairs, someone collapsed on the platform or, sometimes, under a train – so it still didn't strike him as anything unusual. But then he heard the controller repeat a previous call and he recognised the voice – it was George – and George was a cool customer but now he could hear the stress in his voice and Lindsey's ears pricked.

'Come in three-oh-three. Three-oh-three, are you there? Three-oh-three, please provide a situation report.'

There was no response from car 303 and while Joe was puzzled at what was going on he needed to be on his own frequency so he turned the radio back.

Joe's radio operator was calling out for car 341.

'That's us,' said Joe before responding to the call.

'Three-oh-three has been dispatched to Granville but failed to call on arrival and is not responding,' the radio blared. 'Expedite to Bold Street, Granville and report situation. We are receiving multiple reports of a train accident. The switchboard is lit up.'

Lindsey hit the beacon and the whistle and Joe did a U-turn and floored it back to Granville.

They travelled part of the way on the wrong side of the road then turned left into Good Street, which ran right up to Bridge Street, which ran parallel to the train tracks. As they approached the corner, Granville Hotel on the right, Lindsey could see something on the tracks. He could see train carriages and he could see lots of wheels. It was like his eyes were playing tricks on him and he couldn't quite make out what he was looking at. He squinted.

When they got closer he realised why.

'That's a train engine on its side,' he said. It had fallen away from them so he was looking at the underside of the engine, all axles and wheels and a pile of twisted cables. He'd never seen a train on its side before.

Another ambulance, had to be 303, was parked up ahead and Joe pulled over and they turned off the whistle and got out. At first, silence. They stood looking at the carnage and Lindsey felt cold despite the summer heat. He took in the scene, scoping the whole area of operation, training compelling him to look for obvious dangers first.

Not only had the train tipped over, but the first carriage had been torn open and there were people milling around. Survivors, they must be survivors. They were trying to help other people get out of that carriage and there were live wires down, sparking. Further back was worse. The Bold Street bridge had collapsed and the third and fourth carriages of the train had been flattened. The passengers under that bridge must have been goners.

He turned to look at car 303. All its doors were open and not an ambo to be seen. Not standard procedure – especially if the control room hadn't been briefed. He supposed they'd gone down to help the survivors.

He turned to Joe. 'Who's the senior out of us? Who's going to call it in?'

Lindsey was, so he got on the radio and when he spoke into the handset all that came out of his mouth was gibberish.

'Repeat, 341,' the operator said.

Lindsey pulled out a cigarette and his hand shook so much he had to hold his own wrist with his other hand to get the thing lit. He took a deep, shaky drag on the cigarette and tried again. 'The train has derailed and brought the bridge down,' he said. 'Repeat, the train has crashed and the concrete bridge has fallen on the train.'

He started reading from the laminated list of job codes he'd stuck inside his white uniform cap.

'Code 19.' Disaster alert. He hesitated for only a second before issuing it – most ambos would go their whole career without calling in a code 19.

'Eighty code 4,' he said. Code 4 was for deceased patient. It turned out to be a good guess; later he learned that eighty-three people had died.

'One hundred code 9.' Rescue required.

'Code 11,' he said. That normally meant power lines so he qualified with: 'Train lines are down.'

'Code 21.' Paramedics required.

The controller confirmed them back to him then asked again about the non-responsive car 303. Lindsey explained that it was empty and that the officers from it had obviously gone to provide urgent medical support to patients.

'Is that you, Rosie?' said the controller.

'Yeah, George, it's me,' he said.

'Stay on the radio, the super wants a word,' said George. Only seconds passed. 'Rose, we've got no other comms to the site, please stay on the radio.'

'Okay, sir,' said Lindsey and for the next five minutes he answered questions about the scene of the disaster and gave updates as more ambulances arrived. And then he was past the fence and down the embankment and under the bridge.

He walked along the left side of the carriage. There were arms and legs protruding from the wreckage and he couldn't help but notice that every second hand bore a wedding ring.

The bridge had concrete I-beams running lengthways and these had cut through the carriages like cardboard. Most of those killed had been crushed by one of the I-beams.

But there were gaps between the I-beams so there were also survivors trapped in those two crushed carriages. Many of the trapped victims had breathing difficulties as seats, rubble and in some cases corpses were pressing down on them. Rescuers started by slashing at seats and clearing away debris to try to gain an extra inch or more of space around the chest so patients could breathe. A lot of people were in that state and some died like that, unable to draw breath, even as the rescuers were working to free them.

It seemed like only seconds passed before emergency personnel were everywhere. Entry to the carriages was problematic due to the confined space – knee-height above the train's floor in places – and the debris everywhere. A line formed and rubble was passed along, hand-to-hand, after it was removed from the carriages. They removed the people that they could while others attended to those who were trapped, some still attached to a crushed limb.

The seats blocked access to each pocket between the bridge's I-beams, so they had to cut through the cast-iron mounts at the base of the seats. And because it was a Blue Mountains train there were four big gas canisters on board that were used to heat the carriages in winter and they were leaking so the rescuers couldn't use the oxy torch. Lindsey went at them with a hacksaw. Carefully. It was close-in work in twisted metal and when he ducked back up the hill to get some gear he looked around and found a spare white ambulance service hard hat and then he was back down into it. It was awkward being bent over or reaching around obstacles and his back injury flared up in the first half hour.

Three months earlier he'd attended a single-vehicle accident at Picnic Point. An overweight biker had crashed on Henry Lawson Drive and fractured several vertebrae. Lindsey had missed every pothole, driving to the hospital under police escort. But when they'd moved this enormous biker onto a gurney, his partner had bludged on the lift and Lindsey's back had felt like it was buckling. But he'd held his end – letting go could have killed the patient – and now he had displaced vertebrae pressing against nerves. Three weeks of medical leave and referrals had done little to alleviate it.

So his spine was shooting spears as he hacksawed through seating mounts in the wrecked train and he stepped back to catch his breath. It was dark under the bridge, and quiet – words were reserved for discussion of tactics. Everyone was covered in black soot and grease and few wore hard hats and Lindsey had to look closely at badges or epaulettes to know who was who. But when he looked down the line at the row of people passing debris from hand to hand, nearly half the people there were Salvation Army. Volunteers.

He resumed hacksawing. They'd selected the particular seat he was working on because once it was free from the mounts it would still need to be wrenched free quite roughly and that particular seat held no survivors. He was focussed on this one task even though he could sense that the whole operation was pretty much chaos. There were firies, cops, ambos and volunteers, survivors and Salvos all helping out. The cops were running the show and one of them yelled out instructions to cut out the seat behind, which held a patient, but the rescue-trained paras knew that doing so would harm the patient so the cop was told to fuck off.

It took half an hour just to cut through the mounts for the one seat. Another man was there helping him and they pulled out the seat and the three bodies in one go. It was a gruesome task and they stood puffing from the exertion. Lindsey looked up at the other man and it was another Salvation Army officer.

'Thanks,' he said. 'Mate, you are a hero. I'm never going to forget you blokes.'

Now that the seat was out a few of them stood and looked at each other and not a word was said, but Lindsey picked up his kit and crawled into the gap left by the seat and into the aisle of the carriage.

A man in his fifties was pinned by the spine, breathing heavily. Other patients were calling out in agony, panicky, desperate. 'Don't worry about me, son. Look after the young ones,' the man said. Lindsey gave him the once-over and his legs were numb; spinal fracture.

He continued on his knees and had to get down onto his belly just to get a few more feet in and all he could reach were limbs that were protruding from the crush. He checked each limb and if it had a pulse he'd call out to the victim to ask if they could feel his touch and this way they started a management plan for the remaining trapped survivors in that pocket.

He worked his way to the other side of the carriage. There'd been people in the aisle and he was climbing over dead bodies and then there was a thunderous whump. A pressure wave pushed into his ears, black and brown soot swirled in the air and he realised that the slab had settled down another couple of inches. He was going to die, squashed in with all those dead people. His heart hammered and he pressed flat against the floor for whatever good that might do and his ribs were being pushed into the floor by his pounding insides.

After a minute he continued and in the seats across the aisle were two schoolgirls lying side by side in their uniforms. Their dark blue tunics and grey pleated skirts were freshly pressed and immaculate and he figured that they attended one of the private schools in the city.

He continued his search for live ones, trying to purge the image of those two schoolgirls, otherwise unmarked, but decapitated cleanly the pair of them.

Later he was called out for a compulsory break so out of the wreckage he crawled. They'd developed a time-saving process whereby everyone walking out took something with them so he waited a few minutes until the next stretcher had been loaded and picked up a corner and helped them carry the stretcher bearing a cooling body into the tent that had been made into a makeshift morgue.

He visited the Salvation Army tent and never was their name more appropriate. The police had set up a full mobile kitchen for their members, but the Ambulance Service had no such thing so they relied on the Salvos. Lindsey's whole body was covered in the black and brown soot and grease from the train carriages and the collapsed bridge but the Salvos' wash stations had basins with warm soapy water and he was able to clean up his face and hands, blasting enough of the metallic soot from his nostrils to enjoy the hot tea and meat pies that they'd laid on for the rescuers.

It was approaching eleven o'clock and had been getting hotter and hotter in the narrow avenue between the wall under the bridge and the side of the train and an ambulance superintendent came up to Lindsey. 'We need ice and lots of it,' he said. 'Go and find some.'

'Right,' said Lindsey and he skolled his cup of water and started to run. The surrounding area was a car park for emergency service vehicles so he kept running, no plan, until he got to Parramatta Road. They'd taken down the power for the whole area so the traffic lights were out, the traffic was crawling and there was a cop on point duty. He saw a nice big ute – almost a pick-up truck – an F100 Ford Utility.

'Mate, I need your help. I am commandeering your vehicle, will you help me?' Lindsey stepped up to the driver's side door, ready to grab him by the scruff of the neck and throw him out if necessary – people were going to start dying under that slab because of the intense heat so he was not in a mood to be trifled with. But the driver, startled by this soot-covered apparition, said yes and Lindsey ran around to the passenger side and told him to drive.

The cop on point duty saw them and held up the traffic in the cross street to make room. The driver was waiting for cars to clear but Lindsey grabbed the wheel and turned him onto the wrong side of the road and told him to push his way through. Lindsey turned on the hazard lights and the driver put his headlights on high-beam and Lindsey showed him how to use his horn like one tone of a siren – the *hee* out of a *hee-haw* – and he got the hang of it and pushed through, still on the wrong side of Parramatta Road, to the next intersection.

Old Mate was doing alright for a civilian but he started to slow down when he saw another cop ahead diverting traffic. 'Keep going, the cop will work out who we are,' Lindsey said and as they flew by he held out his hard hat showing the Ambulance Service badge and the cop waved them through.

They continued until they reached a service station with an ice machine and Old Mate followed instructions and backed up to the machine. Lindsey went to the counter, asked for the key and told the attendant that he would take all the ice and to bill the Ambulance Service and he'd sign something if he wanted. 'Don't worry, take anything you want, champ,' he said.

The ice was in four-kilo bags so pretty easy to handle and he roped in a couple of bikers to help load up the ute. It didn't take long to clean out all the ice and he was glad he'd picked the F100 as it had a large load space and they'd filled it right up.

Back at the scene assorted rescuers formed another conga line to ferry the ice down to the tracks. The ice was deployed along the inside of the tunnel and in front of the Fire Brigade's large air-blower which had been rigged to draw out the hot air and trapped gas.

There was a split in one of the bags of ice so he popped a cube into his mouth and in the dirty, sweaty conditions it was heaven. He filled his pockets with ice cubes and went back under and now, in there with the rescue workers, were priests administering last rites. He moved along telling people to open their mouths and he got a few funny looks but there was no time for niceties and every mouth got a cube or two of ice.

A man was trapped and the firies had brought in the heavy gear to cut him out. Lindsey and another ambulance officer attended to his IV line and patched up some of the injuries peripheral to his trapped legs.

The man was conscious and for some time Lindsey just kept the man company, engaged him in conversation while the extraction took place around them. He was married and Lindsey asked about his kids and they discussed his career, loves and losses and he fetched an ice cube for the man to suck.

'I didn't know I was going to die today,' the man said.

'Not today, mate, we'll get you out,' said Lindsey. 'One day I'll bring you ice and it'll have Jack Daniels with it.'

He didn't get to keep his promise. The man with the crushed legs died later in the day, eased from life in a morphine torpor.

At his next break he again took the corner of a stretcher. There were thousands of onlookers by now and they were careful to cover the bodies as there was a ghoulish vibe to the crowd; some had binoculars and others had brought down a picnic lunch. As he tried to gulp his hot coffee he spotted a civilian off to the side who seemed to be acting funny and he watched him for a minute and realised he was picking up money. They'd been walking over coins and notes all day and no-one had given it a second's thought unless it was a wallet or purse that could be handed in for identification. Then Lindsey saw this civilian going through the pockets on a body so he yelled at him and started towards him but a big hand grabbed Lindsey by the shoulder from behind and a voice said, 'Don't worry, mate, we've got this one.' The owner of the hand strode past him and he was about six foot four, wearing a suit. Two more burly suits followed and when they picked up the thief his feet didn't touch the ground as he was carried off.

Parts of the carriage were so far under the slab that they couldn't be accessed but it was past midday now and they'd probably found all the survivors. Most had been removed but there were a few victims still trapped and he overheard the medical teams talking of the need to amputate limbs to get them out. He read later that some victims weren't released until the evening and some of those died of renal failure anyway, soon after being released. The cause was later found to be crush syndrome: suddenly freeing a trapped limb released the by-products of destroyed muscle tissue into the blood, overloading the kidneys.

Lindsey's normal shift was due to start at 2 p.m. so the super asked him to leave the scene and report to his station to do his shift. His mind was focussed solely on the job at hand and he stood with his mouth gaping for a few seconds trying to process what he'd been told. Then he realised that the few survivors left were all being managed and that the rescue could continue without him.

He walked off the site, covered in filth, and caught a taxi home. He showered and changed and then drove into the city and back to the control room. He worked the rest of his shift in a daze. And then he went to a bar and drank Jack Daniels and beer, but no amount was enough and he got home and lay in bed and didn't sleep, staring into the darkness and remembering.

He didn't sleep for a week. When he finally slept, the nightmares started.

16

I am touring the scene of a crime. As you do.

Gladesville, a block back from Victoria Road and its strip of suburban shops. Here was a massage parlour called Kerrie's Oasis until 14 February 1994 when the proprietor was murdered on-site and the premises set alight.

The former massage parlour is now occupied by a financial planner. I feel like a prowler as I snap photos from the front of the building, debating whether or not to go in. I force myself out of my comfort zone and walk up. The sign says 'Reception' and the young woman is quite happy to fetch the boss when I say I'm researching the premises. He stands there in the tiny reception room – a room where once a 21-year-old unknowingly awaited the arrival of an intended murder victim.

I ask him if he has any knowledge of the history of the building. He doesn't pause for long – he'd heard references to someone dying here. 'Why, what do you know?' The receptionist's interest is piqued and I tell them the story.

'Where were they killed?' the receptionist wants to know. I gesture and show them but later I realise I've told it wrong. One was killed in the room next door, not here at reception. I thought the other was shot in the hallway but she was actually killed in the back room, the financial planner's boardroom.

The planner shows me around and lets me take photos of the hall and rooms. They've completely refurbished since moving in two years prior but I want to see the layout, to visualise what happened here. It helps but only in a spatial sense – I am no closer to visualising the Lindsey I thought I knew prowling this hallway with death in his eyes and blood on his hands.

I take one of the planner's cards and the receptionist gives me the phone number for the property agent in case he has more information. I take the number and thank them profusely for their time but already I feel like I'm trespassing and I've seen enough and I never ring the property manager.

17

They met on the phone. He'd spent the day in the control room at Quay Street, assigning jobs to ambulances from different stations. It had been a particularly challenging day juggling heart attacks, car accidents, assaults and a suicide.

Late in the day things had been calm for about half an hour when one of his phone lines lit up again. This time it wasn't another triple-0 emergency, but a call back from the female voice who'd been routing his calls for most of the day.

'It's Lydia. I wanted to make sure you were okay,' the voice said.

'Oh, I'm alright. Why do you ask?' Lindsey replied.

'Well, you've had your hands full, haven't you? What with the double fatal and then the three different cardiacs inside of an hour. And the whole time you managed to stay polite on the phone. I was impressed. A lot of the other blokes get worked up and start swearing and yelling at me to hurry up when it gets crazy like that, but you didn't. Thank you.'

Never one to miss an opportunity, he asked her out for a drink and they met face to face that night. She had a sparkle in her eye and with her blonde coiffed bob she could pass for the TV newsreader Katrina Lee. She was a stunner. It was August 1977, the month Elvis died, and Lindsey decided within a week that he was going to marry this woman.

The courtship was slow at first. Even though they were into each other, Lydia was cautious and kept it platonic. Later she told him that she'd been seeing another man. It had been one of those on again, off again affairs that was never going to go anywhere and once she and Lindsey started sleeping at each other's places she told Lindsey that she wouldn't be seeing the other man anymore.

She'd never met anyone like Lindsey. He was comfortable around guns and sometimes it got a bit edgy, but it was fun-edgy and that was part of the attraction. His family were raucous and some of their hijinks she thought were crazy but hilarious at the same time. Sometimes they'd meet for a picnic and there were so many uncles, aunts and cousins that they'd take over the local park for what would become a mini sports carnival. She'd seen nothing like it.

He was twenty-three and she was twenty-two and they were both headstrong characters, but they got each other. Lydia's mum fell in love with Lindsey as well – he charmed the pants off her.

After one long night out they drove to Stanwell Tops and parked at the lookout. They had sex while the sun came up and that was how they christened Lydia's Fiat 125. By now nothing kept them apart.

Granville was six months behind him when they met and when he woke howling she was there to hold him and he slept again.

•

Any emergency personnel who attended the disaster received the standard Granville Medal that came in a box with a certificate. They were mass produced and bore no personalised inscription. They also gave out heroic medals – recipients nominated by people at the scene – and there were special ceremonies to present them to the select few. Lydia called down to him from the triple-0 switchboard to tell him that he was on the list, recommended for one of the heroic medals. One of her friends worked in administration and she'd called Lydia in excitement to let her know that she'd seen Lindsey's name on the list.

But Lindsey had been at loggerheads with the superintendent over his back injury and medical leave and he told Lydia that he'd be surprised if he ever actually received it. Sure enough, when the awards were announced his name was absent and he found out later that the super had vetoed his award.

> It was typical of the Ambulance Service and its culture to veto that gong. I had expected just that to happen. I was gusseted with all the other guys for the Granville Medal. As I left the service, no doubt mine lies in someone's drawer gathering dust.

•

THE FATALIST • 77

The orthopaedic surgeon had recommended exercises and chiropractic treatment and if that didn't work he'd need surgery one day.

He followed the treatment plan but the demands of the job took their toll and management refused to grant any more medical leave and declined his request to move into a less active role. The culture in the Ambulance Service was similar to that of the armed forces. The chain of command was clear and non-commissioned officers were required to be respectful and obedient towards their superiors – only the salutes were missing. And so the soldiers went out to battle every day and took it on the chin and there was tremendous mateship between ambulance officers, who were bonded by adversity. And no matter what it was – handling the corpses of men, women or children, even babies – if it got to you, you'd go to the pub and drink. Drink until you were beyond caring, unconscious, or in a bar fight. And just as soldiers in the Great War knew that if they failed to go over the top they'd be shot by their own officers, so it was with the ambulance officers. Or so management appeared to believe.

A back injury, despite being the most common for ambulance and rescue personnel (as for nurses), was assumed to be fictional. Late in 1978, lifting a cardiac patient onto a stretcher in the patient's home had sent his back into spasms. It was worse the next morning and he could not get out of bed without assistance. Lydia helped him onto the couch where at least he could reach the phone and call his supervisor. He took anti-inflammatories, applied cold packs – the usual procedure. Usually he could be mobile again in a day or two, and the symptoms would subside inside a week if he looked after it. Two days later he took an extra dose of anti-inflammatories, topped up with codeine and struggled in to work. It was no good. Getting through the car park into the station and sitting down was enough to drench his shirt in sweat. He felt nauseous and nearly fainted from the pain. A colleague helped him back to his car and he got home and back onto the couch.

The next day the pain was even worse. By late afternoon he was lying on the hard floor, trying to self-manipulate his lower vertebrae to get some relief when the doorbell rang. He could not get off the floor. Lydia was at work.

'Who is it?' he called out.

'It's your station manager, Rose,' the voice said. Lindsey was surprised. It was rare for senior staff to show concern for the welfare of a grunt, but he supposed the super had heard about the state he'd been in the previous day.

He dragged himself along the carpet to the door and reached up to unlock the door.

'What are you doing on the floor, Rose?' asked the station manager.

'It's my back, sir, it's killing me. Normally it starts to come good by now, but it's getting worse. I'm going to see the doc tomorrow,' he said. He'd rolled over onto his back, with his feet on the floor and knees up so he could look up into the man's face while they spoke.

'Rose . . . You're not fooling anyone. Clearly you saw me from the window and decided to put on this charade for my benefit. Why don't you get up off your lazy bum and get back to work? You know how much it costs in overtime to fill your shift while you're swanning around here faking injury?'

Now it made sense. How naïve he'd been to think concern for his welfare had brought the station manager around.

'Boss . . . honestly. Nowhere I'd rather be than back on the job. I can show you—'

'Don't want to hear it, Rose,' he interrupted. 'You have a think about whatever your problem is and then come and see me in my office and we'll have a little chat about it, okay?' Lindsey swallowed his anger. He'd been about to offer up his medical records but there appeared to be no reasoning with the man – the super would probably find some way to discredit the surgeon's report anyway.

A week later he went to the super's office as requested, medicated to the eyeballs. As expected, he received a bollocking and was threatened with suspension if he was caught faking injury again. Lindsey explained his medical condition and said he was preparing to lodge a workers' compensation claim to cover his medical bills.

'If you do this, Rose, I'll make sure every possible hurdle is put in the way of your claim. And you know what that means,' said the super.

Lindsey knew alright; the claim would never be approved and he'd be subject to even more harassment from management.

He and Lydia talked about it. Lydia had left the service herself by now and she was supportive so the next day he handed in his resignation. Stuff them if he was going to be put through the wringer. When he resigned he was spitefully informed that doing so proved that he must have been faking all along.

•

Officers on the edge

'It is only a matter of time until more staff suicide as a result of the bullying and harassment by senior staff . . . or until someone goes to HQ with a shotgun and makes them pay for what they have done.'
   Unnamed suspended officer, 8 years service
   (John Kidman and Louise Hall, *Sydney Morning Herald*, 13 July 2008)

The newspaper archives reveal a long history of poor culture in the NSW Ambulance Service and repeated claims of harassment and bullying from a nepotistic 'old boys club'. Recent reports suggest the problems persist to this day despite a parliamentary inquiry in 2008 which made recommendations to address 'extremely serious cultural problems within the Ambulance Service'.[5]

•

It didn't take long to qualify for his taxi licence and he drove long shifts to keep the cash coming in. He gave away the flying lessons. After he'd earned his restricted licence in the single engine he'd done a few more hours in a twin engine, not enough for endorsement, and more recently he'd started taking lessons in a helicopter. He'd thought he might do medivac work one day. But the lessons weren't cheap, $140 an hour, and with his ambulance career over there wasn't even a good reason anymore.

While he was still hurting from his treatment at the hands of the Ambulance Service, at least he was shot of the bastards. So a modicum of calm came into his life and when he asked Lydia if she would marry him she agreed.

Lydia had a better paying job working for Honeywell in North Sydney. He wasn't earning a lot in the cabs and he wanted to buy an engagement ring for Lydia. He couldn't save fast enough and he had some gear he didn't want to move into the marital home anyway so he sold it. Then he had enough to buy a decent stone. They announced their engagement to the family on Christmas Day 1978.

•

Lydia told me that Lindsey's mother didn't approve – didn't think she was good enough for her Lindsey. Glenda, apparently, never let Lydia forget the sacrifices Lindsey had made for her including selling his rifle to pay for her engagement ring. Of course 35-year-old memories can be problematic; Lindsey's recollection is that he never owned a weapon until a few years later when he started doing security work.

18

He'd still catch up with Russ V. at the Stop at Rest if he had nothing else on and they'd still talk about restoring cars, like that old wreck Russ had bought from Lindsey, or about the stresses of being an interstate truck driver. One night Russ introduced him to a cop he knew, Connor. Lindsey was fed up with the taxi driving, he needed something better. How about joining the cops, said Russ. So Connor asked a few questions and all was fine until he asked about Lindsey's glasses. The prescription was strong and his eyesight was only going to get worse. 'They won't take you. No chance,' said Connor.

But Connor had a suggestion: work for a private inquiry agent. Similar skills, no eyesight test.

In January he passed a job interview, gave up the taxi driving and commenced work with a mercantile agency serving court documents – summonses and the like – for a man named Mark Lewis.

Mark Lewis was the owner and licensee of Pierce Investigations. Lindsey applied at West Ryde Court House for his private inquiry licence, as sub-agent to Mark Lewis, and within weeks he was process-serving all over Sydney.

He was keen to learn and quickly discovered he had a knack for tracking down people who might not want to be found. And after the years in the Ambulance Service and all its horrors and head cases – and ten years of martial arts training – he had no fear of any deadbeat who might try to pick him.

'Here's the first two rules for you to remember,' said Mark Lewis on Lindsey's first day in the office. 'We keep the cops on-side and keep your hands off the female staff.'

Within a week Lindsey learned why he'd made the second point. Mark Lewis had been married since he was twenty-one but now, in his early forties, he leered at the young women in his employ – all of whom had been employed for their looks – and then it was inappropriate comments and wayward hands.

By the end of the second week Lindsey was screwing the girl on the switchboard.

•

'Hang on. I'm pretty sure my timeline has you starting work with Mark Lewis shortly before you were married. So you were cheating on Lydia?'

'Well, I was shagging that switchboard girl within a fortnight – jeez, she had great tits – but I never cheated on Lydia. You must have something wrong.'

After the visit I review my source material. The wedding date had been double-checked and the date he started with Mark Lewis stacks up.

Three months later, my next visit: 'I checked. You started with Mark Lewis in January 1979 and were married two months later.'

He looks at me with his hands open, bottom lip out, eyes wide – as if flummoxed.

'Like I said, I wasn't married yet so I never cheated on Lydia,' he says.

I can tell now when he's decided to clam up. Pursuing it further will be pointless.

•

Lydia and Lindsey were married at Stanwell Tops at dawn at the spot where they'd christened the Fiat. A dawn ceremony was a huge inconvenience to everyone, but once they were all there and the sun came up it was worth the effort. Lydia looked glorious in her cream gown and her heels dug into the soft lawn at the lookout as they looked out over the ocean, a thousand miles of pewter.

The reception was at the house of one of Lydia's cousins and they rode there in Bill Rose's MG – the one Lindsey had helped repaint as a teenager. Lydia had lost weight for the fitting of her wedding dress, but as the day approached she put some of it back on quite quickly so Aunt Marjorie had gone and bought them a pram as a wedding present. Lydia just laughed because to her it was a giddiness that was typical of his family.

He moved into Lydia's place, her grandmother's old house, on Kenyon Road in Bexley. Lindsey was just shy of twenty-four and Lydia a year younger. They worked hard and kept up with the family functions and still there was time for late nights out, the occasional harbour cruise and weekends away in Tasmania or the Blue Mountains. They were good for each other – at first. Twelve months later everything was very, very different.

19

Ivan gets mail from all over the world. Just people who have heard about him and write to him to ask about what it's like. You'd be surprised how many women write to him.

There are two rooms for visits in Supermax and they usually escort the two sets of visitors together. The white-haired man I'd seen at my first visit is one of Ivan Milat's brothers, older. He's a regular visitor and, by the third time, we nod in recognition and chat briefly. He is urbane, articulate, and wears a tweed jacket and smart leather shoes. He'd visited when the Supermax first opened and as we wait in an antechamber he tells me he'd been trapped in here for twenty minutes on that first visit because they couldn't get the door open again.

Ivan's visage is startling when he is led out in the orange canvas. His hair is receding but what's left is long, almost pure white and spikes out, electrified. His face is clean-shaven and pinkly youthful in contrast. He smiles a lot and appears pixie-like, turning his head in that talk-show-host kind of way when addressing one of the guards.

Lindsey tells me that when he lived at Brighton-Le-Sands he'd visit a friend at Long Bay and this friend introduced him to Ivan.

CM: First impressions?

LR: Just another bloke. It took years to get to know him.

We discuss recent media about Ivan. He'd been moved into an observation cell because of publicity about privileges accorded him and the politicians had moved in to shut down what pundits were calling a scandal. Lindsey rolls his eyes as he tells me about what he calls typical corruption of the process.

A tabloid newspaper had run a front-page story highlighting Ivan's access to a sandwich-maker and a television in his cell. An Opposition spokesperson described the cells of the HRMU as 'holiday units' and a victims' support group expressed concern. Premier Morris Iemma, no less, announced that the sandwich-maker and television had been taken away. There was little need to add that privileges such as these were part of an agreed protocol to help the prison manage difficult inmates.

Ivan threatened to kill himself if he didn't get them back and was placed on suicide watch. Four weeks later the Department completed its 'review', the media storm had blown over and the items were returned.

For four years, Lindsey tells me, he spent every day sitting next to Ivan at a computer and most nights dissecting his case. Ivan was seeking leave to appeal his convictions and Lindsey helped him put together his submission. Lindsey was convinced there were irregularities with Milat's conviction and that there were legitimate grounds for appeal. But Ivan was difficult: he had to be in control of everything. And for all his powers of persuasion, Ivan could barely write a legible sentence, so Lindsey would take dictation, typing, and tell Ivan when something didn't make sense and suggest a better approach. Ivan would always disagree and argue the opposite. They'd print out a draft to be reviewed overnight and the next day Ivan would hand over the edits; they'd invariably be the changes that Lindsey had suggested the previous day.

Eventually his stubbornness overcame Lindsey's guidance and the submission that went out was incoherent and Ivan's last legal avenue closed. It was Lindsey's only failure, he tells me – he'd helped three other inmates with their legals over the years and those others had all succeeded.

Not one day in those four years did Ivan give away any clue that he was guilty, he says, but when the appeal was finished they were talking about 'Helicopter John' and Ivan let something slip. John Killick had escaped from Silverwater prison in the helicopter that his girlfriend had hijacked but was rearrested after six weeks on the run. Great plan, said Lindsey, but he wouldn't have been landing in North Ryde as Killick had. Even though he'd made it out of the area, that was a high-risk landing zone. He described to Ivan a place he knew up north: in the bush, but with a clear landing zone and plenty of options for leaving the area quickly.

'If you were to land a helicopter up there, you might disturb some sleeping spirits,' said Ivan.

'Does that mean what I think it does?' asked Lindsey.

'Oh, yes,' said Ivan.

He had to admit that Ivan had had him fooled alright.

They'd been close for those years, but soon after that conversation, now that the legals were finished and Ivan had no use for him, they had a falling out and have barely spoken since.

For the rest of the visit he tells me more about the next phase of his life, his work as a private inquiry agent. He doesn't get far before we run out of time but over the next few months he sends me long letters with dozens of stories.

20

Lindsey's responsibilities expanded to include security details and repossessions. He worked long hours but most evenings he'd be home in time to see Lydia and if he felt like a beer he'd bring home a couple of tallies. Friday nights he took to the Hurstville Legion Club as it was next to the ambulance station and frequented by ambulance officers, police and firies and he felt at home with them.

Repossessing a car necessitated mastering the art of breaking in and driving it away without leaving a mark. Even with his existing tradecraft it took him months to master and they were in a perpetual arms race against the motor industry. There was no legitimate way to learn how to beat new locks and new alarms when they were released. Lindsey's mate Mick worked for NRMA Roadside Assistance and Mick was pretty handy but even he couldn't keep up. So whenever new technology came out it was the Marrickville car thieves who Lindsey would visit.

The new Yellow Light alarms had been giving him grief and he mentioned it to Dimitri and before he'd even sat down Dimitri walked out the door. He was back inside of five minutes and dropped the control box for one of the new alarms down on the bar table. He'd lifted it from a car on the main street of Marrickville, 6.30 p.m. on a weekday, and he pulled the rest of the alarm system from his jacket. Lindsey could usually break into a car, rap the tumblers in the ignition and be away inside of two minutes. But Dimitri from Marrickville left him for dead.

•

Very early in my agent days I was repossessing TVs for Radio Rentals. One little old lady at Roselands I called to see asked me in and made me the most excellent cup of tea. She had a little money but was mostly confused. I explained to her that my instructions were to take her TV, no matter what. She was so upset, it's all she had.

I asked her to make another cup of tea and took her set out to my car. I had a car load of TVs, back seat and boot. I selected a good set I had repoed for another company and took it in, set it up and wiped it down. Then I wrote out a hire agreement, all legal and correct, got her to sign it and gave her a note explaining the monthly payments etc.

When I returned to the company I told one of the girls what I had done, gave her the hire contract and I paid two months rental and the stamp duty. She was a good scout and did not tell her supervisor, just processed the deal and that was that.

A few months later I wrangled that dear old lady a TV for free. I had a sense not to do the wrong thing by my client so worked it out so the client still got paid. I never told any other agents about this as it would be taken as a sign of weakness, not kindness.

•

He doesn't pretend he never made a mistake – he does admit to failures – but during one visit to Supermax, after a fabulous run of heroic reminiscences, I tested the waters: 'Wouldn't you say there's a tendency for people to slant their personal history to reflect themselves in the best possible light? Especially people in here, who have more reason, more temptation, to rationalise – even justify – their behaviour.'

'Absolutely, it's human nature. But remember I was an investigator for many years. It's part of the job, it becomes your permanent mindset, to report events objectively. Even where I'm relying on my memory, I'm compensating for this tendency. What I tell you, you can believe it.'

•

He was repossessing a four-wheel drive in Condell Park. He'd learned that the most effective way to repossess a vehicle at the hirer's premises was to remove the rotor button from inside the distributor cap, disabling the vehicle, before approaching the hirer. If the arrears were paid then he'd reinstall the rotor button; otherwise, the tow truck would be called.

He'd popped the door lock easily enough and released the bonnet and was walking around to access the distributor cap when the shooting started. He looked up and the hirer was on his front lawn. He looked Italian and he appeared to be shooting an M1 carbine.

Lindsey dived behind the four-wheel drive and had enough cover to work back to his own car and into the cabin. 'Shots fired, shots fired,' he yelled into the handset of his two-way radio and ducked as another shot rang out.

It seemed like only seconds passed before cops came running out from everywhere and the crazy Italian was quickly overpowered.

He walked into the muster room at Pierce Investigations the next morning and two other agents were typing up their reports.

'Oh, officer down, officer down. I'm hit,' said one.

'Sit tight. I'll call for back-up,' said the other.

'No, no. Just leave me. Save yourself, Starsky.'

'Very funny, fellas,' Lindsey said. 'Very fucking funny.'

•

One of his first surveillance jobs was a cheating husband. The target was a musician and he had a regular gig at the Summit – the revolving restaurant at the top of Australia Square in the city. He'd finish the gig at two in the morning, cab it to Kings Cross and settle in at the Bourbon and Beefsteak until breakfast. That's where he was meeting his lady friends.

For the first few nights Lindsey ate dinner at the Summit with Marie, another agent. Marie showed him the ropes. It was surprising how a few small adjustments to hair and costume could mask one's identity. Marie would arrive at the Summit first and it was a test for Lindsey to spot her; sometimes it took him two laps to recognise her.

It took about half an hour for the restaurant to do a full turn and for the small stage to come back into view, but as he could hear the guy singing he could relax and it was one of the more pleasurable jobs he'd had, chatting over wine and watching the city lights passing by below.

Once he'd confirmed the routine he'd skip the Summit and sit alone at the bar in the Bourbon and Beefsteak waiting for the target to turn up. One morning the muso walked up to the bar, sat next to Lindsey and struck up a conversation. Lindsey introduced himself as John Bishop, his standard cover name – if anyone rang the agency and asked for a John Bishop the staff had a look-up sheet to know which cover name belonged to which agent.

So whenever the muso saw Lindsey he'd join him for a drink and he was an okay guy and eventually Lindsey came right out and told him that he was working for the man's wife.

At first he thought Lindsey was joking but the penny dropped and then the anger surged and Lindsey braced, his arms ready to block. The muso wanted to swing, but he saw Lindsey looking pretty handy and backed down. A few drinks later they were laughing together about it, but the crunch came and the muso asked, 'Well, John, what are you going to do about it?'

In the end he told the muso that he wasn't going to tell the wife, but he was busted and he needed to sit down with her and sort it out. The wife had paid a retainer upfront, but he made the muso pay the rest of her bill as a condition of Lindsey's discretion.

•

Another client was an insurance company and the job was to investigate a claim from a mid-sized construction firm which, for months, had been losing heavy equipment from job sites: generators, a bobcat, jackhammers and more. He interviewed the principal and the foreman. All the claims seemed legit but something nagged at him and it all seemed too familiar. He'd performed similar investigations before and he knew other agents were working other claims for this same insurer.

He didn't have any leads on the thefts so he spoke to these other agents and then to the insurance company and asked to see the details of the claims from the other clients: both were equipment hire firms.

He worked his contacts. Eventually he got a hit at the Sawdust Hotel in Gladesville. Robbo worked as a prison guard at Long Bay and he must have enjoyed his work because he spent most of his spare time at the Sawdust, which usually contained more crims per square inch than any other pub Lindsey could think of. Robbo gave him the name of a bloke he thought might be involved.

The paper trail confirmed it. The suspect was a subcontractor and he had links to every job site that had had a problem. Lindsey knew a couple of the subbie's mates, so in no time he was on his tail.

A few days of surveillance led him to a warehouse in Yennora. Getting access was the challenge – there were guard dogs, alarms and a foot patrol. But he took his time, planned his entry point and when he got inside it was full of machinery and he took down serial numbers. There were matching serial numbers in the client file; he had found the thieves' holding yard.

Two days later he was home, late afternoon. Lydia was cooking dinner and there was a knock on the door. He recognised the outfits – plain-clothes cops – could spot them a mile away.

They were from the Motor Squad, the first one said. They'd been led to believe he'd been investigating some stolen machinery. He confirmed he was indeed working on such a case and they wanted to establish his credentials so he retrieved his private inquiry licence.

'So, what can you tell us about this matter?' asked Cop One.

Well, nothing, client privilege, he said, but the cop told him the name of the company and the name of the operations manager who'd engaged him, so he came clean and told them yes, that was his client.

'This matter is under investigation by the Motor Squad and we'd ask that you drop your enquiries,' he said.

'Well, actually my enquiries are nearly finished. I know who's been stealing the gear, where it's stored and how they've been shifting it. We would have been in contact with you in the next few days anyway, once we'd collated the evidence.'

The cop looked at him, turned to his barrel-waisted colleague, who raised an eyebrow and stroked his moustache. Cop One turned back to Lindsey.

'Okay.' Exhalation. 'We have been pursuing this matter for some time and we are close to securing sufficient evidence to lay charges and we don't need you either tipping off the offenders or getting in our way.'

'I don't really see your point. I'm trying to get my client—' and now Cop Two spoke up.

'You'll drop the matter or we'll be recommending your licence be revoked for obstructing a police investigation.' He stood with his arms folded casually but there was flint in his eyes as he adjusted his belt and sucked in his gut.

Lindsey didn't take kindly to being threatened – and the bad cop routine was laughable – but he also knew how easy it would be for them to get his licence revoked and then he'd be back in the cabs at best. His mind drifted over his shoulder to the lounge. His .38 snub-nose was stashed in the cushions. These pricks.

'Okay, officer. Thank you for the heads-up,' he said. He hadn't argued the point but he hadn't given in to the intimidation either. He looked Cop Two in the eye and the cop knew that was the best he was going to get.

'Thank you, Mr Rose,' he said.

He watched them drive off, closed the front door and pondered the matter over dinner. It was possible they meant what they said, but then why hadn't they asked for any evidence he might have already collected? Why hadn't they even asked who he suspected so they could confirm their own investigations? It stank.

He was at the Stop and Rest that weekend to have a beer with Russ and his mate Connor was there. He was still stewing over those pricks from the Motor Squad. He asked Connor if he could help.

'Too big for me, mate. Leave it alone.'

The next day Lindsey walked into Police HQ and asked to speak to a senior policeman. They'd not met before but they had a mutual acquaintance and Lindsey thought he'd listen. The desk sergeant gave him a funny look – suspicious at the familiarity – but he made a call then escorted Lindsey upstairs to the senior's office.

How could he meet his obligations to his client, Lindsey asked, if the Motor Squad had warned him off?

The high-ranking officer sat quietly, listening, then thanked Lindsey for raising it and assured him that he would look into it and give him a call.

After a few weeks he'd heard nothing so he got on the phone and eventually spoke to the senior officer.

'Tell your client that this is a police matter and you can't help him,' said the man and he wasn't going to discuss it any further.

Lindsey put down the phone and stared into space.

Again he asked Connor about the Motor Squad. This time Connor laughed. Okay, he said, let me tell you what goes on behind the scenes. The cops knew they got a raw deal, he said, and were paid far less than they deserved, so in certain situations they'd even up the score a bit.

Detectives relied on informants and often they let their informants get away with a bit of drug dealing, or car theft, as long as they got information out of them. And after a while you'd get to know your informant pretty well and, after all, you were in the shit together so you'd have a beer with the guy and then you'd meet some of his mates and you might help him out if it looked like he was going to be raided. So of course you'd ask for a bit of taxation as a way of him showing his appreciation. And if you were busting some other drug dealer – either because he hadn't been green-lighted, or because you needed some convictions – and a bit of whippy turned up, then that was fair game and more cash for 'the bag'.

The contents of the bag were periodically shared; divided up proportionally, according to rank. The sergeants held the line and it was up to them to blood the junior detectives: if they wanted to make it to full detective they'd have to go on the bag and if they wanted to stay there they'd have to earn their keep.

Lindsey had got to know a few cops over the years and there was one in particular who had a nice house and a *very* nice car and seemed to be doing very well considering he and his wife were both on police wages. So even though none of this was a complete surprise, he was still taken aback at how organised it all was. Connor described it to him like it was their natural entitlement and while Lindsey could see his point, it didn't sit well with him and his respect for cops fell a few notches. At least a crook was just a crook: he wasn't walking around with a badge pretending to be a pillar of society.

Any remaining doubts he might have had were gone. He explained the situation to the claimant who had lost two fifty-thousand-dollar bobcats.

'I don't believe it,' he said.

'I'm telling you, the Motor Squad are running the show, and they've got senior police running interference for them.'

'What am I supposed to do, then? I'm covered by insurance, but every time this happens I lose revenue while I'm waiting for the claim to come through.'

'Hire more security. There's not much else you can do other than wear it.'

'This is bullshit. I'm calling Jerry.'

Jerry ran one of the two big equipment hire firms in the state.

A week later Lindsey spoke again to the man who'd lost the two bobcats and he'd taken Jerry out to dinner. Jerry had franchises all over the state so how come he wasn't getting ripped off too, he'd asked. Jerry let him in on a secret – he paid a monthly stipend to the Motor Squad.

Police charged in car theft clean-up

At least half-a-dozen police officers have been charged following a 14-month police operation against car theft involving inquiries in three States.

Three NSW policemen have been charged with criminal offences

. . .

One of the NSW officers was a detective-sergeant.

(Malcolm Brown, *Sydney Morning Herald*, 10 July 1989)

The detective-sergeant mentioned was the former second-in-command of the NSW Motor Squad and he was later sentenced to four years in prison for accepting bribes from car thieves in 1984.

This, my friend, is the real world. Before I started doing this type of work the most I had was a speeding fine. Sure I did a few black bag jobs for corporate or solicitor clients. But that was a game. Find out who, what, where, put in a bug, etc. But, mate, I was honest. I was an investigator with a statutory authority. Fucking police corruption is what's spoiling the world.

•

As Lindsey tussled with the Motor Squad, Lydia moved into the IT response team at Honeywell. It was a demanding role at times and towards the end of 1979 she was asked to go to Melbourne for a few weeks to run an operation down there. Lindsey kissed her goodbye when her taxi came and said he'd try to come down and visit as he sometimes got a job that took him close enough.

He never did make it to Melbourne and she returned to Sydney in time to head straight back out for her office Christmas party. At seven the next morning she hadn't returned and he was in the driveway about to drive to work when a taxi pulled up.

'Where have you been?' he asked. He made a mental note of the taxi's plate.

'Oh, I just stayed at a friend's place,' she said.

'Don't lie to me,' he said. But she pursed her lips and marched straight past him and inside.

He drove to Mark Lewis's offices in West Ryde and put his other jobs on hold. A contact at the taxi company tracked the cab for him so he knew where she'd been picked up – Artarmon.

He drove to Sydney's leafy Lower North Shore and made his enquiries in and around Artarmon and it took the rest of the day. When he returned home that night Lydia was there and he laid it out for her. Here was a copy of the receipt for the night she'd stayed at the Artarmon Motor Inn, the room number and what they'd had for breakfast. And a name.

'So tell me. Who is this Ben prick?' he asked.

Lydia played it casual. 'Look, it wasn't really a big deal. And it's all over now anyway.'

'Tell me,' he said.

She told him. Ben was the manager she'd travelled with and they'd been invited to the Melbourne office Christmas party. Here she was in a new element, performing in a stressful role with this handsome executive, and of course they got drunk and the night sparkled so she spent the first night in his hotel room. And the next.

And then he'd come up for the Sydney office party and she hadn't planned it but they carried on after that one as well and she'd gone back to his room at the motel. Lindsey hadn't done anything particularly wrong, she said; she was just impulsive and that's the way it went.

His head dropped. She waited. He looked back up and her jaw was firm and he just nodded.

He slept on the couch that night and the next day he packed a bag and went to work. In the evening he had a function to attend at the Hurstville Legion Club – he'd always got along with the other members and he'd recently been elected to the board of directors. They were short-staffed so he was serving behind the bar when this pretty young thing walked up and ordered and he could see the edge of her ambulance officer uniform peeking out the top of her jacket.

'Ambo, hey? You must have seen some terrible sights,' he said as he poured the drinks.

She gave that thin smile that he'd worn many times himself and shrugged.

'Terrible, terrible things,' he continued and she was starting on a well-practised response with that familiar look on her face and he couldn't keep it in any more. His face seized up into a wheezing laugh and her eyes and mouth were wide open now and he laughed even harder.

'It's alright, love, he used to be an ambo.' One of the members had dobbed him in.

Later he joined her group. Her name was Liz and they talked and at the end of the night she took him back to her place and the sex was good.

He was still furious with Lydia and she asked him to come back but she wasn't in a great rush to apologise. Stop making such a big deal about nothing, she told him. For a few nights he crashed with a mate – a transit cop – who had a place at Lakemba, but Mark Lewis had him on the armed response team and he needed to be closer to the city so he found a share flat in Lewisham and cleared his stuff out of Lydia's house in Bexley. When he updated his licences and registrations he used his mate's Lakemba address – subterfuge, the life of a PI.

Lydia was offered a better job in Melbourne and she took it.

•

At this point in his life Lindsey has been more a force for good: volunteering, helping people as an ambulance officer and performing acts of kindness for those around him. He never lost that willingness to help people – even through the life of his criminal career – and to this day there are people who know what he did but still feel a powerful love for the goodness that they saw in him.

If categorisation is helpful, I wonder, should we look at him as a good person who performed evil deeds or as an evil person who also did good? I don't have the answer yet. First I need to understand how he could have devolved from this life he had to the furthest extreme of criminality.

In our conversations he has provided only glimpses of his reasons for what he did: 'She ruined my business . . . He bashed my mate. He had it coming . . . I'd do it all again.' But without context they have no meaning. Up to this point in his life he believes himself to have been a 'cleanskin'. I want to understand how and when he crossed over – was it a conscious decision to turn to crime?

In the early '80s something changed in him – a tipping point was reached, he says. Again, I'm telling these events in order of occurrence, not in the order of my discovery. He's alluded to this from our first meeting but it's not until mid-2013, near the end of my research, that I get the final details. It's in his twenty-ninth letter to me – he's clocked up more than four hundred pages now – and here they come, what Lindsey Rose believes were the straws that broke his camel back.

21

Mark Lewis had a job for him on Belmore Street, Burwood. The tenant had stopped paying rent and Lindsey was to go and change the locks. He knew the block of units as it was only two doors down from where his gran now lived. She'd moved there from Enfield after everyone moved out and she was too old to look after the house by herself.

He figured it would be a half-hour job at most so he'd knock it off on his way to serving a summons in the same area. He scoped the unit from across the street. Blond brick units, block of four, a movement in the kitchen window. He knocked on the door and took a step backwards – prepared, as always, for the tenant to try it on.

This time the tenant opened the door, didn't pretend to be anyone else and invited Lindsey into the lounge room. He acknowledged that he was indeed behind in his rent but that he had already told the agent that he'd have the money by the end of the following week.

'I'm sorry, sir, my client has asked me to change the locks. Would you like to pack a bag while I do this? I'll need you to be off the premises before I leave.'

The man's wife came into the room and looked to her husband. 'Come on, you can't just kick us out,' the man said. 'What about the rest of our stuff?'

'Look, my client, your landlord, has informed us that you've failed to keep many previous undertakings to pay the outstanding rent. My job here is simply to change the locks. I can't help you with your property, but in my experience if you make up your arrears quickly your landlord may be willing to give you access to the rest of your property. I'll give you a bit more time to pack if you need it.'

The man was in his mid-fifties. Heavy-set but with a belly. He stood there and his eyes bulged and his lips curled and Lindsey didn't pick him as a fighter so he was caught by surprise when the man's fists, a left then a right, both connected with Lindsey's mouth. Lindsey grappled his arms around the man and put him in a bear hug.

'Stop it, you idiot,' Lindsey told him. 'Stop struggling, I'm just trying to talk to you.'

They wrestled for maybe thirty seconds, the man screaming blue murder and his wife watching and waiting, before the man stopped struggling. Lindsey let him go and stepped back so he'd see him coming if he took another swing.

'I'm calling the police,' said the wife, fraught.

When the uniforms arrived the wife told them that Lindsey had attacked the man. Lindsey told them it was bullshit and the cops took statements from each of them.

His lip was split and fat from one of the punches when he arrived at Pierce Investigations the next morning.

'Gave you a hard time, did she?' asked Mark.

'Yeah, no. Had a problem with that tenant at Burwood yesterday. Took a swing. Then can you believe the dumb cunt's wife rang the cops and complained about me? Look at this lip. I can hardly eat a fucking sandwich.'

Lindsey explained the whole story and Mark mumbled something about keeping your hands off the punters even if it was self-defence.

Weeks later he received a court summons. He was to be charged with assault. He blew his top. He wasn't in the wrong – the tenant had started the whole thing.

So he went to court confident that it would be thrown out – there was no other evidence against him, so presumption of innocence . . . The cops didn't even turn up and the wife gave evidence of Lindsey's 'attack'. She said Lindsey had verbally abused her husband, started the fight, thrown punches – all lies. But the magistrate bought it and Lindsey was found guilty. There was a fine, $200 plus costs, which hurt a little, and the only saving grace was that he got a section 556a (guilty, but no conviction recorded).

So the cops had stitched him up – and the magistrate – after that bitch of a wife had put him in; more bullies in a long line that had fucked him over in his twenty-four long years.

All the resentment and helplessness of his childhood flooded back. These people, these 'authorities', had abused their power over him – as Maxie and his bully mother had and the Ambulance Service super who'd suspended his pay on suspicion of faking an injury which he'd only got because of that cunt who'd bludged on the lift.

It didn't come to him in a flash, but he was so bent out of shape he went about his business like an overwound top. And the next time he had a beer with Russ, Lindsey offloaded all of his frustrations and then it was Russ's turn. Russ was struggling to meet the repayments on his truck and he'd recently taken up with an older woman with three kids. Gabby was a nice girl and Russ had taken on the kids and cared for them like they were his own but money was tight and life was tough.

For years Russ had been working for local identity Bill Cavanagh – started as a yard boy and worked his way up to purchasing his own rig – but he was a hard man to work for, Bill Cavanagh. Lindsey had heard from other drinkers at the Stop and Rest that he walked around with all this cash, boasted of paying no tax and he was hard on the drivers and his other employees at the yard and was often slow to pay wages.

Russ could do with another earn, and it didn't have to be legal.

'You've got a shotgun. We could knock over some place easy enough. What do you reckon?' said Russ.

What did he reckon? He'd been a cleanskin and been loaded up on an assault charge so a fat load of good it had done him trying to do the right thing, that's what he reckoned. And to top it all off, the love of his life had gone and cheated on him. So what good was the world? It was every man for himself.

Sure, he said to Russ, let's go rob some joint – best to get hold of an unregistered weapon first.

PART 2

Evil is a kind of cosmic sulking. It rages most violently against those who threaten to snatch its unbearable wretchedness away from it . . . [T]o vanish from the scene would be to let the cosmos off the hook. People might then mistake it for a benign sort of place.

TERRY EAGLETON, *ON EVIL*[6]

22

A week later he was driving through Bankstown after midnight and the neon sign for Greenacre Firearms caught his eye. It took only a few minutes to disable the magnetic alarm on the back door and he was in. But the weapons were all locked in a steel strongroom. It was a lock he couldn't pick and the owner wasn't silly enough to have left the key on the premises either. He left with a couple of replacement pistol grips.

•

Things with Liz had kicked along for a few weeks and they went looking for a flat together. They moved into a place on King Street in Kogarah. 'This doesn't mean it's serious,' he told her.

•

'Bill owes me for last week's wages,' said Russ. 'He reckons I stole dogs and chains from the yard and he won't pay me till they're paid off.'

'Did you?'

'No, mate. No. I was on the Brisbane run when he reckons they went missing.'

'Did you tell him that?'

'Jesus. No, I told him it wasn't me and when he didn't believe me I told him to get fucked. He went apeshit.'

'You can't leave it like that. If he makes you pay for them it's like admitting you stole them. Maybe you should try and explain it to him one more time. He might see sense when he's calmed down a bit.'

'Yeah. Maybe,' said Russ.

•

Three weeks later Lindsey had a job at Liverpool so he dropped in to the Stop and Rest and one of the truckies told him that Russ had been bashed and was in hospital. He went round to the house and his missus, Gabby, was a mess because Russ was in intensive care and they recommended that the kids stay away, that's how bad he was, and she was stuck at home and didn't know if he was going to live or die.

Lindsey rang up Liverpool Base Hospital, asked to speak to the sister on duty and got the full story. Indeed, Russ was in a critical condition and it was touch and go. He went to visit but there wasn't much he could do for Russ. He hung around for the rest of the day and when visiting hours finished he went back to the Stop and Rest to drown his misery. Russ was well liked down there so the bashing was the talk of the pub and Lindsey gave the locals an update on his condition.

'Yeah,' said Russ when he was out of intensive care, 'it was Cavanagh alright.'

He'd gone to talk to him at his house but Bill wasn't for listening and Russ had gone all big on him and Cavanagh had walked back behind his front door and locked it against Russ's shouting.

The bashing had come a week later. It appeared that Bill hadn't taken kindly to feeling threatened.

He paid two guys, brought them up from Melbourne, two professional thugs, and they were the ones who'd done him over so badly.

So Russ was going to live but it would be a few more weeks before he'd be back on his feet. Russ's truck was repossessed and with his truck went his livelihood. Lindsey chipped in to help Gabby with some of the bills, but she despaired of finding a way out and Russ was still in hospital.

Lindsey dropped in to the Stop and Rest and settled in. Cavanagh was there and later on, when everyone was a bit pissed, Lindsey moved out of the saloon bar and took a seat at the far end of the public bar. Bill Cavanagh was talking to a few of the other hard-arses and he was laughing it up. Lindsey tuned in to the conversation to make sure and there it was: Bill was gloating about Russ and what a deadbeat he'd been and how he'd got his just deserts. He sat there in the smoke-filled bar and thought of Russ and all his hard work down the tubes, his family broken, and he nearly went for Cavanagh then and there.

Joey came over and sat down. Lindsey had known him for a few years and he was well regarded among the truckies at the Stop and Rest for his distinctive red Kenworth W900. 'What's up, Rosie?' Joey asked.

'That bastard Cavanagh,' he said. He knew Cavanagh would never face charges for the assault – he had the local cops stitched up – and Lindsey felt blood pound into his eyes, fit to burst, as he continued, 'I'll fucking kill that fucking cunt.'

Joey kept his mouth shut.

23

Russ was still recovering from the bashing when Lindsey dropped by his house with beers.

'It's fucken hot in here, Russ. How do you put up with it?'

'Can't afford air-con, Rosie. Not exactly flush at the moment.'

It didn't take many beers for them to hatch a plan. They'd rip off an air-conditioner and install it in the house themselves. There were a few new housing developments close by and it wouldn't take long to find one with a unit on-site, waiting for installation. The plan still had legs when they sobered up, so one night they went to a promising site and Lindsey brought his 12-gauge. It was registered to him for security work, but he wasn't planning on firing it.

Bolt cutters got them in the front gate and they drove into the middle of the work site. Russ kept an eye out while Lindsey walked around with his penlight, looking for a unit that was either freshly installed or about to be. He was around the side of a storage shed when he heard an engine and saw headlights so he clicked off his torch and walked slowly back towards where they'd parked, shotgun at the ready.

A security guard had his gun out, pointed at Russ, and Russ was standing there with his hands in the air like some kind of western.

Everything speeds into a hot blur as Lindsey walks out of the shadows with his shotgun and chambers a round. Loud and firm, he tells the security guard to place his pistol on the ground. The guard stiffens with the shock, then bends quickly and does as he's been told. Russ can't believe it and walks over and picks up the guard's pistol and hands it to Lindsey.

'You're not going to get hurt if you do as you're told,' he hears himself say. Then he walks over to the security guard's car, rips the handpiece out of the radio and pockets the car keys. 'Lie on the ground,' he says and they leave him lying there, unharmed.

The red shift of the confrontation subsided as they drove out into the night.

It felt like a clean getaway – they were driving a stolen car and the security guard couldn't have got much of a look at their faces in the darkness.

They hadn't scored an air-con unit, but the security guard's .32 would come in handy.

•

Another cheating husband. The wife worked at Chase Manhattan Bank and the husband was also in the banking game. He drove a black, late model BMW. It seemed he was pursuing his dalliances after hours and during the day he parked in his employer's underground car park in the city. Lindsey decided the BMW would need a tracking device so he wouldn't have to spend hours staking out the city car park. The wife could give him direct access to the car when the husband was out so a device hard-wired to the car battery was the go.

It was a simple job. When the tracker showed the BMW on the move he'd hit the road and once the signal stopped moving he could be at the rendezvous within minutes.

Within a week he sat down with the client and gave her an overview – her suspicions were justified. He slid over the report, photos included.

There was no emotion on her face and she only brushed the edges of the pages as she turned them, as if she were handling a dog turd.

'Thank you, Mr Rose,' she said. 'That's exactly what I asked for. But I wonder if you'd be so kind as to furnish some additional information?'

'Everything I gathered is there in the report. What else do you need?'

'Details,' she told him. 'Who are these women? What are their names?' and red blotches rose up on her throat as she went on. 'How often does he meet them and whereabouts do they meet?'

'Ma'am, I can do that for you, but that'll be a lot more billable hours for you. Are you sure you—'

'Oh, yes. I'm sure.'

Three weeks later he handed her the expanded portfolio without a word. There were all the gory details and she nodded and wrote out a cheque for his invoice on the spot and he had a four thousand dollar pay day.

And once the business was dispensed with she dropped her guard a little. 'I suppose I'll be leaving the bastard now,' she said.

'Well, you might want to speak to a solicitor before you tip him off,' he said.

She wanted to know more so he took her to dinner and gave her a few pointers and it was advice given out of goodwill but he earned another contact out of it. From time to time he'd ring the divorcee from Chase, who now drove a black BMW, and she was sometimes able to provide intel from the bank's records to help him complete a repo or a skip trace. It usually cost him a dinner but she was good company so that was hardly a chore.

•

Russ still had his cash-flow problem and Lindsey said he'd help out. They decided that driving interstate, stealing a rig and ripping off the parts was a pretty safe earn. But they needed some readies to fund the operation and they settled on holding up Clever Dicks Amusement Centre in Liverpool. Lindsey organised the wheels – a blue Commodore, a recent model, a nice one, from the Westfield car park at Parramatta – and picked up Russ on the way. He took the .32 that he'd taken from that security guard and they waited until closing time, ten o'clock. Russ waited in the car while Lindsey ran in and pointed the pistol at the manager, who was in the process of shutting up shop. The manager did what he was told and lay down and Lindsey tied up his arms and legs and went for the till. It looked like about twelve hundred dollars and he yelled at the manager where was the rest, but that was it.

He vowed to get better intel on his target next time. It was barely worth the risk of being caught for such an amount. But it would help.

Q: So was that your first armed hold-up?

A: If I can remember, as true as I can remember, that was the first time I actually held up anybody.

. . .

Q: Yes. Your next?

A: There's quite a few other matters after that and I would have to say with some contrition that I was active as a villain at that stage but I can't particularly . . . get into them – I can't remember. There were other robberies in between that were stealing cars, stealing trucks. The next main robbery would have been another armed robbery in Wollongong.[7]

They drove back to Russ's place, swapped the plates, packed bags, left a couple of hundred with Gabby for groceries and drove through the night to Melbourne.

Over the next few days they cased truck yards in Melbourne and then Adelaide. They never found a suitable target so they ditched the blue Commodore, upgraded to a green V8 Commodore and drove back to Sydney.

•

Back in Sydney, Lindsey had a truck repossession and the driver was a subcontractor for Bill Cavanagh. He needed some intel on the target, so he turned up at Bill's yard on Jedda Road and stated his business. Bill was wary – he recognised Lindsey as Russ's mate. Lindsey kept it professional and gave no hint of his hatred for the man; it was easy to look Cavanagh straight in the eye, knowing one day his comeuppance would arrive.

Yes, Bill knew the driver and wasn't surprised that he was behind on his payments. The bloke would be back in the yard the following day. Lindsey thanked Bill Cavanagh for his time and made a note in his day book to call in again the next day to collect the rig.

The next time he was in the Stop and Rest he passed Bill on the way to the saloon bar and their eyes met again. Lindsey was about to nod hello but Bill looked up and called out to another drinker. Bill had brushed him – didn't want to be seen talking to a repo agent, apparently. *Fine, if that's the way you want to play it, you cunt.*

•

By now Lindsey was subcontracting to half a dozen agencies. Scott's Investigations liked his work and he got to know the owner, Bill Glare, a former police academy instructor. One day, over lunch, he asked Lindsey if he wanted to open and manage a new branch at Queanbeyan. Sure.

He'd be moving away from his associates – three hours down the Hume – but he didn't even hesitate. He told Liz he was going and she wanted to come too and he wasn't fussed so he took her along. They rented a townhouse in Scullin. Liz had quit the Ambulance Service but she was also a trained nurse and found work at the Queanbeyan District Hospital.

An investigations business doesn't need much office space – most of your work is on the road – so Scott's leased a one-room suite in the Queanbeyan shopping district for him and they arranged the phones and the fit-out.

A new town and his first step was to phone up his best contact in the area, one John Cavalier. They'd met several times when John was in Sydney for PI jobs.

John was an experienced operator, did jobs for a few other agencies in Canberra and Queanbeyan so he had plenty of local knowledge and a contact network to call on. He loved a long lunch and most Fridays it was down to the Pot Belly, an olde English–style pub, from noon until midnight. It was really an informal small business network with the local accountant, panel beater, printer, signwriter and brothel owner.

The signwriter's name was Peter. He and Lindsey ended up drinking together at a pub in Ainslie and he helped Lindsey with repossessions from time to time.

Early on, Peter told him about his life and the adversity he'd overcome. He'd been a specialist rigger and he'd fallen from the hook of a crane. The scaffolding he fell through broke the fall, but he still suffered horrific injuries and wasn't expected to live. He'd taken up karate during his years of rehabilitation and eventually got himself back to square one and then on to a high-ranking black belt.

Lindsey worked hard, but the turnover built up slowly. Scott's wasn't paying a retainer for him to be starting up the Queanbeyan branch for them, so money was tight. And Bill Glare had this arrogance about him which irked Lindsey, so when Scott's neglected to pay Lindsey his commission one week he was particularly annoyed.

John Cavalier worked freelance and Lindsey mentioned this problem with Scott's over a beer one night. He could almost see the clockwork turning in John's head, working out how much business Scott's were taking off his hands, and John suggested that he and Lindsey go into partnership together.

He didn't have to be asked twice and they sketched a business plan to start up their own firm. They based the business in Belconnen and John already had a business name registered, JG Investigations.

> A   We did security. Service of documents [court documents, summonses and writs] . . . missing persons, debt collection and repossessions.
>
> . . .
>
> Q67   Was that a successful business?
>
> A   Very.
>
> Q68   Right.
>
> A   . . . [It] was quite a good business . . . two guys that have been in the game a long time putting their heads together and coming up with . . . [what] I thought was a pretty winning formula.[8]

Before he locked up Scott's office for the last time he rang a twenty-four hour recorded time service and left the handset off the hook. Bill Glare would get a nice surprise when he received the phone bill – the time service he'd dialled was in California. *That'll teach the arrogant prick.*

•

Lindsey was driving back to Canberra from a job when he saw a broken down panel van with a courier logo on the side. He pulled over and the smell of the countryside hit his nostrils as he stepped out. Pungent. The driver was short, dark hair, olive skin, mid-twenties. And nervous.

The van's bonnet was up but the driver didn't know what he was looking for and Lindsey walked up – need a hand? The driver stretched his arms out with the palms up. What do you think, he said. Lindsey tried the key and the starter motor was turning over but the engine wouldn't start. He walked back around to the bonnet and then the wind shifted and it wasn't the countryside that was pungent. He realised why the driver was nervous.

'I'd be able to help you shift your load if my car was big enough. I can tell it needs to be moved because I can smell it from here,' he said.

'Any help will be much appreciated,' said the young man. The accent was Italian and he was better dressed than your average courier driver.

Lindsey had a look and found it was an electrical problem. Some temporary rewiring and the van started.

'How about I drive with you to the next town to help out if you have any trouble,' said Lindsey. The driver played it cool. 'Trouble? Bah, no need. But thank—'

Then Lindsey opened his jacket and showed him his holstered roscoe. 'It's okay, I know your business. Let me go with you in case you have more trouble with the van – that wiring might not hold up for long.' The Italian raised his eyebrows and shrugged his agreement.

They made it to the next town and a sympathetic mechanic. While they waited Lindsey learned that the Italian was from Griffith and his family was Calabrian.

Later Lindsey was told that those courier vans had the green light all over New South Wales – they could do two hundred kilometres per hour without being pulled over – but they only moved gear when *their* cops were on duty. That's why the Italian had been so nervous. He had to complete the run before the window of bribery closed.

So Lindsey was in well with one of the Calabrian families and he even got some moonlighting work out of it. They had him do a couple of break and enters and one long night he and Gunther lifted a competitor's crop from bushland off the Brindabella Road west of Canberra. Gunther was another truckie from the Stop and Rest – good mates with Joey – and he and Lindsey cleared a quarter acre of mature plants and carted the whole lot back to Griffith in the back of Gunther's brand new Scania 2-series.

There were other advantages. On his first job with John in Griffith, the local cops had pulled them over and inspected their guns, gear and licences right there on the side of the road. The purpose was clearly to annoy and humiliate and the cops then told them to 'get out of town' immediately. Lindsey proceeded down the main street into town to finish his business and then left.

If that cop had pulled me over again there might have been a dead cop in Griffith.

Soon after, the Calabrians put the word about that Lindsey and John were 'not against the family' and so the cops knew to leave them alone.

His last contact with the Calabrians came the first time he went to Long Bay. He received a message via the prison telegraph to say they would help him out with his legal fees. He never took them up on the offer. Didn't think it was right. Not after what happened to Bill Cavanagh, who he knew to have been in their employ.

•

Liz didn't appreciate the long hours – especially the road trips.

The last trip had lasted several days. He'd had a repossession at a property out near West Wyalong. The poor cocky invited him for dinner and to stay the night. It wasn't cost-effective to book a trailer or a tow truck for a full-sized header with a comb trailer so it took him all of the next morning to drive it to town on the main road at its top speed of twenty-five kilometres per hour. And after impounding the header he'd had another job in town but there was trouble. He had to skip town to avoid a ute full of angry locals. He drove to Parkes where he was booked on a flight to Sydney for a court appearance the next morning. He was giving evidence on a fraud case.

He'd made it to Parkes in time but the flight never turned up. Ansett told him it had been cancelled and no-one else was flying that day. He would be in all sorts of shit if he didn't make the court date and he couldn't even drive the rental car back to Sydney because it had already been reallocated. They had no others available and he didn't fancy giving the locals at West Wyalong another crack at him so returning there for a flight wasn't an option either.

He was still pondering his fate when a single-engine Cessna landed on the strip and taxied around to the terminal and he saw it had State Bank of NSW painted on the side. He had a chat to the pilot who was doing a cash and mail run and would be heading in the right direction in an hour or two. But there was no way he could give Lindsey a lift: company policy.

'Mate, fair enough, but would you please just check with me before you fly out again?'

Lindsey had a contact at the State Bank, their manager for realisations, and he got on the phone.

When it was time for the pilot to leave he said: 'I don't know how you did it, but I've been told to take you with me.' Eureka.

From the next airport he caught a Hazelton flight and arrived at Mascot in time for court. After that hectic week he'd returned to Liz and the townhouse in Scullin.

And there she was, carrying on: 'Where have you been and why bother even coming home at all?'

'You are not my wife and don't nag me,' he said. But Liz saw their relationship as something that he did not and her onslaught continued.

So I told her to fuck off. She took it badly, stormed out and took my car – not hers – and drove at high speed into the fountain at the front of the war memorial.

•

Lance was one of the local drinkers down at Ainslie and they were talking about money. Lance had a cousin he'd fallen out with who lived near Wollongong. Her family ran a business and kept a large amount of cash on the premises.

When Lindsey had a few jobs in the area he took a few days away and spent a few hours watching this house in Fairy Meadow and got a feel for who lived there and their movements. It was a plain brick house, single storey, but on a large corner block and with a double garage at the end of the backyard. It was a better house than most of the other ones in the street, which were mostly smaller and weatherboard.

On Tuesday, 5 October 1982 he was set to go. No-one should be home in the afternoon so he strode up to the front door and picked the lock and was in. He walked down the hallway and he'd planned to scope the whole place first, but then the woman walked out and saw him. He pulled out his gun and pointed it at her and she started to argue so he punched her in the face – hard enough to shut her up, that was all, an operational necessity. She went down and started whimpering. He told her to be quiet and walked her down the hall to a bedroom with the gun pointing at her and tied her up on the bed. Then a sock tight around her mouth so she couldn't call out.

He walked through the whole house and started looking through all the cupboards and behind furniture for a safe. He was halfway through when he heard something and there was the woman. She'd managed to wriggle her legs out of the bindings and she was nearly out the back door.

This time he whacked her with the pistol and tied her up again, tighter this time, and he found cash stashed in a desk out the back. There was nothing else worth taking. He walked out with eight grand. He'd worn gloves and he knew how to dump the stolen car and not leave anything traceable. Even though she'd seen his face, he was out of area and the police didn't have him on their radar so he was untouchable. And for every break, enter, steal he clocked a point to himself on his mental tally. One more back at the corrupt system of the world and the bent fucking cops who had tipped him over the edge.

When he got back to Canberra he walked into the Ainslie bar and gave Lance half the cash, as promised.

They stayed, drinking, and Peter the signwriter walked in with two of his truckie mates. When they saw Lindsey, one of them elbowed Peter and grinned.

'What's up, fellas?'

'Mate,' said Peter, 'have you seen Liz lately?'

'Not for months. Borrowed her car once.'

'Yeah, right. Well, I've got some news for you. I saw her at the shops on Monday and she's just had a baby. A boy. And I think we know what that means.'

'What's that, then?' Both the truckies were grinning now.

'What do you reckon? You're a daddy, Rosie.'

'Bullshit,' he shook his head. 'Is that what she said?'

'No, no, she didn't say,' said Peter. 'But think about it. You busted up in January. Baby born in September.' The truckies nodded in agreement. They'd started drinking together when he was still with Liz so they all knew her. She wasn't the most together girl he'd ever been with, but neither was she the type to have cheated on him. Surely they had the timeline wrong.

'Whatever you reckon, guys,' he said and changed the subject.

He never saw her again, so he never did find out for sure if he'd been the one who'd fathered that child.

A month later Peter and his missus had a daughter of their own and they had a little ceremony in Peter's front garden and Lindsey was her godfather.

•

How does it feel to walk into someone's house, armed, assault them and leave them there tied up and bleeding? How do you feel, for that matter, after you've walked out of a blood-splattered house, leaving the remains of two people whose lives you've ended by propelling lead projectiles into their craniums? And what of the state of mind necessary to embark on such courses of action in the first place?

I ask Lindsey. When you killed those two people, were you nervous? Was it upsetting?

Not at all, he told me. Committing those murders, it was just another job. He determined the objective, planned the operation and carried it out. Matter of fact, just like that.

So how does it feel to walk out of a house a murderer? If you're Lindsey Rose, it seems you feel nothing more than the satisfaction of a job well done.

I wonder, is that even possible? Other times he's fired up, passionate and angry about the victims who 'had it coming' and who set him on the path. But the execution of just another job . . . stone cold; in this he never wavers. How does someone end up like that?

24

Towards the end of 1982 JG Investigations was making good money – they'd been in front within weeks – but though he enjoyed the Friday long lunches with John and the gang, they were becoming any-day-of-the-week long lunches. It had been giving him the shits for a while. He felt like he was carrying a larger share of the workload and John just laughed him off. So finally he told John to stick it up his arse and left.

After nearly two years in the ACT it still didn't feel like home. He'd been talking again to Lydia – though they'd been separated for two years they'd never discussed divorce – and he rang to see how she was going. She was doing well with Honeywell, wasn't seeing anyone and had no plans for Christmas. He drove to Melbourne, wined her and dined her and on Christmas Eve they spent the night together. In the morning, Christmas Day, they agreed he'd move into her place and they'd try to patch things up.

But first he had a job to do back in Sydney.

•

Back at the Stop and Rest, Russ, Joey and his mate Gunther had been talking about it for months. Before he bought his red Kenworth, Joey had worked for Rothmans and knew that two semi-trailers full of smokes left Sydney each week: one bound for Queensland and the other for Victoria. And Joey knew a Lebanese bloke, Tony, who had contacts to offload them.

Lindsey and Russ visited the depot in South Granville.

There was a public laneway with a footpath that ran beside the fence at the back of the depot, so Russ would drive there then Lindsey would walk down the laneway and they got to know the routine. They decided the roads heading south were too busy but there was plenty of empty highway on the northern route so that was the one they'd target.

New Year's Eve, 1982, Lindsey saw that they'd started loading a prime mover – a blue Mack with a silver trailer and no insignia (to deter theft)

– and it was due to leave the next day. They came back that afternoon to check on the progress but as they turned in to the street the semi came past them and shit, they weren't ready for it. They hightailed it back to Russ's place, picked up their weapons and gear and rang Joey to let him know that they were a go and then they were off.

The Rothmans truck had a head start of more than half an hour. Lindsey would have taken the Pacific Highway, but Russ knew the truck routes and told him it would be taking the inland route out through Windsor and then up the Putty Road. They knew they wouldn't catch it before Singleton; Lindsey took them at ten over the limit through the suburbs and when they got to the highway he opened up a bit more.

They'd been driving for more than six hours and they'd had concerns all the way about the different ways they might lose it, but past Armidale they continued and then, just past a small town called Llangothlin, they saw tail-lights.

'Is that it?'

'Looks like it. Yep, that's it alright.'

The time on the dash showed half past midnight. 'Happy new year, Russ,' he said.

'Yeah, you too. Happy days.'

He called up the driver on the CB and told him they could see sparks flying off the back of his trailer.

So the blue Mack pulled over and the driver and his offsider climbed down from the truck to have a look. Russ walked up and pointed a pistol while Lindsey stood in front with his shotgun. The offsider was young, a teenager, and they ordered them both down onto the ground and tied them up. They locked the driver in the boot of the car and the young bloke – the man's nephew, they found out later – in the back of the truck's cabin. Then Russ drove the rig and Lindsey the car and they went all the way back down south to the meeting place at an abandoned property off the Putty Road.

They stopped for petrol and gave water and food to the driver and his nephew. When they got to Windsor Joey and Gunther were there with three pantechnicons. They transferred all the boxes of cigarettes into the three smaller trucks. The papers later reported that the haul was worth $600 000.

Once the transfer was complete they put the driver and his nephew in the back of the truck, drove it back out to the New England Highway and left them there, locked up, with a six-pack of beer.

Back at Windsor, Lindsey pulled over at a payphone and rang the police to let them know where the truck was parked so the man and boy could be rescued.

They still had a night's work ahead of them. They split up and took each of the smaller trucks to a prearranged destination. The cartons were unpacked and those pantechs were back on the streets doing courier work the next day. Tony looked after retail and it seemed like most of the smokes ended up in Lebanese corner shops. Lindsey's cut arrived in dribs and drabs and he'd cleared a couple of thousand when Tony and his mates were raided by the Drug Squad and that was the end of the money. Lindsey and his crew never heard from the cops about it so Tony's mob must have kept their mouths shut.

•

Two weeks later he shifted to Melbourne and in with Lydia – she was renting a little place in North Balwyn – and they warmed to each other again. He found a job as the national credit manager for a mid-sized advertising firm.

Keeping regular hours helped a little with domestic life. Then Lydia told him she thought she might be pregnant, so it wasn't such a shock when the doctor confirmed it. They hadn't been trying, but nor had they made much effort to be careful and they calculated that it must have been the Christmas Eve bonk that had done it.

They'd been enjoying each other's company and Lindsey was cautiously optimistic that things might work out and became excited about the prospect of fatherhood. He imagined that having experienced how *not* to raise a child would make him a better parent. He didn't want to think about the so-called child to Liz – couldn't imagine her coping – and he wouldn't put it past those blokes at the Ainslie to have made the whole thing up anyway.

He concentrated on his work and Lydia was working and making preparations for the baby and when Anzac Day came around Lindsey drove up to Sydney for the annual get-together with his uncles, aunts and gran and their friends the Fowlers. Lydia stayed in Melbourne.

•

Donna was the first person he noticed when he walked into the Enfield RSL. Aged seventeen, she had grown up and was a proper woman and quite a good sort now. He thought about it but quickly decided, no, she was off limits. He nodded hello and she kept to herself but soon after he looked over and she was looking upset so he went to her. In the previous eighteen months, she said, her grandfather and two of her uncles had all been diagnosed with cancer, had surgery and treatment and died anyway. And now her mother had been diagnosed and been given less than six months to live.

For hours they talked and she cried and tried to make sense of the world.

'If you accept that she's going to die and let her accept it as well, she'll have no hope,' he said. 'She's young enough. Be positive, make her feel positive and she'll have a chance to recover.'

'How can— I'm losing everyone around me. I cry every night. How can I act all happy when I see Mum and how sick she is?'

'Compartmentalisation,' he said. 'Put the bad thoughts in a box and file it. How do you think an ambulance officer can treat someone in agony, maimed, possibly dying? You need to compartmentalise your emotional response so you can do your job and actually help them.'

By the end of the afternoon Donna's spirits had lifted and she promised she would try to do what he'd said.

•

On 2 May he turned twenty-eight and he put his hand on Lydia's tummy and the baby kicked with such ferocity that they laughed and joked that it was Godzilla hiding in there. The nickname stuck for the rest of the pregnancy.

But Lydia was a little anxious and it set her on edge and that set Lindsey on edge. One day he was in the backyard repairing the lawnmower. He was good with small engines and he had the mower in pieces when Lydia came out and started haranguing him for something else that she thought he should be doing. She's walked out just to start a fight, he decided, and he gave her the warning. The next day she started on him again, so he packed a bag, loaded up the box trailer and drove back to Sydney.

He moved into a safe-house, his unit in Campsie. He'd cultivated it over the years and built a shadow identity, Gary Rose, with a driver's licence, passport, Medicare card, insurance and he'd even rented a TV so Gary Rose would have a record on the database of the Credit Reference Association.

> I was working on a black bag job for the next three months. I can't tell you what it was or someone is going to get in trouble.

•

If he was in the area he'd visit his gran at her flat in Burwood. Uncle Max had moved in with her now. The other uncles had taken to drinking at the Burwood Hotel and it had gradually become his local too. So after he'd seen Gran he'd wander down, just a block down Burwood Road. Sometimes Morris, Walter, Stanley and Maxie would all be there.

So it felt like home and he resumed taking on jobs for Mark Lewis at Pierce Investigations. And all the while thoughts about Lydia and the baby ran through his head. He wanted to have this child in his life and he kept trying to figure out what he should do. Three months later he was still in this funk about it and if the baby came early enough he could miss the birth. So he drove back to Melbourne and moved back in with Lydia. He wanted to stick around for the birth and help out afterwards. He didn't tell her that it wasn't going to work out between them.

In mid-September Lydia's waters broke on the hallway carpet and Lindsey told her, joking, that was a dumb place for it and later they had to replace the carpet after it had soaked for a day in amniotic fluid. The baby was born at the Francis Perry Women's Hospital, only two kilometres north of the Melbourne CBD, a little girl. Lindsey had delivered other people's babies in the backs of cars and once on a kitchen floor so it wasn't a novelty but he cut the cord and looked into his daughter's slow blinking eyes. Finally in this pointless corrupt world there was something worthwhile.

Penny was healthy and slept the right amount and she melted their hearts. But it wasn't enough to mend the relationship. They had no support network in Melbourne so they decided the three of them would move back to Lydia's house in Bexley. Once they were settled there, he told Lydia, he'd move out for good.

So on a late spring day they sat together in the courtyard of their North Balwyn cottage having breakfast while Grace Brothers Removals packed up their house and Penny, only two months old, slept in her bassinet.

Back in Sydney it took a while to unpack everything and then there was some extra maintenance to do around the house. He enjoyed the time with his daughter and he and Lydia weren't intimate, but they'd arrived at a kind of unspoken truce – there were still flare-ups but they tended to fizzle out fairly quickly now. The right time to move out never seemed to arrive, so he stayed. Lydia didn't complain – Lindsey was paying the bills.

He ran into an old colleague and started picking up jobs from WatchGuard at North Sydney to supplement the income he earned from Mark Lewis's contracts.

•

He was parked uphill from a target's premises typing up his reports for the night. He had a wooden board that he'd shaped to slot into the glove box and the portable typewriter sat on the board and that way he made the best use of wait-time. Repossessions were usually done after hours and on a good night he could get through twenty reports this way.

He'd completed half a dozen reports when a gold LTD drove past and his eyes lit up.

Custom Credit at Homebush was a regular client and Lindsey used to take the manager, Barney, out to lunch once a month. A gold LTD had been missing for more than a year, had more than four thousand dollars owing and was on the books of three different agencies.

He checked the registration number and sure enough it was Custom Credit's missing LTD – the Holy Grail of repos. He threw the typewriter and paperwork into the back seat and set off in pursuit. He followed the car to a shopping centre car park in Hurstville.

He broke in, picked the ignition and he was gone. He wasn't far from his own house now so he parked the LTD there; he could collect his own car the following day.

The next morning he organised lunch with Barney and picked him up in the LTD. Didn't bat an eye. In the restaurant they sat at a table near a window and during lunch Lindsey asked how much an agent would expect to receive if that fabled gold LTD was ever recovered. It was a big number for those days – more than a grand. Lindsey pointed out the window to the car they'd arrived in and watched the penny drop and fuck did he laugh.

Barney paid for lunch that day and eventually he was promoted to regional director. Lindsey was his lead agent for that area – from Homebush to the Victorian border – and eventually he earned thousands on Custom Credit jobs, all on account of the gold LTD that he'd only acquired by luck.

•

Now that he was back in Sydney he went out to Mount Pritchard to have a beer with Russ. Lindsey was shocked at what he saw. Russ had never fully recovered from the bashing and that extended stay in hospital. He was running off the rails – driving again but taking more pills, hanging around with drug dealers – and when Lindsey saw the state of him it made him furious at Bill Cavanagh all over again. He realised that he had unfinished business to attend to.

25

'This is the most I've written for years,' he writes at the end of one letter, more than thirty pages long. 'More than I write to my lady friend.'

So at the next visit I ask about this lady friend and he tells me some more about Donna and that's when I first learn about the Fowlers and their Anzac Day ritual at the Enfield RSL.

In May 1998 he was in Long Bay, awaiting trial, and a letter arrived. He hadn't received mail from anyone other than his lawyer since he'd been arrested the year before, but he was only mildly curious until he saw that it was from Donna.

He tried to remember the last time he'd seen her. It had probably been an Anzac Day at the Enfield RSL club – must be ten years ago, when he was waiting for charges in Queensland to be finalised. She'd been with her new husband, the one they all hated. Lindsey could spot a problem a mile away and Donna's new marriage fit the bill. Her father Jim had been opposed to the marriage – he came right out and said it to Lindsey while they waited at the bar for their beers to be pulled. Lindsey offered to take care of the guy, but Jim declined. He obviously thought he meant to rough him up a bit, but Lindsey had had something else in mind.

What must Donna think of him now? He opened the letter, half expecting hate mail. Nothing could've been further from the truth.

Donna's mum had just died. After that day at the Enfield RSL, when they'd talked about the cancer diagnosis, Donna had suspended her studies, supported her mother, told her what Lindsey had said and after months of painful treatment she came out the other side and was happy and well for another fourteen years beyond the six months she'd been expected to live. But in February they'd found the cancer in her liver and within weeks she was gone.

Two hours before she died, Donna and her mum were in the back of an ambulance.

'Lindsey was a paramedic,' she said.

'I know, Mum.'

'I wish he was here,' she said.

'Oh, God, me too,' said Donna.

'Do you know where he is?'

'You know where he is, Mum. He's in gaol.'

'Yes, but *where?* Which gaol?'

Donna didn't know.

'But you still think about him, don't you? I mean, remember all the nice things about him?'

'Yes, Mum, I think he's the best friend I ever had. He looked after us,' said Donna.

'That's right. Well, go find him then, baby. Stuff what anyone else thinks, go find him and when you do, give him a hug for me.'

She'd written it right there in the letter. Two hours later her mum was dead. Liver failure and she'd bled out and gone into cardiac arrest. They'd tried to resuscitate her with the defibrillator and the room at the A&E had been showered with her blood. But before that awful finish, her thoughts had been of Lindsey.

He put the letter down and tried to control his emotions. His cellmate was watching him.

'Read this.'

The cellmate sat there reading, cocky at first, then poring over it, his fingers arched over his brow. Finally his face creased and the tears began to flow and now Lindsey could let go and he was sobbing too. As he wrote back to Donna the next day: 'so there we were, two tough guys in gaol, crying over a letter!' He also wrote that the staff in casualty should never have offered resus or let Donna and her father witness their beloved bleed out in front of them. If he'd been there – and he'd done it with complete strangers – he would have removed them from the room whether they'd wanted to go or not.

26

Bill Cavanagh rates a couple of mentions in Bob Bottom's book *Shadow of Shame: How the Mafia Got Away with the Murder of Donald Mackay.*[9] Apparently the police investigators received information that Bill Cavanagh, alias Bill Collins, was involved with the Calabrian mafia including the notorious drug lord Robert Trimbole. The Calabrian mafia were found by the Woodward Royal Commission to have commissioned the hit on anti-drugs campaigner Donald Mackay, who was killed in July 1977. And Mackay's widow received a letter from a woman who believed that 'Collins' was the driver for a three-man team that murdered Mackay. Bottom found no record in the police running sheets to say that the allegation about Collins was investigated.

•

It was guys like Cavanagh who made the world the unfair place that it was, decided Lindsey; the place where the little guy always got screwed over. Why not make the world a better place?

He looked through the *Trading Post* that Sunday night, rang a few sellers until he got the right vibe and made arrangements to visit the next day.

Now he had a plan in train the anger left him, all of it converted into this trajectory from which he would not be diverted, and he felt calm, in control. Just another job.

•

He'd picked up a medium-term contract in credit control with Lindeman's Wines which had a factory and offices at Lidcombe. Lydia was working at Lidcombe too, so for a few months they'd had a routine. Each day they'd drop Penny at the babysitter in Homebush. Then Lindsey would drop Lydia at work, drive up the road to Lindeman's, and the reverse in the evenings.

This particular day, though, he did the drop-offs then rang his office to say he'd be out all day. Then he drove out to Camden to buy the .22

calibre rifle. It wasn't the cheapest or the safest way to acquire a weapon, but it was about the easiest and he wasn't in the mood to muck around. He checked it out on the spot and the firing pin seemed to be lined up okay which was the main thing and he offered the full price. He held up his gun licence, still folded up, and the seller waved him away so he drove out with the rifle, anonymous.

He'd brought a box of .22 cartridges with him so he pulled over a kilometre down the road and walked out into the bush and fired a couple of rounds into a tree. It worked fine.

Hoxton Park wasn't too far off his route home so he drove along Cotteril Avenue and scouted for an observation post for the Cavanagh property. The whole area was semi-rural and no-one just parked their cars beside the road so he kept driving past Bill's house and had a look at the cars in Bill's front yard. He pulled up over the next rise to look at his street directory and decided there was no suitable vantage point. He'd be better off tailing Cavanagh from work or from the pub.

He drove back to Bexley and locked up his rifle in the back shed. It was still too early to pick up Lydia, so he decided, for a change, to pick up Penny from the babysitter's first. When he arrived, he was ushered inside and found the house to be well-appointed. He'd never been inside; Lydia had always gone in. And there was his daughter, in a bouncer, surrounded by Lebanese kids who were running around happily and speaking Arabic. He didn't have much time for Lebs as a rule – loud, arrogant and bloody crooks half of them – but Lydia had convinced him these ones were okay.

He was offered a Lebanese coffee – the strong one in a tiny cup – and he did enjoy a strong coffee and he had time to spare so he sat and had coffee with this lady. As they chatted he looked around the room and there were three degrees on the wall. Wow. And when he looked they all belonged to this lady – her husband's degrees were hung in his office. And when the husband got home he was wearing a three-piece suit – wow.

Later he realised how stupid and parochial he had been to make assumptions about this family that was looking after his daughter. These were absolutely wonderful, gentle, educated people. Not like regular Lebs, he thought.

•

When Penny and Lydia had gone to bed he went out to the shed to shorten up the rifle. The barrel came off with the hacksaw and he took a few inches off the butt as well. Now it would fit nicely into a small carry bag.

The next day he told Lydia that she could keep the car for the day and on her way to work she dropped him near Rockdale station – Lindsey and his carry bag. The commuter car park near the station was an easy target and he was on the road in a Cortina within minutes. It wouldn't be reported stolen until the evening so he drove to Lidcombe and did a normal day's work with Lindeman's. Then he drove the forty-five minutes to Hoxton Park and picked up Bill's trail. Bill left work at 5 p.m. and stayed at the Stop and Rest until about 9 p.m., when he drove home.

The next stop for Lindsey was a workshop in Bankstown. An old mate had left the key out and Lindsey let himself in, fired up the lathe and machined a silencer for the rifle.

Q127   OK. And how did the silencer attach to the firearm itself?

A   In engineering parlance it's called interference fit. In other words it just slid on but it was such a close tolerance it hasn't slipped on the end of the barrel, it adhered to [it].[10]

Then he drove the Cortina back east – past midnight now – and just for a laugh he parked it back in the same commuter car park in Rockdale, walked for ten minutes down the Princes Highway towards Kogarah and hailed a taxi to take him home.

•

It wasn't until the weekend that he got a chance to retest the rifle.

Q145   Well can you remember how it went?

A   It worked well. It fired. That's what I wanted it for, the projectile come out and I don't know whether it . . . I think I fired at a tree stump or something and I noticed that the projectile was tumbling when it actually hit the target.

Q150   Would you have regarded it still as a usable firearm?

A   Yes.

Q151   And would you still regard it as being dangerous?

A   Definitely.

Q152   Okay. Now you said you made the silencer, how did you get the background to be able to do that?

A   From my trade as a fitter and machinist.

Q153   Okay. Was it hard to make?

A   Simple.

Q154   Right. What were the ingredients, what did you, how, what did you make it from?

A   Metal, would have had a screw cap on the front and inside the silencer I put, I would've put leather as the medium to slow up the sound.

. . .

Q156   Okay, and was that successful once you put the silencer on this rifle?

A   To a degree, it took away about eighty-five per cent of the noise.

•

His gran had bought her meat from the same butcher for more than a decade. It was just inside the front entrance of Burwood Plaza and Lindsey bought his meat there too. Opposite the entrance to the shop was a green public payphone which Lindsey would use for sensitive calls. Or he'd give out the number to undesirables – if the undesirable had connections and traced the number back to source, all they'd have was a public phone in a shopping centre.

The butcher knew he was a PI with the cover name John Bishop and he would take messages and ring them through to Lindsey's home or office. Whenever Lindsey paid for his meat there'd be a little bit extra for the answering service and at Christmas he'd buy the butcher a hamper for his family.

On his way through Burwood he stopped at the green payphone opposite the butcher's in Burwood Plaza and he rang Peter the signwriter in Canberra. They had discussed Cavanagh before and he'd told Peter:

one day I want to go around there and rob that fucking cunt. So Lindsey spoke to Peter and asked after his god-daughter, who was a little sweetie. She was fine because Peter looked after her well even though he had to do it by himself because the mother 'was a rat' and had gone off with some other bloke. Lindsey told him that now he had the equipment ready to do that job they'd discussed and for the right price Peter agreed to help.

•

More trips to Hoxton Park ensued.

A   I went to see what time he left the local pub, what time he got home and who else was in the house and what was going on there.

. . .

Q168 Okay, and what was the reason for that?

A   Just to see where he went, what time he went, if he, if he frequented any other places, just to . . . a general check on his movements.

Q169 But why did you want to know what his movements were?

A   So I could shoot him.

. . . then he rang Peter again and told him the date.

•

Peter flew in from Canberra on the morning of 20 January 1984 with a return ticket. Lindsey picked him up from Mascot in his own car, a white 1967 Valiant Pacer, bearing a set of unregistered number plates that he'd acquired on the quiet from a wrecker's yard. He reimbursed Peter for the airfare and paid him the agreed sum for the job. Peter was still skinny. He had fair, collar-length, wavy hair and he was only about five foot seven but he was tough and he could be trusted. It was eleven in the morning and it was another hot, midsummer day. They drove west and Lindsey started to talk to Peter about where his thinking was at with this job . . .

Q204 Okay so where did you go next?

A   Can't remember. I know we didn't drink so we didn't go to the pub. I can't remember.

Q205 Okay, you seem very specific that you didn't drink. Why do you say it like that?

A Well there's no way that I'd be drinking alcohol if I was going to do what I intended to do.

Q206 Why is that?

A I think that's pretty obvious . . . you don't know what you're doing if you're drunk, y'know.

They stopped at a takeaway shop and ate hamburgers and drank cold Cokes and he told Peter the rest of the plan. The next stop was his mate's workshop at Campbelltown. Lindsey pulled out his cut-down rifle and checked the action, attached the silencer and loaded it with a full magazine. And he had a .32 for back-up. He loaded this one as well and holstered it against his ankle, under his jeans.

He had surgical gloves for Peter and himself and he had a few tools and his Maglite in case he needed to break in and he rechecked them and packed them so he could walk straight from the car into Bill's place when they got there.

Cavanagh's house was brick with a big front yard. There were steps up to the verandah and there were glass sliding doors as well as a wooden front door. They parked out the front and all was quiet at the house so Lindsey took the loaded rifle and they walked up the front steps to the front door. It was open so they walked right in.

A young woman walked out into the living room. It was Carmelita. He'd met her briefly once, when he'd been to interview Bill, but he had no idea she lived there – such a young girl, early twenties, with this old bloke in his late fifties – so it just hadn't occurred to him that she might be there in the house. She was wearing a towel. She recognised his face and there was no hiding the rifle so it was going to be a problem. Lindsey pointed the rifle at her and guided her to the bedroom. He pulled the phone out of the wall and he tied her up on the bed with the telephone cord, wrists and ankles.

She was panicking at the sight of the gun and being naked with these two men and she started breathing fast and talking fast and half of it was Filipino and even what she said in English he couldn't understand and he didn't care. She wasn't calling out but she was still making noise so he tied a gag around her mouth to shut her up. Lindsey told Peter to stand out of sight until Bill arrived home.

They waited, standing. Ten minutes passed and they calmed down from the shock of seeing the girl and Lindsey thought Cavanagh would probably have spare cash stashed somewhere in the house. So they started going through the house for anything of value. They messed it up as they went and then a phone rang – there was another handset in the front room. They looked at each other and checked on Carmelita and let it ring out.

27

Our correspondence touches on criminal psychology and Lindsey's had some medical training from his Ambulance Service days so he's no novice – he knows more than I – and he's quite willing to step outside himself.

Aug 2008:
You implied that I was using the Ambulance Service as an excuse. A catalyst, yes, but not an excuse. Reluctance on my part, in the past, to be open and frank stemmed from me not wanting to appear to be making excuses. If you form the opinion that I am making excuses then you are going to miss the essence of what I am trying to communicate to you and my new open and frank disposition will be fruitless. If you are intending to analyse my psychopathic behaviour you will need to take a leap of faith and believe me when I say I'm not making excuses, merely trying to explain why I lost social responsibility.

I could, at this juncture, attempt to explain away my psychosis by saying I'm mentally disturbed: I've been diagnosed by a forensic psychiatrist and that's the end of it. But is it? Did I wake up one morning in 1984 a psychopath, get a rifle, manufacture a silencer, drive out to Hoxton Park and kill Bill Cavanagh because I woke up a psychopath? I think not.

Was I always a psychopath, say from birth? I think not. Then when did I become psychotic?

As you well know I am not qualified to comment on this subject as an expert (psychiatrist) however I am qualified as a psychotic.

There are different levels of psychotic behaviour, even us psychos know this and even categorise ourselves – though this can only be done when one is banged up with other psychos. Ha ha.

Was Wade Frankum [Strathfield massacre] a martyr, a psychopath, misunderstood? Are the hundreds and hundreds of people (myself included) so far out of the norm? I think not. Us so-called psychopaths and our psychopathic behaviour at its different levels is becoming rife in our society. Youths who commit suicide, if not for the suicide, would become a candidate for the list below: murder-suicide, murder.

You have different levels of psychopathic behaviour and it manifests itself in different ways:

Category 1: The criminal. He seeks gratification and so robs and steals and batters and kills if it will help get him what he wants.

Category 2: The mental breakdown guy. This guy is beaten down to the point where his synapses go faulty and he falls into a deep hole. Some climb out of the hole, but most, even if they give the appearance of normality, are never the same and their life is ruined. The bastards have won.

Category 3: The suicide guy. This person is weak. They have had enough but they don't have the fortitude to go on. The bastards have won again.

Suicides, murder-suicides, murderers all had something in common: they couldn't take it anymore.

Category 4: The murder-suicide. This guy has had enough but has a strong personality and is going to kill the bastards first.

Category 5: The murderer, the strongest personality. Sure of his convictions and those bastards are going to pay. If I kill myself, they win and I will not let them win at any cost. Life in gaol, it doesn't matter, he suicided in his own way.

Category 6: The terrorist. They aren't so different to the other groups, just they are an organised group of people sick and tired of being downtrodden. It wasn't even about religion, that's just a prop to hang it on. They are led by some form of organiser who selects the mission for each individual. Thus, the weaker is selected for simply suicide; walk up and push the plunger. Stronger might fly an aeroplane into a building, while the strongest are reserved for ongoing missions.

And in amongst the categories is the loner. No amount of intel can find this ticking time bomb and he is the most feared as he can pop up anywhere, any time and commit the next massacre.

The police contribute to this as well as the judiciary. The level of corruption is unbelievable. To Mr Straighty 180 it does not exist, but exist it does. It flourishes.

28

Half an hour of waiting and Peter calls out and Lindsey takes a position in the hallway. Bill Cavanagh comes up the stairs and he steps inside the front door carrying two jars of oysters. When he sees Lindsey standing down the hallway with a rifle he stops. Lindsey aims at him and tells him to put down the jars but Bill is too slow for his liking and he just fires and the first shot gets him in the middle of the forehead, virtually between the eyes, and Bill goes down. One of the jars of oysters smashes and the other one rolls away and then Bill's lying on the floor. Lindsey's treated gunshot victims as an ambo and here was another one but he was the one who'd done it and now he'd really done it and look what the bastard made me do and everything is a blur.

They're in the bedroom and Bill is there so he's dragged him in here and you can't leave a man like that, because Bill is making this sound . . . and more shots and then there's yelling, where is the money, no-money-no-money and the girl is on the bed and more shots . . .

Q303 When you shot Carmelita, what was your intention?

A   My intention was to shoot her so she couldn't identify me.

Q304 And were you aware that shooting her the way you did that she might die.

A   Yes.

Q305 Was that your intention?

A   Yes.

. . . there must be money here somewhere. There's a desk with a roll-top and he shoots out the lock and Peter rips it open and it's a fucking organ and they can't stay much longer . . . and he's storming, throwing things. Bill's Chevy C20 ute is parked on the front lawn and they check it for cash too but still nothing. Then they're in the car and going down the road and he gets his breath and his focus. Already the memory of what they've done is jerky and spastic and he wishes he could go and ask the person who'd done it what had happened.

Q442   Okay now you said you drove slowly and carefully, why was that?

A   Well I'd just committed a murder and I didn't want to exceed the speed limit, be pulled over by a traffic policeman, so I drove on the speed limit and concentrated on what I was doing.

Peter chain-smoked and passed lit cigarettes to Lindsey as he drove them wordlessly down the Hume Highway and back to the workshop at Campbelltown. It didn't take long to switch the plates back to his legit set and the old plates went on the floor of the Valiant. They removed and bagged the clothes they were wearing and changed into fresh ones.

He'd filled up with petrol at the start of the day so it should be a straight run to the airport. Back north past Hoxton Park again, Newbridge Road and right down Henry Lawson Drive and they stopped at two different council bins and offloaded bags of soiled clothes along the way. In the dark the traffic was light and even though Canterbury Road might have been faster he knew this way best. On Stoney Creek Road he'd pass within two kilometres of Austral Street, Penshurst where his daughter, little Penny, four months old, was with her mother and most of the family because they were celebrating Lydia's mother's birthday.

Just past Padstow Heights they crossed Salt Pan Creek and the left lane was close to the edge and the railing was low. There were no cars in sight so he slowed to a crawl and Peter threw the licence plates and then the shortened rifle out over the dark water. The night was still warm and they got a whiff of the cooler air coming off the water and Lindsey drove on.

They arrived at the Domestic Terminal two hours and seventy kilometres after Hoxton Park. Lindsey stayed in the car, told him thanks heaps, mate, then Peter was gone.

Half an hour later, after a shower back at home, he drove back to Penshurst. He kissed Lydia on the cheek, wished her mother a happy birthday and poured himself a glass of red wine.

CM: Lydia remembers you being at the party. But after all that driving, surely it was well past midnight by the time you got there?

LR: DO NOT believe what Lydia tells you. No party took place.

29

In my local library I find a book titled *A Mind to Crime*.[11] The authors, Anne Moir and David Jessel, performed a meta-study of research papers relating to brain chemistry and crime.

That roughly 90 per cent of crime is committed by men is suggested as evidence of biology at work – men have different hormones to women. Androgens – the so-called male hormones, of which testosterone is one – are blamed.

High levels of androgens can allow for high achievement through ruthlessness and single-mindedness. Too much can result in antisocial, aggressive, destructive behaviour.

Adrenaline is discussed: most of us would be too terrified to rob a bank, or even start a fistfight, because adrenaline kicks in and we feel overstimulated, anxious, nauseous. The 'alarm bell' of adrenaline fails to ring in the violent criminal.

I write to Lindsey about these theories and he doesn't fall over himself to agree but he does concede some recognition in his own circumstances.

> You say 'surely it must be something biological.' I agree, which manifests itself psychologically, different in some people to the next – reference to my comment that all us psychos are not the same.

Moir and Jessel also push a barrow about criminal responsibility: if criminality falls from a chemical imbalance in the brain then is medical treatment more appropriate than incarceration? I am seduced by the proposition and for too long my research goes down that path – only later do I realise I wanted to find a defensible 'excuse' for the behaviour of such people (for Lindsey). But – other than for diminished responsibility due to a forensically scheduled mental illness – there is no excuse. For at the end of every 'blame my brain' argument lies the same dead end, the same wall – the wall saying that free will is a thing.

30

He walked in to the Stop and Rest and when he saw Russ he nodded. He went to the bar and bought a beer for the both of them and he kept a straight face right up until he sat down and said it to him. 'Job done, son,' he said.

'Nice work, Rosie,' said Russ. He smiled and clapped a hand on his shoulder. They drank on together into the night. The buzz was still going in the pub with the news that Bill had been shot – a lot of people hated his guts and weren't so disappointed about it. As for the girl who'd been killed along with him. Well. It didn't really come up.

The Bill Cavanagh murder dropped off his radar soon enough. He heard the cops interviewed all and sundry, but Lindsey's name never came up so it looked like he was in the clear.

Relations with Lydia had continued in the holding pattern. The contract at Lindeman's finished and he was still taking PI jobs and now he was also going to UTS – working towards an engineering diploma. And he was renovating Lydia's house, mostly at night. The wallpapering was finished. He was preparing the floor for sanding, on his hands and knees, knocking the nail-heads down to avoid ripping the paper on the sander. Eventually he was down on his stomach; he hadn't had a full night's sleep for weeks and the next thing he knew it was 7.30 the next morning and Lydia was looking down at him with Penny, six months old, on her hip. He looked up from the floor with a deep pattern of floor boards across his cheek. Penny was frowning at him, befuddled.

'The engine in my truck is on the way out,' Russ said.

'Get a new one. I'll help you put it in if you like,' said Lindsey.

'I can't afford it and I can't get another loan.'

'Okay, I've got a better idea.'

He'd done work for this mob who did engineering and truck hire and they'd always had Volvos. He'd thought their security was a bit ordinary, so they hatched a plan. They'd take a Volvo prime mover from this joint – Eric Newham Holdings at North Ryde – and get a new engine for Russ.

•

Bolt cutters got the front gate open and his picks got them into the office where it wasn't hard to find the key to the N12. Russ led and Lindsey followed in the stolen rig and they had a safe spot pre-planned, out past Badgerys Creek. Far from prying eyes they swapped the number plates and removed the signage then they drove on to a farm down the south side of Brisbane, mates of Russ. They swapped out Russ's worn-out engine for this new one and upgraded the tyres and they were pretty pleased with themselves when they fired her up and all systems were go.

Russ's mates stripped what was left. There was a small earthmover on the property and it was half a day's work to dig a big enough hole to hold the chassis and they buried it.

•

He didn't like to bring his work home with him so Lydia rarely knew anything about the jobs he was doing (legal or otherwise). Mark Lewis won a security contract for the Royal Easter Show and a few of the agents lived on the south side so for them it was a long day to drive between West Ryde and Moore Park at the start and end of shift to check their weapons in and out. Bexley was much easier for everyone so Lindsey kept the weapons and the register at home and at the end of each day the agents would come to his house and he'd sign the weapons back into the register and secure them.

Q50   OK, are you able to give me an example of some of the firearms that you possessed during that period?

A   Fifteen shot Parabellum, .357 revolvers, .38 revolvers, five shot revolvers that were worn on ankle holsters and also small calibre automatics which I believe were .32s, I can't quite remember the brand of the weapon. Also Webleys ... At one stage when I was doing patrol I had a 12 gauge shotgun which I had locked by padlock into a bracket beside the seat of my car which is my personal car fitted with radios and doing security patrol work and I carried this shotgun as a backup.[12]

Halfway through the contract, a weekend, Lydia screamed out 'What the fuck is all this?' and he raced into the bedroom. She'd been putting the washing away and found the cache of weapons where he'd 'secured' them: in the sock drawer.

Lydia was working again now and looking after the baby as well and exhaustion set in. Finding weapons in the sock drawer didn't improve her mood and she was fed up with the sight of his mates. Russ was living in Brisbane and driving the Brisbane–Sydney route. He would drive on pills for a week non-stop then sometimes crash at their place, the spare bed, and sleep for two days straight. And if Russ needed a car, he would drop them all off in their car, run his errands and then pick them all up at the end of the day. One day Russ was in the back room when Lydia came out and she ended up screaming in his face, so he just packed up his truck and left.

Lindsey ran a few more operations with Russ, including a factory break-in, and one night they filled a car-carrier with brand new Commodores from the GMH holding yard at Pagewood. But Russ was getting ratty and unreliable – too much speed – and then they argued about Gunther.

Lindsey had warned Russ to be careful. Russ was involved with a speed operation and Gunther was in on it too. Even though Gunther had held up his end alright on the Rothmans job, Lindsey thought he was a risk. He wasn't strong and Lindsey thought he could be turned by the police. One day Russ was delivering to Paddy's Markets and dropped a pallet through the floor of his truck. It took him an hour to patch it up, then he drove around to visit one of the dealers. The cops had just raided the house and Gunther was standing next to a cop car with his arms folded while everyone else was in handcuffs. Russ kept driving. He had a kilo of speed in the cabin of his truck. 'Boy, you got lucky,' Lindsey said. 'I told you Gunther was a dog.'

Russ tried to argue that it didn't prove anything – that Gunther was just standing there. It didn't matter to Lindsey whether Russ really believed that, or just didn't want to admit he was wrong; Lindsey was jack of him, and they never spoke again.

31

At 11 a.m. he received a page to contact an Alexander, Brisbane area code. He knew the name and trawled the memory banks. That's it, he was a solicitor – he'd booked Lindsey for jobs in the past. He rang straight away. Alexander's client's daughter had been snatched, apparently at the behest of the ex-wife. The Federal Police were involved but the client didn't think they'd get a result and would he fly straight up and take on the job?

It would be a pain in the arse as he'd have to rearrange other jobs, but Alexander was a real pro and Lindsey was flattered to be asked ahead of every PI in Brisbane. He couldn't say no.

He was only twenty minutes from Mascot and he had a go-bag in the boot so the only thing he was missing was his pistol. It was locked in the safe, half an hour away, and he couldn't get it on a plane without an interstate permit, which would take too long. Leave it. Straight to the domestic terminal, booked a flight and he just had time to ring a couple of sub-agents to take over his other contracts. Flight to Brisbane, taxi to Redcliffe and he was at the client's address by 2 p.m.

Police cars, marked and unmarked, and a crime scene van were parked along the street. As he paid the cabbie a federal agent, senior constable, walked up.

'Can I ask who you are and your business here?' he said.

'I'd like to speak to the senior officer in charge,' Lindsey said. The constable straightened up but then smirked when he saw Lindsey's business card. A private investigator, ha, the smirk said. And from Sydney.

'I'll pass on your card,' he said, eyeing Lindsey's tailored suit. 'For whatever that's worth.'

Ten minutes later a well-built man in his fifties stormed out the front door, yelling. This was the client, Ray, and he was apoplectic after hearing that Lindsey had been kept waiting. He threatened to throw the Feds out of his house before he calmed down and showed Lindsey inside.

The place was a mess – huge holes in walls, smashed furniture, blood-stained ornaments. There had been a serious fight and people had gone crashing through gyprock walls.

Lindsey reinterviewed each witness: Ray, his wife, their housekeeper and the driver/gardener. The staff wore well-pressed livery. Ray had made money in carpet then a fortune in real estate. He was also connected, judging by some of the high-profile names he'd dropped when he was threatening the Feds with eviction. That must be why the Feds were involved in what would normally be a straightforward matter for the state cops.

The stories all lined up. Two men had kicked in the front door, assaulted the client and his wife and taken the kid – a seven-year-old girl. Both burly and with broad Australian accents. One five foot eight, the other six one. Jeans and long-sleeved shirts. On a February day in Brisbane.

Ray was on his second marriage; the child was from his first marriage and he had sole custody on account of the mother's drug habit. The ex-wife had remarried a man named Hughes who was operations manager for a trucking firm in Kingaroy. That might go towards explaining the long sleeves – all the witnesses remembered them. Lindsey made a bet with himself that the two kidnappers were truckies and the long sleeves were to cover tattoos.

He spoke to the officer in charge. Maybe they could set up a liaison protocol. No dice, the officer said. The Feds had a non-disclosure policy on operational matters. The usual shit. He just nodded and walked away.

He was given a photo of the girl – cute blonde thing she was – and her mother. Ray, his wife and the help were taken to the police station to look through mug shots and Lindsey made some phone calls. He had a list of suspects that needed checking out and he couldn't do all the searches himself. He hired a car and visited his mate Gavin. Gavin was a cop, worked at the Brisbane watch-house in the city.

Even though the ex-wife was the obvious suspect, he had to tick all the boxes and there could have been inside help so that meant checks on the housekeeper, driver, pool cleaner, lawn-mower, cook and, of particular interest, a nanny who had quit just a few weeks earlier.

Gavin started running checks on his police computer while Lindsey kicked off his own searches on the phone. He'd need help with some of the legwork so he rang Chris Manne, a PI he'd worked with before. He left Chris with a list of names and instructions for searches to be performed on each of them.

In between phone calls he ducked up to the top floor of the watch-house – to the bar.

The next morning he was in Ray's Cessna 210, flown by Ray's pilot, on his way to Kingaroy and the last known address of Ray's ex-wife. North-west, half an hour flight time, and he could see the whole town on approach.

He signed up for a hire car at the airport and they assigned him a Datsun 280B. No good if he had to keep up with someone, but it was all they had.

First stop was the local police station. It was a block back from the main drag, but from the front lawn he could still see the massive peanut silos. Kingaroy, the peanut capital of Australia.

'My name's Lindsey Rose and I'm in town investigating a kidnapping,' he said to the desk sergeant, handing over his ID.

The sergeant nodded when he read the private investigator's licence. 'Welcome to Kingaroy. I don't believe we've ever had an investigator introduce himself here at the station,' he said.

'First time I've had a job in Kingaroy. I always present myself at the local station when I'm in a new jurisdiction. Makes life a bit easier for everyone if the local police know I'm active in their bailiwick.' More to the point, if the shit hit the fan the local sergeant was likely to get mighty pissed off if he discovered there was a surveillance operation happening in his town. Better to have him on-side from the start.

The sergeant offered to help and Lindsey told him the story and the sergeant pulled up the ex-wife's file and verified her home address, work address, car rego and criminal record.

'I've had a couple of calls from HQ about this one,' said the sergeant.

'Yeah, thought as much,' Lindsey said. 'The Feds are on the case as well. They're stonewalling me, though.'

'Don't worry, son. If you need any help, just give me a call,' said the sergeant.

The home address was a large block on the north side of town. The neighbours ran tidy five-acre blocks but the Hughes property was a mess – car bodies, truck parts and rubbish everywhere. Lindsey parked out the front in view of the neighbouring houses and stood gazing intently at the property. Then he went to his car and fiddled about, slammed the boot and walked down to the homestead. The front door was open, the shed doors were open and it was clearly abandoned. He made a big racket knocking on the open door, calling out and standing right back scratching his head and looking – as if they might be hiding on the roof – and soon enough one of the neighbours was watering her front garden, rubbernecking.

He waved hello with a smile and walked over for a chat.

Oh, yes, she knew Hughes and there was no love lost. Always with the noisy machines and his truck driving in and out and he was vulgar as all get-out too. And that's when they weren't having parties that went all night and into the next day and she thought there might even be druggies there.

Lindsey looked around the yard and the shed and there were boxes for spare parts, old parts and invoices. From the oil and air filter boxes it was apparent that Hughes was working a Kenworth K124 and doing all his own servicing on the property. There was no truck registered to Hughes in Queensland so he made a note in his day book to check the motor registries in New South Wales, Victoria and South Australia.

The next stop was Hughes's work address, Inglis Transport.

'Yep, he used to work here. I think he had a blue with the boss. He just stopped turning up. Yep, a white Kenworth.'

The ex-wife's work address was McKechnie's music store in town.

'Who's asking?'

'It's a private matter, but I'd just like to speak with her. I'm an authorised inquiry agent. Here's my ID. Is she in?'

'What's it to you?' The music store manager had his arms crossed now.

'Like I say, it's a confidential matter, and as a duly authorised representative—'

'Oy, are you listening to me Mr Private Eye? What's. It. To. You?'

'Sir, you'll be wanting to lower your voice or we're going to have a problem.'

The manager blustered a little longer, and even though the fight had gone out of him he still wasn't going to provide any intel.

'Thank you for your time – sir.'

He checked into a motel and made some calls. The other PI, Chris Manne, had interviewed some of the other hired help and turned up nothing untoward. Lindsey rang sub-agents in Sydney and asked them to use their interstate contacts to try to find where the Kenworth was registered.

In the evening he took his darts to the local pub and joined in a game. He trod lightly but the information came easily. They knew Hughes, alright. He wasn't well liked and a couple of the drinkers thought he was dangerous. No-one had heard about the kidnapping.

Next stop, the RSL club and he bought a beer for the local sergeant but learned nothing new.

Kingaroy was a bust. He made a final call to Ray's pilot and arranged to be picked up the next morning and flown back to Brisbane.

In Brisbane a contact got him access to credit histories for Hughes and his wife. They'd had loans with Custom Credit but none of them related to the Kenworth. He must have paid cash for it and this profile he was building said Hughes was probably doing illegal runs.

He rang Barney – Barney of the fabled gold LTD – in Custom Credit's head office in Sydney and made arrangements to see copies of the paperwork for Hughes's loan. It was an old PI trick that the cops didn't know about – the loan applications had names of referees and witnesses.

He narrowed it down to two live leads. One was an address in the Sydney suburb of Berala, the other in Cootamundra – another country town, this one four hours' drive south-west of Sydney. It was thin but his sub-agents hadn't turned up a registration for the Kenworth and he had little more to go on.

So Ray's pilot flew him in to Bankstown and he hired a car.

The Berala address was dead so he hit the highway and drove through to Cootamundra non-stop. The property was out of town and it was the ex-wife's aunt who opened the door and invited him in for a cup of tea. She wouldn't hear a word until he was comfortably seated on the back verandah and the tea and scones had been served.

'A bit of a lost soul, that one,' said the aunt. 'I haven't heard from her for, oh, not since before her cousin Josephine was married so that would be, let me think . . . Eighty-two, it was. So more than three years now I'm afraid.' And the address she gave he already had so he enjoyed the tea and the vista, which was dusty green pastures and thinly scattered gums into distant low hills, and he had run out of leads.

The white Kenworth was still his best bet and his mind turned to the years he'd spent repairing trucks. He'd known the workshop foreman at Kenworth Trucks, Homebush.

Back to town, payphone and Kenworth had the same foreman. Sure, he'd help look for this Hughes gentleman on the computer. He came back on the line and said that for two years Hughes had had parts delivered to the Kingaroy address but there was a new address for the most recent order. Bingo! The new address was in Griffith – a rural property to the south, closer to Darlington Point.

He hightailed it to Griffith in two hours. It was the one town where he would not be visiting the cop shop to make his presence known. The Griffith detectives were as bent as shit and even though he had the blessing of the Calabrians, he didn't want to risk them stamping all over his case or alerting the target.

He found the property without tipping his hand and hid his car off-road a mile distant. He changed into his camo gear, loaded up, walked into range then crawled the last eight or nine metres to his chosen lay-up position – slightly elevated, in scrub with cover. He could see the rear yard and there was a sedan parked at the side but no Kenworth and no movement. He swept with binoculars every ten minutes and he sweated through the afternoon and still nothing moved.

Night fell and he only had nuts and beef jerky to eat so he tossed up whether to come back in the morning but decided he'd come this far and he'd stick it out overnight. The house was dark and it was quiet in the scrub so he'd hear anyone coming and going. He dozed in fits and starts until the pre-dawn light came.

Now he intensified his focus. Anyone who'd slept at the homestead had gone to bed early and would likely be up early. He didn't have to wait long. A woman came out to hang washing on the line and there was a small blonde girl at her feet playing with a kitten. He followed them closely through the binoculars until he was sure.

Stiff as he was, it was a slow crawl out and a long walk back to his car. He drove to a roadhouse at Darlington Point and made the calls.

The Feds arrived inside of two hours and he gave them a briefing then the Special Ops team raided the house, arrested Ray's ex-wife and recovered the girl. Hughes wasn't on the property, nor, it would seem, anywhere in Griffith. A female agent took custody of the girl and after several phone calls they let the family pilot take them both to Redcliffe and he was done.

•

He'd been away for nearly two weeks and he'd only contacted Lydia twice: once to say that he'd be gone for a few days and another from the airport in Brisbane on his way home. When he returned to Bexley the reception was chilly.

'You like the pay cheques but not me working the hours. Make up your mind,' he said.

'Oh bullshit, Rosie. How hard is it to pick up the phone for five minutes and let us know you're still alive?'

'Like you give a shit. Besides, I was on a sensitive operation. We rescued a little girl who'd been—'

'What about your own fucking daughter?' Lydia interrupted. 'Hmm? Your own no-father only child? What about her?'

That throb began in the base of his skull and he grabbed at the most hurtful thing he could think of: 'Well, now you mention it, actually, she's not my only child,' and he threw it in her face, told her that he'd fathered a son with Liz when he'd lived with her in Canberra.

'Oh, I'd be surprised if that were true. Surprised if you could even get it up for that slag.'

•

Three days later he flew back to Brisbane with his invoice and a written report of the operation and he debriefed Ray, his wife and the solicitor, Alexander. The girl had settled back in just fine, smiles all round. Ray put a little extra on the cheque and Alexander had some news.

Hughes had been arrested by Victorian police on his way back north in the white Kenworth. The police found a hidden compartment in the Kenworth's fuel tank. So Hughes, operating out of Griffith in an SA-registered truck, must have been transporting hooch for the Calabrians. Lindsey was glad he'd kept a low profile on his way out of Griffith – that was one conflict of interest best kept under wraps.

It was only a short drive to his parents' house and he picked up a cinnamon bun for his mum on the way. Bill Rose, his Pa, was home as well and it was no surprise to them for Lindsey to turn up unannounced so they put on the coffee and sat on the front verandah and Glenda smoked her menthols between slices of bun.

They talked family updates. Her sister, Lindsey's Aunt Stella, had married a GP and Glenda thought she was a stuck-up bitch for marrying beyond her station and now their mother – Lindsey's gran, Ethel – had bequeathed all of her jewellery to Stella. The Dulux plant was going to close and it looked like Max and Stanley would be out of a job and Morris's drinking was getting worse and he'd been hospitalised for a few days with some stomach problem that sounded to Lindsey like pancreatitis.

But she spoke in a lullaby cadence, telling these well-practised anecdotes. She walked back inside to fetch some biscuits midway through a story and when she came back out she was on the next one so she'd obviously kept up the patter while out of the room with no audience.

Lindsey looked across at Pa, who was studying his coffee dregs, and his mum's voice blended in with the background noise of hot buzzing insects and distant traffic and she sat back down and stopped talking and the next cigarette burned away in the ashtray untouched.

He excused himself and did the bathroom cupboard inspection and this time there was diazepam as well as the temazepam. Right there in front of her, he asked Bill how many a day she was popping and he said he didn't know but it was all prescribed by a doctor so he assumed it was okay – she was a lot less volatile now than in the old days. Lindsey thought back to the despotic Glenda of his childhood and looked now at this aging woman prattling away, stupefied by pills, and they were not the same person. His feelings for her now were as for an unwanted child: no love, but a responsibility that he would not shirk.

Lindsey shook his head. 'You're addicted to these things, Mum. You've got to try to get yourself off them. Pa, take her to a different doctor – she needs treatment for this.' And that sparked up Glenda.

'You can't take my pills away from me. I get these cramps and headaches if I don't take them so they keep me well.' He knew those were withdrawal symptoms she was describing and his suspicions were confirmed.

'An overdose could easily kill her,' he said to Pa after Glenda left the room and Bill agreed to do something about it. Lindsey wasn't optimistic but he had to let it go as he had business in Sydney to attend to.

32

Now that I've turned back from the 'blame my brain' blind alley, my reading goes mainstream. It is the psychology that draws me. What contortion of the mind leads one person down the path but not another? And I still haven't reconciled the Lindsey I knew (and now the Lindsey who appears to have been a competent professional in multiple disciplines) with this cold-blooded killer.

I am way down the curve and when I stumble across the *Diagnostic and Statistical Manual of Mental Disorders* (DSM)[13] I need to do more reading just to understand its significance. The DSM is published by the American Psychiatric Association and it defines disorders of the mind with labels and categories to be applied by the psychiatric profession.

Psychology seems to use a similar but slightly different set of labels and it feels important to understand the difference – to have a basic grasp of these fields – before I can begin to understand where Lindsey fits in these categories and diagnoses. I need help.

I approach the University of Wollongong. Dr Mitch Byrne, an expert in clinical and forensic psychology, kindly gives me his time, a targeted overview and a reading list of foundation texts (criminal psychology 101). When I describe Lindsey's 'career', he talks to me about psychopathy and describes it as a spectrum along which all of us lie. Based on the scant evidence I've provided he guesses that Lindsey is quite high on the spectrum. He gently quizzes me, asks after my own mental well-being, then (apparently satisfied) he offers some words of caution: 'He's not your friend; he's most likely using you to further his own interests. Be wary. For example, he might want to get back at someone and you shouldn't help him do so.' It's a confronting idea and I am tempted to disagree, but I thank him and we move on.

At the end of the hour I leave with scribbled notes, the reading list and a new question that needs an answer: is Lindsey Rose a psychopath?

33

Lindsey sat at the bar working on his case files at The Oaks in Neutral Bay. It was a short drive from North Sydney and he could usually find a park among the hordes of BMWs and Mercs. It became a habit to sit at the end of the bar next to the red phone. He drank OJ while he worked. The bar staff were used to him and they didn't mind the twenty dollars he gave each of them for taking messages for John Bishop.

His pager beeped. It was Mark Lewis and when he rang back, Mark had that tone in his voice.

'Rosie, I've got this job for you. Repo on a truck.'

They'd recently had a falling out. He hadn't taken Mark's calls while he was away on the Kingaroy job and Mark had blown his cool. Lindsey told him to shut up or he'd belt him and Mark sacked him on the spot. It wasn't the first time and it only ever lasted until Mark got desperate enough to call on him again.

'I don't have time for it, Mark. I've got jobs on with three other agencies. What other agents have stamped all over your repo, anyway?' If an incompetent agent had tipped off the hirer it could mean a protracted investigation – or mission impossible.

'Rosie . . . Rosie, no-one's been on it. I told Citicorp I'd have the truck in their yard by Monday morning and my other agent's bunked off. You'll give us a hand, won'tcha?'

Scott's Investigations had the Citicorp contract, but sometimes finance companies liked to try out other agencies. Mark must be trying to win a contract, which was why he'd overpromised on this job. Dickhead. Lindsey checked his watch. It was 10.30 a.m. He made Mark promise that he'd be paid immediately, took the details and rang off. A three-tonne flatbed in Five Dock.

Lindsey rang his contact at Citicorp and gleaned a few more personal details about the hirer. A few phone calls later he knew where the hirer worked and the address in Drummoyne. He drove straight over and the truck was parked outside. He disabled it, rang the heavy-duty towie and while he waited he typed up the report.

The towie was close and the truck was ready to roll and he was up Victoria Road to West Ryde in ten minutes and dropped the report on Mark's desk at 12.08 p.m. – an hour and a half after the job had been issued. 'I'll have that cheque now, thanks,' he said.

Mark flipped through the report, read the costs on the last page and wrote out a cheque.

'I have some other jobs on the books—' he began.

'Mark, I'm still not over our last bust-up. It's payroll today and I have to submit invoices this afternoon. Can't help you.' Fuck him.

•

He got back to Bexley after midnight and the next morning Lydia was at him. Barely awake and she was hassling him for getting into bed reeking of smoke and booze and he snapped. He slapped her – as hard as he could – and she was holding Penny in her arms and *oh, that was hard,* and Lydia started to go and he grabbed Penny before she could fall and sure enough Lydia lost consciousness and her head caught the corner of the bedside table on the way to the floor.

He put Penny down – she was screaming – so he could move Lydia onto the bed in the recovery position and she was already coming around. He picked up Penny again and comforted her and told her everything was alright and she calmed down for him as Lydia gained her bearings. Lydia was sitting up on the bed and her face was split from the blow and there was another gash from the bedside table so there was blood. She was simply stunned. It was the first time he'd ever seen her lost for words.

He found a cloth to press to the wounds and considered his position. She'd pissed him off so much that he'd slapped and injured her. Clearly, things had gone too far. It was time to leave for good.

He collected his clothes and loaded them into his four-wheel drive. And when that was full he hitched his box trailer to the back and loaded up more clothes and his tools until it was full too. Lydia followed him around the house asking how he could do this to her and then just leave her there, bleeding, but she knew that once he'd made up his mind there was no stopping him. Lydia and Penny watched him and he said no more than six words to them that whole time so he could focus on the job at hand. It needed to be done because the decision had been made.

Two hours later he finally left them there crying, and Penny – he just couldn't look at her.

•

Lydia, with the makeshift compress bound to her head, packed a suitcase for herself and a bag for Penny and drove to the hospital. After they'd sewn up her head with twenty-seven stitches, they stayed the night at a women's refuge. Just in case he came back.

34

He and Craig walked up concrete stairs to someone's unit for the poker game. He'd moved in with Craig, one of the other senior agents at WatchGuard, after he'd moved out of Lydia's. Most of the attendees were other WatchGuard agents or cops who were on the payroll. Craig was the organiser and Lindsey had been attending for a few weeks now.

There was chat and beer before the game started and when he sat, the detective sergeant from a North Shore station was sitting opposite with that fat head of his.

There were two types of serving police seen at a mercantile agency. The first were detectives who'd put in some extra hours between their shifts – the agencies used them for legwork to help out the more experienced agents. They were straight cops trying to make a few extra bucks to get ahead and, even though moonlighting was officially banned, they generally got away with it.

The other type were only ever seen on payday, collecting cheques made out to cash. These were the bent detectives. The problem for your bent cop was that he made a lot of extra money and he wanted to buy nice things: a flash car, overseas holidays or a better house than a cop's salary would warrant. But unexplained spending was what Internal Affairs looked out for, so that was a problem. One solution was to let it be known that you were moonlighting for a mercantile agency. Get on the payroll, do the occasional job, and IA were likely to leave you alone.

The detective sergeant with the fat head was in the latter category and he drove around in a late-model Mercedes and thought he was bulletproof. The game was raucous so colourful banter was the norm but Lindsey didn't think 'North Shore' was in a position to be as lippy as he was and he seemed to serve it up to Lindsey more than most. A fortnight earlier he'd told North Shore at the end of a hand, 'I'm sick of listening to your shit,' and walked out the door.

But he'd returned anyway – the game was enjoyable and the conversations were wide and varied and he'd gained contacts and sometimes a few tricky cases were solved along the way. A senior solicitor had attended one game and a lot of his clients were property developers.

'You would have done better when Landa was the minister, wouldn't you?'

'Actually, no. Landa was pretty clean,' said the solicitor.

'Bullshit, they've started an inquiry. They reckon he was taking pay-offs for land releases hand over fist.'

'Nope. He was done in because he was about to expose Wran over a Landcom fraud.'

'Done in? He had a heart attack playing tennis, didn't he?'

'Heart attack? Yeah, brought on by a dose of poison. The police knew to look the other way. Craig can tell you. You knew the officer leading the investigation, didn't you?'

Craig nodded then shrugged. 'Well, it wasn't so much an investigation as—'

'Exactly.'

But this week the conversation was more mundane and they were discussing the payment of tips. Sometimes an agent would receive a cash bonus – a wad of canary notes on the side – after a wealthy client had a good result. It reminded Lindsey of another perk of the job.

'I was repossessing a car on the northern beaches and the woman who answered the door was dressed for the beach and she was a stunner. I kept it professional, but she invited me in to talk it over and then she offered me a drink and I knew it was on.'

The other players were tuned in while the next hand was being dealt.

'Well, we had a few drinks and one thing led to another. Mate, was she a good root. Anyway, I stayed the night and when I woke up she was still asleep and there was her car key right there on the bench.'

'You didn't!'

'Oh yes, I did. Well, I thought about it for one second. She was a nice bird, blah, blah, blah, but I had a job to do. So I made a hundred bucks on the repo and got a night of nookie along with it.'

As the laughter subsided, the detective sergeant spoke up.

'Hey, Rosie, I heard when it came to sex you were usually the one who was paying.'

No pause – he flipped the card table and he was going to wipe that shit-eating grin off North Shore's face once and for all. He got in a few good punches before the other players grabbed him. North Shore was out the door and running down the stairs and Lindsey felt the grip on his arms loosen, shook them off and gave chase. He caught up quickly and launched himself from a landing, tackled the guy on the stairs and pounded his head into the concrete floor. The other players pulled him off again and marched him up to the unit in a full nelson and okay, fellas, he said, it was all over now.

They sat Lindsey in the kitchen and gave him a scotch then the detective was carried in and *Oh, shit, he's a mess* and someone called an ambulance.

Pounding his head against the concrete had done the most damage and he needed pressure on a haemorrhaging wound and Lindsey asked the owner of the unit for a first-aid kit and some ice for the largest haematoma.

He applied the basic first aid, wishing now that he hadn't done quite so much damage – the detective's head was like a busted melon – and when the ambulance arrived Lindsey stood quietly in the corner until they were done.

So for a week they called him Rocky until he told them to knock it off or cop a fat lip or worse and at the next poker game the North Shore detective was absent and Craig announced that he wouldn't be back.

After that night of violence, the poker game introduced a new rule – all pistols were locked in the safe until the end of the game. Lindsey imagined the consequences if he'd been arrested that night – he'd been carrying his unlicensed Beretta 9 mm.

•

North Sydney was short-lived and he found his own place at Cammeray. He'd been shagging Cathy for a few months and, more recently, Fleur and Narelle on the side. They'd all been to the house at Cammeray and it was getting complicated – he'd had to usher Fleur out the back door when Narelle came knocking and Cathy didn't know about the other two.

So after only three months he gave up Cammeray and moved with Cathy into a leafy unit at Wollstonecraft, right on Shirley Road. Fleur and Narelle didn't get the new address but he kept them on the backburner until one of the agents at Pierce Investigations asked him to come along to this swingers' club he went to in Surry Hills. It sounded pretty sleazy but eventually he relented.

'Okay, it's fifty dollars a head, booze included. But you can't turn up without a bird.'

So he rang and left messages for Fleur and Narelle and to his surprise they both said yes and his mate's eyes lit up – sure, bring them both, even better.

So, a group of five, they arrived at a nondescript office building and took the lift to the eighth floor and walked the stairs up to the penthouse and were introduced to the German couple who ran the place. The fit-out was luxurious, a bit more classy than he'd expected, and they were led to change rooms and everyone walked out with a towel on and nothing else and most of the other patrons just walked around naked. There was a bar and lounges and a spa room and other rooms with wall-sized screens running videos. They sat on a couch with their drinks and there was a couple screwing on the next couch, another pair in the spa and on the floor nearby was a threesome in progress. Well, it was a bit of a laugh and Fleur and Narelle were both into it so it became a monthly habit.

•

What involvement did Lindsey have with his daughter while all this was going on? Lindsey told me very little. Partly it's because he's protective of her privacy (he never forgets I'm writing a book), but eventually I conclude that he didn't see as much of her childhood as he might have liked so there are not so many stories to tell. One story he does tell me supports that conclusion.

He claims that he went to pick up Penny for a visit and when he arrived she was on the front steps crying. Her mother had upset her. Eventually, Lindsey told me, he rang Lydia up to tell her: 'I'm going to ring back in six months and give you time to stop all this bullshit.' She had no way to contact him and six months later (diarised) he rang again to ask if she was 'over the bullshit'. She started to give him grief so he yelled, 'Speak to you in another six months' and slammed the phone down. Another six months passed and he rang again. This time, according to Lindsey, Lydia begged him not to hang up and he resumed visits with his daughter.

I don't bother to say again 'to spite your face' because I already know what he'd say: he had to teach Lydia a lesson, no matter the cost.

35

He'd first met Alan Thomas in the saloon bar of the Burwood Hotel.

Lindsey had seen him around and assumed he was a cop. One evening he was drinking with his uncles Stanley and Maxie when Thomas walked in with a group of civilians. Lindsey struck up a conversation. Detective Sergeant Alan Thomas worked in the Fraud Squad out of the Remington building on Liverpool Street in the city and he liked a drink and a punt. He also taught karate up at the Masonic Hall and the civilians he'd walked in to drink with were his students. Lindsey wanted to know more about the karate and then Alan was full of questions about the jujitsu and judo that Lindsey knew because it was quite different from karate. By the end of the night they'd arranged for Lindsey to come to Alan's next karate class.

After a couple of classes Alan showed them how a knife-hand strike – more commonly known as a karate chop – could be used as a potent weapon in unarmed combat. Lindsey started calling him Choppie.

So Lindsey had another drinking companion, a cop, and he would ask Alan for advice on some of his legal matters. At first it was basic stuff like speeding fines but as the trust grew he'd ask Alan's advice if there'd been some argy-bargy on a repossession and how the cops might look upon certain situations.

And one afternoon he was caught by police after breaking into a factory yard in Smithfield. He couldn't tell them who his client was and he was about to be charged with break and enter.

He kept his mouth shut until he could get Alan on the line and Choppie came to the rescue. He'd been at home and he'd had to drive across town so he wasn't happy. But he spoke to the local detectives and after a brief negotiation they showed Lindsey the door with no further questions asked. It cost him a gorilla.

When they got to know each other better, Choppie introduced him to some of his cop mates and told them Lindsey was like 'one of them' and Lindsey had already worked out that they were happy to have a bob each way. They were friendly with an agriculturalist and sometimes one of them drove bags of pot into Sydney in the boot of his patrol car.

•

Lindsey was pulling in about a hundred grand a year: half from WatchGuard and the rest from XD Investigations, Pierce Investigations and private clients. That went a long way in 1985 but it was never about the money and when he had it he spent it. And if there was a black bag job, or some other kind of illicit earn, he'd go along with it even though he didn't need the money. It was something to do.

•

A client wanted intel on a solicitor's intentions for the handling of a corporate case. Lindsey donned a grey dustcoat and a Telecom ID badge and walked straight into the building when the solicitor was out for lunch. He spent a few minutes in the comms room with a handset, for show, then went to the target's office.

Hard-wired microphones were always the best as they avoided the need to regain entry to change batteries. Battery operated bugs also had the problem of moving off frequency when the weather changed or when components heated up and expanded. But if there was no other power source you had no choice and with a battery-powered mike you had more options for hiding the bug so he'd sometimes go that way anyway – especially if he had routine access to change the batteries.

He quickly scanned the room and there was a suitable power supply so it was one listening device installed inside the double-sided power point near the desk and the other into the telephone handset.

The listening post was in an office across the road and he set up two scanners. One was tuned in to the frequency of his bugs; the other scanned all frequencies. It was a trick he'd been shown, to keep an ear out for other signals. If he picked up a signal from the same premises on a different frequency, he'd know someone else was listening.

It was common to encounter agents working for the other side. On one operation the target had employed his own agents and Lindsey was tailing them. Of course, those agents had a second team who were tailing Lindsey and Lindsey's second team were tailing their second team. Lindsey rang one of the opposing agents who was working for McGrath Mercantile in Carlingford and they met over a beer. It was farcical, he said, these four teams of agents tailing each other around the city. So they cooked up a scheme whereby the target's agents dropped off and Lindsey would give them enough of the information to satisfy their client and he could gather intel on the target unimpeded.

But there were no other agents under his feet for the job listening in to that solicitor's office. The listening post was set up with voice-activated tapes, the bugs did the trick and the client had his ill-gotten intel. Another successful black bag job: no invoice, just a legal yellow envelope full of high denomination banknotes.

•

He arrived at West Ryde to pick up some jobs from Mark Lewis. One of them was a fax from Tim Bristow's agency: a car repossession that Bristow didn't have the manpower for. He called up Bristow's office and clarified the details. The client had recently separated from her husband, name of Butler, but he was short of cash so had gone and pinched her car. The agency had checked the legals and they were clear to take back the car. She knew where he lived so it might be an easy lift.

He rang to put his preferred tow-truck outfit on standby and drove around to her old fella's place. It was early afternoon and there was the car parked right in the driveway. He rang the towie first, walked over, slipped the bonnet and removed the rotor button.

The tow arrived in half an hour and this was usually the tricky part – a hirer would often be alerted by the sound of the truck hooking up, or the winch, and reactions ranged from weeping to violence.

This time it was the latter. Out he came in a blue singlet with the smoke still lit in his mouth. Lindsey stood between Butler and the car so the towie could get on with his work.

'Why don't you fuck off, ya fucken scabs,' said Butler.

'Mr Butler, we are authorised—' started Lindsey, but he was drowned out by indecipherable abuse. He squared his shoulders, raised a finger in front of Butler and tried again.

'I am authorised to remove this vehicle. If you have an issue with that, I'd be happy to call the police and wait for them to come over and sort it out. Of course, no guarantee they won't want to charge you with car theft, I suppose.' He stood with his arms crossed as Butler walked towards him and pulled back his fist sharply as if he was going to swing. Lindsey didn't flinch. Butler grimaced. He could see Lindsey was tough enough to take him, but he needed to save face. So he shoved Lindsey hard in the shoulder – hard enough to force a backwards step. 'Prick,' he said.

Lindsey smiled. 'You don't want to do that, Mr Butler,' he said, and started walking towards Butler then feinted forward at speed. Butler nearly tripped over in his haste to back away. He slunk back to his house with an eye over his shoulder, shouting filth the whole way. Just another day on the job.

The car looked worse for wear so Lindsey asked the towie to stop at a servo on the way back to the client's address. He added air to the tyres, topped up the water and checked the oil. Then he used the payphone there to ring the local cops and log the righteous repossession – standard procedure in case Butler tried to call up and claim he'd been robbed. It was nearly dark when he got the car back to the client. She was grateful, quite timid and living by herself. Now that she had her car back she was going to drive back to her hometown, Yamba, and try to get her life back together.

He asked where she'd be staying then rang the cops in Yamba and explained the situation and asked them to keep an eye on the place in case the husband came for her. It was a small town and the cop he spoke to knew the family so he was satisfied that she'd be looked after.

He felt sorry for the lady so he billed her $200 – of which $50 went to the towie – which was the minimum he could have charged for the time and effort. But because it was a subcontracted job, Bristow's firm took a commission and the next day Lindsey was in Mark's office and Bristow was on the phone.

'What's your game, Rose? You trying it on, are you?' said Bristow. Lindsey immediately knew what Bristow was thinking – that he'd faxed him back a fake invoice to justify holding back some of the cut. No point playing dumb. Bristow was sharp, but he was also under pressure, awaiting trial on charges of conspiring with bent cops to supply Indian hemp,[14] and it was all over the news.

'Mr Bristow, the lady's had a hard time and the job was pretty clean so $200 was all I billed the client. You can ring her yourself and check if you like,' he said.

'Well, *Mister* Rose, while you're trying to get your dick wet, I'm trying to run a business. What you billed is way below par and I haven't even covered costs getting that client and farming out the job to you clowns. You're a joke, Rose. What business do you think you're in, hey?' said Bristow, booming down the phone. Lindsey paused. Bristow was mates with crime boss Lenny McPherson, had done time for assault and been involved in all manner of high-profile investigations. He was a pretty hard man, but Lindsey didn't think he was quite so hard as he would have people believe when he named his boat *The See You Off Club*.

'Have a go at me, will you, Bristow,' he yelled back down the phone. 'What are you going to do, break my arms and legs? Hey?' Then he slammed down the receiver, fetched and holstered his pistol and drove around to Bristow's offices at Dee Why.

The drive – half an hour driving fast and tight – did nothing to calm him down. He double-parked out the front, walked right in past reception, saw an open door and there was Bristow behind a desk in his office and Lindsey recognised a cop, off-duty, lounging in a chair to the side.

'You'd be advised to clear off if you don't want to get your fucking head blown off,' he said to the cop, with his hand inside his sports jacket. The cop didn't need to be asked twice and slowly pulled himself up out of the chair and showed his palms as he slipped out the door.

Lindsey turned to Bristow. 'Okay, here I am,' he said. 'You've got a problem with me, so come on, let's have it.' Bristow was sitting in his chair with his hands flat on the table, stock still, and Lindsey realised that as he'd been waving his hands around he'd pulled his hand out of his jacket with the pistol in it.

To Big Tim's credit, he kept it cool. He was no stranger to having a gun pointed at him, but Lindsey's antics had certainly focussed his attention. Some of the colour had drained from his face, but still he spoke in a steady voice. 'Mr Rose ...' he paused. 'Mr Rose, thank you for dropping by. I'm just trying to run a business here. There is no profit for me going after sub-agents. Let's just call this matter a misunderstanding, shall we?'

Lindsey pointed the gun at Bristow's face and said nothing. He could see Bristow resisting the temptation, just, to duck out of the way. No doubt he had his own revolver within easy reach, in his desk or on his person, but Lindsey thought he had Bristow's measure. He lowered his weapon, holstered it, turned his back, stopped to straighten his jacket, then walked out the door without saying a word. When he got back to his car he pictured Bristow, looking all of his fifty-odd years, still sitting at his desk with a face like the skin off burnt milk.

CM: By chance I spotted Tim Bristow's biography in the second-hand bookshop and bought it. I'll let you know if you rated a mention.

LR: Bristow would probably not have remembered me. The only way he was going to was if he continued to stand over me. Then he would have got the Bill Cavanagh treatment and remembering me would have been a moot point.

Years later he discovered that he and Tim Bristow had something in common. Lindsey did some time on the door at the Manly Pacific and word got around and one late evening the owner, Andrew Kalajzich, offered him the hit on his wife. According to his biography, Bristow received the same offer. Both declined. Perhaps they both discerned Kalajzich's lack of discretion. He finally engaged a hitman via the friend of a friend. When the hitman pulled out, one of the intermediaries decided to do it himself, despite having no experience with firearms, and was finally successful after five aborted attempts. Andrew Kalajzich served twenty-five years for the murder of his wife, Megan Kalajzich, shot in bed as he lay beside her.

36

At the State Library I spend two days gutting some of the criminal psychology texts recommended by Mitch Byrne at the University of Wollongong. I'm still coming to grips with the overall field – what causes some people to become criminal – and there's a tipping point where I start to see the same threads appearing in disparate material.

Since the eighteenth century the prevailing theory for understanding the cause of criminality has veered back and forth between 'nature' and 'nurture'. Psychological theories have now come to the fore. They include those of Freud but are dominated more recently by the work of Hans Eysenck, who argued that people were more likely to perform criminal acts if they had high scores in the personality traits which he labelled psychoticism, extraversion or neuroticism.

Eysenck is confident that genetic factors contribute more than half of the risk of an individual becoming a criminal, but it is the interplay between biological and environmental factors that determines the overall risk. It is a surprise to me that genetics plays such a large role – but there have been large-scale studies involving twins separated at birth which makes the case compelling. I think back to Lindsey's mother, when she tried to run over Morrie Pinfield in a murderous rage, and it feels like a piece of the puzzle has fallen into place.

37

Lindsey saw his mum just after Christmas. She was still in the grip of prescription drugs and he was pissed off that Pa wasn't dealing with his mother's addiction; someone had to sort it out and no-one else would if he didn't. Seven years as a private inquiry agent, he was at the top of his game and he had no worries about finding work if he moved to Brisbane. The only reason he hesitated was his daughter, Penny. It had been more than two years since he'd left Lydia and only in the last few months had Penny started having sleep-overs again. Every two or three weeks he'd collect her and spend a day and a night with her and he made a point of planning the day each time so he'd take her somewhere fun, memorable. She was a forthright three-year-old and he enjoyed their time together now that he had this little person he could have a conversation with.

He would be in Sydney once a month anyway, he decided, so he packed up the flat at Wollstonecraft and moved in with Mum and Pa. Their little house was near the beach on Elizabeth Avenue, Clontarf, half an hour out of Brisbane. The weatherboard was white and the roof tiles were red, like just about every other house in the street.

Within a week he had a list of all the local GPs and chemists – and a couple further afield – that Glenda had been patronising and when she refused to listen to him he brought out the list and threatened that if she didn't let him manage her medication he'd drive around to every provider in the area to make sure she was cut off, and he meant it. He couldn't watch her all the time and knew it could take years to wean her off the pills, but this was the first step. He had a management plan in his head and started her off with a dosage that was only one level below what he estimated she was on. Slowly, slowly, to start with.

He had contacts in Brisbane from various jobs that had crossed the border north and he did a lot of driving that first week, visiting all his contacts and trying to organise some work. Things were 'a bit quiet' and he took it at face value at first, but after three weeks of getting the same answer he began to suspect that he was being fed a line. He spoke to Barry, one of the other agents from XD Investigations, and described what was happening.

'You're being stonewalled in sleepy hollow,' said Barry, laughing. The Brisbane operators liked to keep things local, he said. It was a much smaller market than Sydney and plenty of NSW ex-police preferred the climate in Brisbane for their retirement job. They probably didn't want Lindsey encroaching on their turf.

He thought back to his beginnings. Rather than present himself as an experienced investigator, he'd start again at the bottom and ask around for some humble summons work. Fidelity Investigations handed him seventeen outstanding summonses and, when he reviewed the case files, they'd all been around the traps. He'd copped the too-hard basket. It took him weeks and he barely covered his costs, but he successfully served sixteen of the summonses. The seventeenth target had died.

He wasn't covering his living expenses so he was on the phone to his Sydney contacts and when he'd booked enough jobs he drove down. He could still earn $2000 in a good week that way, compared to the $200 a week he was making in Brisbane.

On his next trip to Sydney he was delivering a repossessed vehicle to Rossmore, only ten minutes west of Hoxton Park where he'd shot Bill Cavanagh. The owner of one of the mercantile agencies ran fifty-odd greyhounds there and he also used the property as a holding yard for cars.

There was activity in the shed. A mechanic he knew was restamping the compliance plates on a stolen BMW – and he was botching it. Lindsey showed him how to chock up the wheel with a block of wood, bypassing the shocks, to get a clean imprint. He'd never done it before – it was just common sense.

Lindsey soon joined the enterprise. They'd buy a few wrecks, preferably late-model, and obliterate the compliance plates after making note of the VINs, months of manufacture and colour of the plates. Lindsey would have a shopping list with him wherever he went and if he encountered a matching vehicle he'd take it on the spot or make a note and come for it later.

Once a car had been 'fixed' with the details from the matching wreck he'd acquire legitimate plates and put an ad in the newspaper: private sale. He sold enough cars to keep him in beer and cigarettes.

'Rosie, we have got to get hold of some extra money,' Mark said. Mark's cash-flow management was flaky at the best of times and he needed to pay for repairs and new equipment.

'So what's new?' said Lindsey. 'Dunno how you've stayed out of bankruptcy this long.'

'Look, you know we've been talking about robbing some joint? Well—'

'You mean, do I remember the fifty thousand times you've hassled me about it in the last three months?'

'Yeah, yeah, shut it. I know this retired bookie, Bill Graf. He owns half of West Ryde. He's got to have cash stashed in his house. Why don't you knock it off?' Lindsey gave him the look, over the top of his spectacles. Mark must have forgotten that he'd introduced him to Bill Graf a few years earlier and they'd met once or twice since. Mark and Graf were both members of the Chamber of Commerce, Lindsey thought they were friends, even.

'Come on, Rosie, if I go down, you'll be on the bones of your arse yourself before too long.'

'Hmph. No chance.'

'Rosie, I need this job done for me. Look at this.' And Mark started scrawling directions on a notepad. He ripped off the page and turned it over.

'And here's what it looks like at the front. Anyway, you can't miss the flagpole, I think it's the only one in the street. He's old, he's had a stroke and he's hard of hearing. Do it one night after he goes to bed and he won't hear a thing. Easy.'

Lindsey gazed out the window, trying to make it clear he wasn't interested. But he knew what a persistent bastard Mark was and he knew they'd be blueing over it eventually and he'd probably sack him yet again and frankly he was fed up with that circus.

'At least go check it out, Rosie. Go on,' said Mark.

'Not likely,' said Lindsey.

Graf's house was a five-minute drive.

•

It was ten in the morning and he parked across the road and the frontage more or less matched the sketch Mark had drawn. Blond brick and all the fittings were white: window frames and security grills, two balconies with wrought iron railings, front fence and gate, even the flagpole, flying a fading Australian flag. Quite a plain house for a rich bloke, but big. A double garage on the left plus two storeys above that and the house took up the whole width of the block. Furthest right was a tiled walkway, slightly elevated, with more white wrought iron rails. It looked more like a small block of units than a house.

Even though he was only a block back from Marsden Road, there was practically no passing traffic and it was quiet. All the houses in the vicinity were behind trees, fences or hedges. So Mark reckoned Graf was half-deaf . . . Getting in would be a piece of cake. But in a big house it'd be hard to find a safe. He could come back tonight and bug the place. He remembered the day a playback hit gold. He'd bugged the target's house and the tape had picked up a conversation that began: 'Hey, what was the combination of the safe again?' They must have wondered how the hell someone had managed to empty their safe. A few grand in cash, that one, if he recalled correctly. Fuck, did he laugh.

He looked at his book of work for the rest of the day and decided he'd do Hornsby first then work his way back to West Ryde and bug Bill Graf's house in the evening.

•

He got back to West Ryde about 9.30 p.m. It was midsummer and the sunlight had only recently departed. He drove past slowly and saw house lights still on. He U-turned at the next corner and drove past again, this time turning into the dead-end street and parking. He was nearly a hundred metres from the house but he could still see the lights of the front room. A tree offered some shade from the closest street light, but a guy just sitting in his car at night was suspicious. He got out and walked briskly up the road. He turned left at Graf's house and carried on down the road. But none of the streets had footpaths. Everyone drove their cars into this neighbourhood so he turned back, started up quickly and drove out again.

Half an hour later he returned. Graf's lights were already out. Barely ten o'clock, the poor old bugger's in bed already. This time he parked around the corner in the marked angle parking outside a bowling club. Only twenty metres from Marsden Road. An easy getaway.

He'd give him twenty minutes, then walk up to the front door and make sure there were no other lights. He put on the rubber surgical gloves and reviewed his tools on the front passenger seat: a small leather pouch with picks and listening devices, his torch – a Mini Maglite, taped up so only a pinprick of light shone . . .

A   . . . and a screwdriver.

Q53   And a screwdriver. Could you describe to me what the screwdriver looked like?

A   It was a yellow handled Stanley screwdriver out of the stock standard Stanley screwdriver set that you buy. It would be the third size yellow screwdriver, meaning that the blade would have been an eight inch blade on the screwdriver with a three and a half inch handle.[15]

He walked down the middle of the road catching starlight. His eyes focussed on the house and his other senses were attuned to the quiet night around him. If he thought someone was watching him he would stop to tie his shoelace then return to his car.

But the street was dead. The front gate was open and the garage door, the roll-up type, was partly open – the gap was about forty centimetres. He walked up the middle of the driveway, right up to the garage door and rolled under.

The pin-light from the torch spied an orderly garage and a brown Volvo. There was no obvious strongbox or safe and he crouched down and looked under the garage door out to the street. Not a soul.

He rolled back out, walked around to the front door and turned around to check and he'd been right – only if someone walked right up the front walkway would he be seen. He held the torch in his mouth, unfolded the pouch and had to pick the lock in the doorknob as well as the deadlock. He had plenty of time so he did it carefully so he wouldn't leave any scratches on the lock casings; it took a good three minutes to be in the door. Adrenaline worked his heart as he pushed open the door. He used the torch to check the door frame and adjacent wall for alarm systems. Nothing. He lay on the ground and scanned the parquet floor by the front door for the elevation of a back-to-base pressure plate alarm. Nothing.

A pin-light wasn't much help navigating a strange house in the dark so he closed the door behind him, clicked off the torch and waited until his eyes adjusted. Soon he could see outlines of furniture, placement of walls. He scouted the ground floor getting the layout of the rooms; the bedrooms must be upstairs. While his plan was to bug the place, first he'd search it for a quick win. Living room. Bar area with a glass-shelved cabinet and a varnished wood liquor trolley with crystal glassware and an ice bucket. Dining room. Methodically he opened every door and every cupboard. He'd found nothing worthwhile by the time he made it back to the bar area. Half an hour had passed.

The downstairs didn't look lived in. Perhaps there was a study upstairs, or perhaps the old fellow spent most of his time in bed. He would have to look around upstairs, where Graf was asleep, to ensure the best placement for the bug. Risky. In the bar area there was a heavy flagon, dark green glass, two pints. He moved it to the floor beside the cabinet – close enough to grab as a weapon if he needed to, but to the side so he wouldn't trip over it on the way out.

At the top of the stairs he turned left. Keep turning the same direction inside a premises and you'll always end up back where you started. He ignored the bathrooms and the hall cupboards. The door was ajar at the end of the corridor and there was Bill Graf, asleep. A warm night but he had a blanket pulled up to his chin anyway. Silently Lindsey checked under the bed and around the skirting boards on the other side of the room. Nothing.

Back out and back past the stairs and down the hall. At the end of the hall is a tidy kitchen and across the room is another open door and there's the faintest of light, perhaps a street light shining through, and *Holy hell* there's someone in the doorway. An intake of breath. 'Don't scream,' he says then the figure leaps towards him. He instinctively blocks with his right forearm and he sees a pair of scissors in his attacker's hands glance off his shirt. He barely feels the sting but later he would find the long, shallow slash wound. He can see now that it is a small woman attacking him, but he has to shut her up and he stabs forward, punching, with the screwdriver and it goes in.

Q281 What was the ferocity of the fight you were having?

A Well she was – you wouldn't believe it – she was like a little dynamo, you know, scared the daylights out of me.

Q282 And she was fighting for her life?

A I think, I think, I think at the onset it was just, from her part just a, an adrenaline rush of, of a stranger confronting her, you know—

He pushes her back into the bedroom and follows and says to her, 'You need to SHUT UP.' She is starting to moan with the wound and the panic, but she swings wildly again, slashing with the scissors. There is a night-light in the room but everything is happening in a blur. They are dressmaker's scissors, chrome, and they haze in an arc towards him. He punches at her again with the screwdriver and she raises her arms and hands . . .

Q236 So you're saying that on the photograph that's now going to be marked by Inspector Baker as number 11, that in your opinion those marks were probably made by the screwdriver you stated you were using?

. . .

A There's another injury there that to me depicts a defensive injury done by an instrument that has got a blade that way.

Q237 So you're saying a squared blade.

A Mmm.

...

Q239 They're defensive sort of marks on her fingers and arms?

A   Yes.

He was back on the street, walking. He felt torch and screwdriver in each hand. He looked down at the blood-stained screwdriver and saw more blood across his arms and shirt-front. His mind was coming back to him, head buzzing, and he told his legs to keep moving, steady, just get back to the car. Calmness came when he opened the door first attempt and sat easily. He placed his gloves and the screwdriver in a shopping bag to keep the blood off the front seat.

As he started the engine he tried to rewind back into the blur. She'd started to scream. The melee was a dim frenzy but he remembered blinds in the bedroom were pulled from the window and that's when she screamed. Loud. Loud, in front of the window – standing there for all the world to see – and just down the hall from Bill Graf's bed. How did he not . . . ? Flight instinct had kicked in. He had to shut her up and escape before he was caught. Twice he'd punched her hard in the face and that had stopped the screaming. She was on the bed, or knocked across the bed to the floor, or both. He'd found a pair of stockings and tied them around her mouth to shut her up.

Stopped at traffic lights he checked his pockets. The leather pouch was still there so it seemed he had made a clean escape. He didn't think the woman would be able to identify him from the struggle in the dim light of her bedroom.

Q519 You didn't leave the premises and knowing that you'd hurt her . . . and call the ambulance did you?

A   No.

Q520 You didn't have care in that regard?

A   No.

Q521 In fact you didn't have care from the moment the confrontation took place, is that right?

A   No, my care for her welfare was virtually non-existent, because I was in a confrontation where I was being attacked with a sharp instrument and then as it progressed my main concern was her being subdued and quietened so I could actually leave the premises.

He drove south – he had a room in a motel in Enfield – and as he crossed Concord Bridge his thoughts turned to the screwdriver beside him and the Parramatta River running underneath. He couldn't get a clear throw to the water and didn't want to stop on the bridge and arouse suspicion. Half a k further he saw parkland, slowed down a little and threw the screwdriver out the driver's side window, across the oncoming lane towards bushes. It was a good throw. He kept driving.

Q356 When did you become aware that the lady who you assaulted had died?

A   I believe it was the next day or the next evening, whatever, news or newspaper or something. I'm not exactly sure. I think it might've been on the radio in the car. I'm not exactly sure where I heard it from.

Q357 And how did that affect you when you heard that she had died?

A   I was surprised because I didn't think her injuries were to the extent that she would've died from them. I honestly didn't.

•

He told Mark what happened. There wasn't supposed to be anyone else there, you said, just an old sick guy that couldn't hear too well and then this woman attacked me with scissors and she wound up dead. Mark shook his head rapidly. No, no, no-one there. No, there shouldn't have been anyone else there, I don't know what you mean.

•

So there was no money from the Graf job and Mark hatched his next scheme. An insurance job. Mark wanted to get out of the private inquiry business and into massage parlours. If Lindsey torched the premises for him it would be more lucrative than trying for a quick sale.

•

Lindsey's mum was more settled, gently being weaned off the pills, and he was getting jobs in Brisbane from Fidelity now so he left the beach and took a flat in Coorparoo, only a five-minute walk from the office. The car rebirthing was little more than a hobby.

Every week he drove back up to Redcliffe to see Mum. Usually she wanted to be taken to the shops and one day Joey, one of his old partners in crime, came walking down the mall towards them.

'G'day, Rosie. What are you doing here?'

'Moved up here to stay with Mum for a while.' He didn't introduce them. Glenda was more interested in the nearest shop front.

'Given anyone the Bill Cavanagh treatment lately?' said Joey.

'Come on, Joey,' he said, shooting a glance at his mother's back. To his knowledge, Russ and Joey – and possibly one of the other truckies from the Stop and Rest – were the only people who knew what he'd done to Cavanagh. Joey would never give him up but Lindsey was surprised at his lack of discretion. Change the subject.

'What about you?'

'Oh, I live here now,' said Joey. 'Moved up about a year ago.'

They exchanged phone numbers and a few weeks later he rang Joey and dropped around to his house. When Joey's wife saw Lindsey she shook her head and walked out to the kitchen.

'Must be some pretty expensive saucepans you've got out there, Joey,' he said. 'From the amount of noise they make.'

On their second beer she came back out.

'How long's this going to take, Joey?' she said and stood there with her arms crossed.

Lindsey sat, took a swig of beer and Joey was just looking at him.

'I'll be off, then,' he said.

•

Mark Lewis rang him up from time to time to bitch about life in general and hassle him to come back to Sydney and finish 'that job'. Lindsey got the hint. He was still shifting a stolen car every week or two and on his next Sydney trip, 7 June 1987, he bought some cans of spray paint from a shop near the city and that night he drove out to 981 Victoria Road, West Ryde – the premises of Pierce Investigations.

He broke some bottles and sprayed some tags along the back walls. Then he made it look like a clumsy break-in, walked into Mark's office, emptied a filing cabinet and tipped petrol over the big pile of papers. He walked up the road where he could watch the fire take hold. The firies turned up eventually, but he'd done a good job and the whole place was gone.

Mark received his insurance payout but for Lindsey it had barely been worth the effort for the size of his share. He'd agreed to it out of habit – just another job for Mark Lewis.

•

Lindsey was back in Brisbane doing phone work from his flat in Coorparoo when there was a knock at the door. He wasn't expecting company and he wasn't in the habit of handing out his address so he narrowed it down to neighbours or trouble.

He opened the door to two uniforms and a suit bearing warrants. Trouble.

Trouble but not big trouble – not enough stripes for a murder bust. Sure enough, the arrest warrant was for the cars and he did a quick mental inventory of the incriminating evidence in his flat as they read it out. No weapons, no drugs. He was probably gone for the stolen cars but nothing else.

He read the warrants carefully but they were all in order, so they searched the flat and collected evidence – his shopping list, rego papers for half a dozen cars, handwritten notes, the cassette from his answering machine – then they took him away to be interviewed.

They charged him with ten counts of unlawful possession of a motor vehicle and three of false pretences. One of his associates had left a piece of paper on his garage floor with Lindsey's details on it and they'd been tracking him. It was pretty solid so he confessed to the thirteen charges. He didn't feel the need to trouble them with mention of the forty other cars he'd shifted.

More paperwork, then he was released on bail and told to keep them advised of his whereabouts so they could tell him his court date.

On his next visit to Sydney he asked around and got an introduction to cops who had contacts in Queensland. How much would it cost to make the charges go away? It was a torturous process and the figure of ten grand came back from the Queenslanders but there were too many arses along the line to cover and nothing ever came of it.

His PI licences were cancelled and he knew better than to keep moving hot cars so both his sources of local income were gone. He went over to have dinner with his mother and Pa and told them he was moving back to Sydney. Hadn't been able to get enough work to sustain himself, wanted to spend more time with Penny – those were the excuses he gave.

He'd probably be going away for a stretch so there was no point taking a lease or a permanent job; he drove cabs and mostly he crashed with Stanley and Max at the flat in Belmore Street, Burwood.

Lindsey's gran Ethel had moved out to a nursing home after a series of strokes. Max was diabetic and didn't always manage his insulin properly so Stanley had moved in to keep an eye on him.

They'd both received a payout when the Dulux plant shut down. Stanley was working for an appliance repair company at Homebush. Max was living on a pension and spent most of his time at the Coronation Club playing the pokies.

•

On a Saturday afternoon in Burwood he planned to relax and catch up with old friends. First he dropped into the hairdressers two doors from the Burwood and, as he'd hoped, Denis was on deck. 'Welcome back, Rosie!' he said and gave Lindsey a tight hug.

By the end of the haircut, Lindsey was back up to speed with the local gossip. Eric's drinking was getting even worse and their favourite barman, Peter, had got back on the smack and died of an OD. Denis agreed to meet him for a drink after work in Lindsey's 'office'.

The 'office' was the small round bar table in the back left corner of the Burwood Hotel's front bar. The beauty of it was that he could sit on a bar stool with his back in a corner with lines of sight across most of the room.

Eric joined him, meerkat skinny, and he was still wearing the same blue bomber jacket that had caused Lindsey to christen him 'Biggles'. Denis knocked off work early to celebrate Lindsey's return.

'Loving the amenity,' said Denis. Lindsey's back-corner office was also right beside the door to the gents'.

'You won't be invited back if you carry on like that.'

'Ha ha. Speaking of invites, when's the next Burwood boys' night out?' said Denis. 'I can't say the Showboat really did it for me.'

'Fuck off, that was a good night,' Lindsey said. The Showboat excursion had been their last night out before he'd moved to Brisbane. Biggles had managed to get his flatmates Steve and Campbell to come along and he'd made the booking for seventeen seats. 'Why don't you organise the next one then?' he said.

'Sure, how about we all go to *Les Girls*. What do you think, Eric?'

'Well, each to their own, I say,' Eric said, stroking his ragged moustache. 'But if that's what everyone wants to do, I suppose I'll go along.'

They stayed and talked and a couple of the other locals drifted in and wanted to catch up with Lindsey and they moved to a bigger table. When closing time came they all wanted to drink on so they went back to someone's unit and that's where Lindsey was first introduced to Oscar, who lived there too.

Oscar was tall and bony with a prominent cleft chin and a crew cut. He wore rings with embedded, polished gemstones and he carried himself as a man of the world. He liked to get around the wineries and later he broke out a bottle of his much revered Mudgee white port and it was nectar for them all after the long night of beer, bourbon and cigarettes.

•

True to his word, Denis organised the night out and the following Friday ten of them caught the train in to the Cross. Carlotta's ribald humour had them in stitches and in spite of themselves they enjoyed the drag queens' outrageous costumes and lip-syncing.

On the way out of the club Lindsey spotted someone he knew and called him over.

'Denis, I'd like you to meet an old client of mine,' he said. It was Keith Williams, the man who developed Hamilton Island into a tourist mecca, and he was at the height of his fame. Denis was impressed.

•

On the kitchen bench he found an overdue notice for Gran's nursing home fees. It was a follow-up notice and the fees were more than a month behind. They were threatening eviction. He asked Max and Stanley what was going on.

'I only just found out,' said Stanley. 'I thought Max was paying the nursing home fees out of Mum's pension, like he always does.'

'So why are you behind? Where's the money going?' asked Lindsey. Max looked sheepish.

'Tell him, Max.'

'Hey, we've got other expenses, you know. Rent, food, stuff like that,' said Max.

'Ahem,' said Stanley. 'Actually, we're behind on the rent as well.'

'Yeah, but Max, you've got money. More than thirty grand from Dulux,' Lindsey said.

'Ah, not anymore,' said Max. 'All gone.'

'What, you've blown the lot already?' Lindsey said. His head was pounding. 'The fucking pokies. And now Gran's about to get evicted from the nursing home because you're blowing her pension the same way?'

'Well, what I am supposed—' began Max.

He grabbed Max by the front of his T-shirt. 'You're a fucking retard, Max. I'm going to kill you, ya cunt.' Max remained passive, rag-doll, and Lindsey released his grip, snatched the overdue bills and stormed out. He didn't mind so much that it was going to cost him money to fix it, he was furious because he felt this need to watch out for Max, this grown man who couldn't look after the most basic responsibility.

•

After a few months he still hadn't received a court date for the Queensland charges. Between taxi shifts he started helping Mark Lewis with his businesses. Relaxation centres were the main game now. Mark and Kerrie's Relaxation Centre had two premises on Victoria Road, both within a hundred metres of the West Ryde print shop, and others at Parramatta and Campbelltown. Kerrie Pang was his new offsider. She had worked in the industry for years and between them they'd developed a formula for how to manage and operate these massage-with-extras parlours and they planned to open more.

Kerrie was also Mark's new lover, twenty years his junior.

When Lindsey asked what had happened to his wife of thirty-odd years, Mark Lewis's character really shone through. She'd had a double mastectomy, a plate inserted into her hip and, more recently, had been diagnosed with terminal cancer. She'd learned of the affair when Kerrie had apparently rung her up, claiming to be pregnant to Mark (she wasn't), and Mark had moved in with Kerrie soon thereafter.[16]

'Classy,' said Lindsey. 'How'd the strife take it?'

'Not great,' said Mark.

Lindsey did a daily round to collect and bank the takings, helped with the bookkeeping and was the designated handyman for repairs or improvements. Dogsbody.

But if anyone came up with a better idea for an earn he was up for it. One night a conversation at the Burwood turned up a mate who had a spare room in his house at St Clair and a willingness to look the other way – for a price. Lindsey fancied himself as a jack-of-all-trades and how hard could hydroponics be, anyway? Within a month he had twenty plants on the go. When they matured, he dried, bagged and sold most of it himself, so margins were high and he could make up to five hundred in a week. Easy money.

38

Mark leased premises in Hornsby for another relaxation centre and Lindsey did the carpentry, plumbing and painting while Kerrie did the dressing, décor and curtains. Kerrie did most of the talking and much of that was complaining about Mark – she'd caught him getting massages from his staff and she wasn't happy.

Lindsey had never had a conversation with Kerrie that wasn't work-related. That came from Mark. Ten years he'd known Mark and they'd never been out for a meal together or a drink at the pub. The closest thing to a social engagement was the time they had to dispose of out-of-date ammo from the security business. They each took a .38 into the bush to go hunting. Other than shooting the shit out of a bunch of trees, they didn't hit anything.

And here was Kerrie, talking about her relationship with Mark, running the man down. Her boyfriend, his boss.

On the second day of the Hornsby fit-out, they started early and by noon they were famished so Lindsey drove them to the nearest takeaway for burgers. Kerrie paid.

She spoke to him of her – 'her' – growing empire of massage parlours and the plans 'she' had for how they'd be run and she seemed to have forgotten her quite recent, humble origins as one of Mark's massage girls. It was all for her kids, she said. She had four children from two previous marriages and a nanny looked after them six days a week during daylight hours on account of her and Mark's punishing work schedule. Once they had enough centres in the black they'd be able to employ a manager and she'd be able to spend more time with the kids.

They worked through the afternoon and at knock-off time she offered him a massage. He was taken aback at first. He rated her about a six out of ten – nothing to write home about – but a nice body, so he accepted. She certainly knew what she was doing and the massage was good and she cooed seductively as she brought him to climax with her hands, and that was very good.

•

Kerrie was behind the desk at their biggest relaxation centre, West Ryde, and she'd been crying.

'Mark and I had a fight and I made him buy me out of the centres. He keeps trying to stop me giving massages. He's so jealous. But I've seen him parked near the house. I'm worried for the kids.'

He nodded and let her talk. She was still managing the centre and it wasn't really his problem but she asked if he'd come over to her house at Cherrybrook to check on her. 'Sure, why not.'

By the time he knocked off and drove out it was nearly midnight. There was no sign of Mark but she invited him in and they had a drink and soon they went to bed together.

> It was a little awkward that first time, she'd been the boss's wife after all, but the next time I relaxed and it was fine. I even felt some fondness for her.

It went nowhere. She'd ask him over from time to time but he didn't want her to get the wrong idea so he'd always decline. Instead, he'd drop in to have sex with her when *he* felt like it.

But she didn't take kindly to being fobbed off and she became more demanding. They'd only slept together a few times when he started avoiding her calls altogether – he figured she'd get the hint.

Now she'd ring him on his car phone when he was doing his night shifts in the RSL taxi. She'd tie up his phone when he was trying to work and he asked her not to call him when he was working but she flat-out refused.

Then he realised what the problem was. She'd been the boss of Mark and because Lindsey worked for Mark she saw him as one of her minions, always had.

One night he finished a shift at 3 a.m., returned his cab to the RSL base at Bankstown and she was there waiting for him. Another time she drove in from her place at Cherrybrook looking for him, knocking on the door of the flat in Burwood at five in the afternoon, and all she found was Max and Stanley.

Eventually, he dropped in to see her and she sat in the front seat of the cab with him so he could monitor the radio for jobs heading back into the city. He told her that this couldn't go on – this business of her chasing him all over Sydney – and it was going to end badly if Mark found out, even though she and Mark were separated. And while he was at it Lindsey explained that he'd been employed by Mark under Mark's private inquiry licence so by law Mark was Lindsey's boss and she never could be.

It was this final point that seemed to pull her up and she stopped calling. He put her from his mind, not imagining that their paths would cross again and that when they did, ruin would follow.

•

After all that palaver with Kerrie was over, he took up with Betty, one of Mark's girls from the Parramatta centre. She was young, oh so young, barely seventeen. She was a knockout alright, but screwed up – probably bipolar. It had started off as conversations and she'd latched onto him like a life raft and he started sleeping most nights at her place.

He came back to his uncles' place in Belmore Street, Burwood to do his laundry one Saturday. He banged on Max's bedroom door and there was no answer so he walked in and Max was on the floor. He tried to rouse him to get some sugars into him but he was too far gone. Hypoglycaemic diabetic coma. When the paramedics came Lindsey rode with him in the ambulance to the hospital.

'We only just got him in time,' said the doctor in A&E. 'He shouldn't be drinking.'

'Yeah, we know,' said Lindsey.

'Has he tried stopping?'

'He's always going to be a drinker. Telling him to stop would be like telling a duck not to sit on the water. He knows it'll kill him – he just doesn't care.'

Max was sitting up with an intravenous drip attached to his arm.

'I'm sorry, Lindsey,' he said. 'All this bother.'

'So you should be, ya dickhead. You know you've got to eat a meal when you take your insulin. It's not that hard.'

'You're right, you're right. I won't do it again.'

'That's what you said last time,' said Lindsey, not unkindly.

'I don't think Mum's got much time left,' said Max. The wandering focus was normal for Max. 'When she goes, I'll go bush, get work on a farm. Remember that time when we were kids? We lived on the sheep farm with Uncle? That's what I'll do, live the real life. I'll be a bushie.' Max was beaming.

'Who's going to take you to the chemist and make sure you don't run out of insulin then?' asked Lindsey.

Max blinked. Still smiling. 'I don't know, maybe I'll just stop taking it,' he said. 'Drop dead, save everyone the hassle.'

•

Max was right about one thing. His mum Ethel, Lindsey's gran, didn't have much time left – she died two months later.

•

He was momentarily between cars and Barry said he had a spare to lend him.

'It's not hot, is it?'

'No, mate, absolutely not.'

So he drove around in this Falcon for a few days and he returned to the car in the Burwood Plaza car park one afternoon and they arrested him.

The Falcon was stolen after all and of course they found his outstanding warrants in Queensland and they told him that he'd been fined in absentia for breach of bail in Queensland even though he'd never received his court date. So it was off to Long Bay on remand until a court date to be fixed where they'd hear the charge for goods in custody (the Falcon) as well as an application for extradition to Queensland.

The cells in June were cold, stark, smelled of disinfectant. It was his first visit to Long Bay as a guest, but he'd visited and he knew people who'd come out so he wasn't fearful, though he knew he had to keep his wits about him. So it was no surprise, his second week in, when some gorilla thought Lindsey had looked at him funny and took a swing.

Lindsey blocked, but the punch deflected into his throat and it swelled up to the size of a grapefruit.

Robbo visited him in the prison hospital. Years before, at the Sawdust Hotel in Gladesville, Robbo had given him the tip-off that led him to the racket that was stealing heavy machinery under the protection of those bent pricks in the Motor Squad. That must have been ten years earlier and Robbo was still a prison guard here in Long Bay. It couldn't look like a social visit but Robbo managed a private word in his ear and told Lindsey all he needed to know about the gorilla who had taken the swing.

A week later Lindsey was working in the prison cafeteria. He took the steel hot water cylinder, used by inmates to make their coffee, emptied out half of it so it was light enough to lift, then threw the other half over the gorilla's head. The burns were severe. When the gorilla got out of hospital he kept his distance. But then he talked and Lindsey spent time in isolation. You shouldn't talk – talking was unforgivable.

He appeared in Liverpool court on his thirty-third birthday, 2 May 1989. For being caught with the hot Falcon he had to pay a one thousand dollar bond and 'be of good behaviour for two years'. For the extradition hearing he made bail, much to his surprise. He made passing eye contact with the cops as he walked out and they too were shaking their heads in amazement.

He went home to Betty and told her only the good news, that he wasn't going back to Long Bay. But in his mind he was preparing for what was to come. He had gear to sell or stow, debts to call in and others to repay, because soon enough he'd be summoned back to Queensland and there, he knew, he'd be handed his first prison sentence.

39

I meet Donna for the first time in person in the car park outside Goulburn prison. She is wearing a bandana on account of the chemotherapy – halfway through a six-month course to shrink tumours in her arms, breastbone and the back of her head. We go through the checkpoints together. She's resolute, less timid than she sounded on the phone.

When we get to the freezing waiting room we sit opposite a slim young woman. She has clear eyes, a barbed-wire tattoo on her upper arm and in the cold room she keeps her arms crossed over her skin-tight blouse and insubordinate nipples.

She asks us if we are visiting HRMU. 'Yes.' The conversation is brief and limited to small talk, but when we get inside to the glass of the visits room she is curious: 'Ooh, who's that? I don't remember seeing him before.'

'Lindsey Rose.'

'Oh, Lindsey Rose. So that's Lindsey Rose. He and my brother Mark often go to the exercise yard together. Lindsey does his garden while Mark does laps.'

'Yes, he loves his garden,' says Donna.

We wave to Lindsey and he is sitting, then standing, facing us, looking over his glasses in some kind of bemusement.

'You know who that is, don't you?' he asks when we get inside. 'That's Mark van Krevel's sister.' I am none the wiser and Donna shakes her head. 'He's that guy that killed a Wollongong councillor. And she's the one that killed their father. Mark reckons his father's the reason he went off the rails.'

Afterwards I look them up then wish I hadn't. Mark was nineteen years old when he walked into Wollongong police station and confessed to two murders. He had bashed to death an Illawarra shopkeeper who he claimed had made sexual advances towards him. He hit him in the head with a wine decanter, disembowelled the body, removed the head and used the man's own hand to paint satanic messages in blood on the walls. And two weeks later he'd bashed and strangled Frank Arkell, former mayor of Wollongong, who was facing charges relating to paedophilia and child pornography.

We've walked in with Mark's sister, Belinda van Krevel. Two weeks after Mark's conviction their father had been killed by Belinda's lover at her behest. It was apparently revenge – Mark's crimes and incarceration were blamed on years of abuse he supposedly suffered at the hands of their father.

The woman dubbed Evil van Krevel by one of the tabloids has already completed her six years for solicit to murder as we chitchat in Supermax.

'Well, she speaks highly of you,' I say to Lindsey. 'Says you spend time with her brother, Mark, in the garden.'

'Yeah. He's got life and he's young. It did his head in so he'd just given up. One of the screws casually asked if I could help. They couldn't get him to have a shower, clean himself, change his clothes, clean the sink, his cell.

'One day we were out in the exercise yard together. Mark just sat there in the bus stop. I took a break from gardening and explained in slow detail what it's like to die of a diabetic illness. The message got through. He took to doing laps of the exercise yard, even running them, and he dropped about twenty kilos, cleaned up his act a bit.'

He turns to Donna. 'What happened to your hair?'

'I washed it and it shrunk.'

He looks at her paternally, pauses, sees nothing else will be forthcoming. 'Uh huh.'

They are close and I feel like my presence makes it three's a crowd and the conversation stays impersonal. World affairs, and he's recently seen a documentary exploring potential future conflicts that might escalate into World War III and 'us guys in here' have an interesting perspective on 'what's going on out there'. Of course, it's Islam that's the problem in the world and 'there are guys down the hall shouting Arabic through two feet of concrete every night and giving me the shits'. Later he smirks while admitting that he has similar shouted conversations with the inmate of his own neighbouring cell.

He asks after Donna's family and it turns out their traditional Anzac Day at the Enfield RSL had fallen by the wayside after the death of Donna's mum.

More talk about life in prison – he has recently been introduced to the new prison counsellor.

'I told her that it all started to go wrong for me when I was abducted by aliens and anally probed.

'The other counsellor managed to keep a straight face to keep it going for a bit and you should have seen this young girl's face when we both burst out laughing,' and he slaps his knee and lays on us that snorting convulsive laughter that he has.

We talk briefly about the book I'm writing. He'd most recently sent me three letters totalling more than forty pages and I tell Donna that all these PI stories he's sent me are real eye-openers and you wouldn't believe some of the tricky repossessions he'd had to do.

> Wheelchair repos were hard. One would try and find soft grass, or at least carpet, before tipping the hirer out of his wheelchair. Even harder were hearing aids. One was not supposed to remove the device from the hirer's ear because it was inserted into the body, one couldn't just remove it – some legal technicality I was told. So the tactic was to speak to the hirer and stop and start your voice, making out like the hearing aid was malfunctioning. When the hirer pulled out the ear piece one simply snatched it and bolted.

I'd thought it was a pretty good story. They both look at me. Pityingly.

'You didn't think that really . . . that was true did you?'

'Well . . .' I mumble.

'You clown. Oldest joke in the book – for a repo agent. Can't believe you fell for it.'

At the end of the visit he gives Donna a long goodbye hug then we're out to the waiting room. Belinda van Krevel is standing with us as her brother is led past, manacled and fingerprint-scanned. The process takes three or four minutes and Belinda is waving through the glass, blowing kisses, 'Be strong', 'I love you', 'Be strong', and a fist-clenched arm across her chest. Mark shambles towards the exit and smiles in a detached way and I think he waves at me as well – just because I am standing with Belinda and watching.

Once we're out I drive Donna to the Goulburn McDonald's where her partner will pick her up. We chat and have a coffee. It'll take them three hours to get home and it's a tiring trip in her condition. She has heart disease – as well as the cancer – and she can only work one day a week now. She's a counsellor for cardiac patients at a hospital. Oh boy.

40

A date was finally set and he drove up to Brisbane to face the charges for the car thefts. Betty stayed behind. He told her he'd be taking an extended holiday.

He made arrangements to stay with his mum and Pa for a few days before the trial and he stopped at the shops in Redcliffe to buy some beer.

Walking back to the car he noticed a red Corolla a couple of rows over. He frowned, kept walking, and put the beer in his car. There was something about that car. It had NSW plates and he looked in the window and it was Betty's car.

He waited and soon enough there was Betty walking back to her car, looking at her feet.

'What are you doing here, sweetheart?' he said.

'Lindsey, I was scared. Someone's been following me.'

'Oh, Betty,' he said. His first instinct was that she was having another episode. 'What did you see?'

'The cars. The same cars. I keep seeing them. Since you left, I keep seeing them and I'm not sleeping.'

He wrapped his arms around her.

He had his day in court and pleaded guilty to the thirteen charges. He received a three-year sentence, eligible for parole after six months. Off to Boggo Road Gaol where he planned to be a model prisoner and only do the six months.

Betty had friends in Surfers Paradise. They helped her find work and she drove the hour and a half up to the prison to see him every weekend.

•

With two months to go he qualified for day release. Boggo Road had been short-lived and he'd been moved twenty minutes down the road to the Sir David Longland Correction Centre. But the kitchen staff, inmate apprentices, just happened to go on strike and Lindsey had been seconded to the kitchen where a skeleton crew cooked hot breakfasts for

450 (inmates and staff) every day. When the dispute was over he was offered any prison in the state for his efforts and he chose Numinbah.

Numinbah Correctional Centre was in the bush – just shy of the Lamington National Park. It operated as a working farm and it was an hour closer to Betty. He handled parole applications on behalf of other inmates and he ran the workshop, machining parts and maintaining the farm equipment and the tractor. It was one big melting pot and everyone got along, apart from the occasional blue, and there was a poker game every Friday night.

On day release, Betty would drive up in the morning then Lindsey would take the wheel and they'd head off for the day together. Most of the other inmates weren't allowed a driver's licence – Lindsey had an exception so he could assist with driving other prisoners to work details. Betty handled it fine. She'd seen worse.

January 1991 he was released on parole and he moved into Betty's place at Surfers. He was in no rush to find work, but when the constriction of the prison jaunt had left him he got his act together and they decided to move back to Sydney. They took a unit on Bondi Beach.

He arranged to meet his Aunt Marjorie for a coffee and she told him that no-one had heard from Max for six months. He'd said he was going up to Queensland with a friend to look for work. Wanted to store his VCR and some videos at her place and told her that if he couldn't get a job he'd come back in a couple of weeks and live with her. She saw him drive off with this mate of his in a blue car.

The family had only recently twigged that he was missing – they'd all just assumed someone else must have heard from him. Lindsey said he'd make some enquiries but the trail had gone cold – no-one knew who the mate was that he'd ridden off with – and he found nothing. The police weren't informed for years – again, the family all thought one of the others must have reported him missing.

•

Lindsey went to the Burwood and sat down with Robbo.

'Rosie, do you remember that guy you scalded at the Bay?'

More than six months had passed, but he certainly did.

'I hear he's being released next week,' said Robbo. 'Under recognisance of his mother.'

'Is that so?' he said.

When the date came he was ready. He saw where the gorilla parked his car, outside his mother's place, and he was waiting for him. The gorilla turned left out of his front gate and straight into a karate punch to the solar plexus which took all the wind out of him. So there was no fight, just a beating. Lindsey left him moaning on the street, walked back to his car and drove away. He could have just as easily knocked on his front door to deliver the beating, but no mum needs to see that.

The next day he had some pot to sell and he walked into the Burwood and Denis was there with another local, Patrick. Denis saw him coming and waved him over and Lindsey bought his drink and sat with them.

'What's wrong with your hand?' asked Denis.

'Busted my pinky in a punch-up last night,' he said. He'd mistimed a punch and the gorilla had a hard head.

'Oh dear, have you been to the doctor? Let me take a look.'

He cautiously brought up his hand with its purple swollen knuckle and Denis examined it gently.

'Ooh, that looks nasty. But are you sure it's broken? Might just be bruising,' he said.

Patrick chipped in. 'Give us a look.'

Patrick fancied himself as a bit of a lad and he reached over to Lindsey's hand and lifted the pinky finger up towards the knuckle.

The pain shot straight through to his elbow and he howled in surprise and leapt across the table at Patrick's head. As the first punch connected the bar table went flying, along with the schooners, and Denis was flung off his bar stool to the floor. Lindsey kept punching with his good hand until Patrick's face was a mess. The bar staff – who knew him well enough – waited until he was finished then shepherded Patrick away.

Hands in the air. 'Okay, it's all over now. I'm calm,' he said and then the bar manager told him to leave and he was barred for a month. He turned left out the door and walked a block down the hill to the

Avondale and ordered a double scotch, a beer chaser and a bag of ice for his throbbing hand.

Denis collected himself and went down to see if Lindsey was okay. They shared a couple of beers and Denis nodded in agreement of what a fuckwit that Patrick was, bending back a broken finger like that.

Lindsey apologised for knocking him off the bar stool and Denis remarked that he'd never seen Lindsey in a fight before.

'I generally avoid a fight when you're around, Denis,' he said.

'And why in particular?'

'Well, you're such a gentleman, Denis, and it's not very seemly, is it?' he said and Denis just looked at him.

After a couple more drinks, he said he had to go so he kissed Denis farewell on the cheek, like he always did, and gingerly waved goodbye out the door.

41

He drove around to Bexley to drop off Penny, age nine. This would be their last visit for some time – she was moving to Perth with Lydia and Ben. He'd had her for an extra night and taken her out to dinner by way of farewell.

Ben's car was in the driveway, so Lindsey parked against the kerb and walked her up. *This'll be fun.* Ben was packing boxes in the hallway and he straightened up as Lindsey walked past and on to the kitchen for the handover to Lydia.

Lydia saw him; he normally left Penny at the gate so she looked anxiously past his shoulder towards Ben.

'Relax,' said Lindsey. 'He can bloody have you.'

He stayed for only a minute, chatting quietly to Lydia about details of the move, before giving Penny a long hug goodbye.

On the way out he shook Ben's hand. 'Good luck, mate, you're going to need it,' he said, glancing back at Lydia. 'You're going to need a fucking big paddle for that one.'

•

Six months out of prison, he and Betty had moved from Bondi to a unit in Potts Point and Mark Lewis was in the middle of another cash-flow crisis.

'Yeah, yeah, Kerrie's moved back in,' Mark said. 'But putting her into that Gladesville business is the biggest mistake I've ever made.' Kerrie was now owner-operator of her own relaxation centre, Kerrie's Oasis.

'So now she thinks she's the Queen of Sheba and she's always in the other centres yelling at my staff or rearranging rosters from one to the other and you know what she's like. Once she takes a set against someone – or has a jealousy attack – she'll just hound them until they leave. So I keep losing staff and I'm just chasing my tail. There's creditors on my back every other day now.'

In the early days he'd often seen thirty grand cash or more in Mark's safe but, for all his business acumen, those days had passed.

'Maybe you should offload a relaxation centre,' he said. 'The one at Campbelltown's so far out you'd save yourself travel time too.'

Mark tilted his head. 'I don't think Kerrie would go for it . . .'

'You're the boss, Mark,' said Lindsey.

'Hang the wolves, I suppose you're right. Know any buyers?' Mark waited for a second, then his eyebrows went up. 'Oh, why don't you buy it?'

Not a bad idea. Be your own boss, don't have to put up with so much of other people's bullshit. And it was about time he started to build some financial security. He could probably scrape together twenty grand if he put his mind to it.

'I'm interested,' he said.

They talked price and Mark wouldn't take less than forty so they agreed that Mark would hold off and see if Lindsey could raise the cash.

•

He thought of Oscar almost immediately – he'd become a regular drinking companion since the night of the Mudgee white port. He was a straighty-180 and he'd just finalised a divorce settlement and Lindsey knew he had some cash from the house sale.

That night they were playing pool at the Burwood and he ran it up the flagpole. Oscar said he was interested in buying a legitimate business but was otherwise non-committal. Over the next few weeks Lindsey kept at him, gently urging, and finally got him to commit to at least come out and have a look at the place.

The premises were well kept and it had a good position with plenty of passing trade and Oscar's eyes twinkled when he was introduced to one of the young massage girls.

A week later they met at Mark Lewis's office, above the print shop at West Ryde, signed a contract and each handed over a cheque. Then it was small talk, shaking hands and walking out the door with a back-slap.

'What did Mark say, rub and what?' asked Oscar on the way back to the car.

'Rub and tug?'

'Yeah, that's it. What did he mean?'

'Rub and tug, Oscar. Use your imagination. The massage is the rub and the tug comes after.'

Oscar was unimpressed to learn the true nature of his new business venture.

•

Detective Sergeant Alan 'Choppie' Thomas was still a regular at the Burwood and when Lindsey asked, Choppie was happy to come out to Campbelltown and offer advice. Under the law you couldn't advertise massage and provide a sexual service, he explained, so the word 'massage' appeared in none of the marketing material and they retained the existing name, Campbelltown Relaxation Centre – as uninspiring as it was functional.

The premises at 219 Queen Street, Campbelltown had a walk-up entry and five massage rooms plus office, laundry, staff room and a lounge.

They were open midday until late and Oscar agreed that one of them should be on the premises at all times. They would each do one week on and one week off and the changeover would be midday Wednesdays.

The punters generally came for the happy endings rather than the massage so on-the-job training was all that was required. Being young and attractive certainly helped and Lindsey found that university students were a great resource and recruited half a dozen. The creepers spread the word and soon they were taking business from the brothel that operated out of the Old Post Office down the road.

He decided the Eastern Suburbs were too far away from everything. Betty agreed to give up the Potts Point unit and they found a place in Burwood. Park Avenue, a unit overlooking the Westfield Mall.

The removalists took most of it and the fragiles he'd move in his VC Commodore. He'd worked into the evening at Campbelltown, so it was past midnight and it was raining as he drove into the underground car park. Someone was already parked in his car space. Terrific.

He drove back outside and parked on the street and was carrying two boxes of Betty's expensive crystal and a desk lamp while trying to juggle an umbrella. The best approach with his hands full was to walk down the ramp, swipe his card to open the boom gate then walk to the internal lift.

Halfway down he heard an engine revving out on the street, then a car slid around the corner and sideways again and the car was coming down the ramp. He'd just swiped his card and he started to run because this car was driving fast and sliding in the wet and it was going to run him over. He lumbered down the ramp, trying not to jumble the crystal, and at the bottom he stepped to the side as the car screamed past. He heard the car descend two levels and then the engine switch off. He waited.

The guy walked up and he was half-pissed. As they got into the lift Lindsey said to him: 'If you drive in here like that again, you and I are going to have words.'

'Oh, yeah? Well, I'm here now,' he said.

Lindsey put down his boxes and started punching him, close-in pugilist-style, and then the lift opened at his floor and he was looking down at this bloke cowering in the corner and 'Stop, enough, stop!' was ringing in his ears. The desk lamp was dangling broken in his hand and the man was bleeding from head wounds and there was broken ceramic lampshade all around. He picked up the boxes of crystal and left him there.

•

When it was Oscar's week on deck Lindsey had spare time and he saw a 1960 FB Holden for sale for next to nothing. The shell was mostly intact and he could see the potential. He trailered it to the underground car park at Park Avenue but soon realised it wasn't a practical place to work, and he was sick of trying to find street parking for his Commodore so he found a shed at Wentworthville that he could rent cheaply. It was the perfect space for fixing up a car – several cars, in fact.

Chinese Phil helped him get the wiring up to scratch and other mates helped with the fit-out.

The FB progressed slowly – he was in no rush – but then the guys who'd helped him set up the shed started asking if he'd help them fix up their cars and before long it took on a life of its own.

He'd been to a barbecue at Easter and met a younger fellow, Zane, who had flown Iroquois during his three years in the army. And he'd recently qualified for fixed-wing so they had plenty in common. They'd become regular drinking companions at the Burwood, so Zane helped out at the workshop when Lindsey was short-handed on a truck repair, and had even donated some tools. A machinist they knew from the Burwood came on board and soon they were repairing trucks, backhoes, compressors, cars, vans, bikes, boat engines and doing some light fabrication work as well.

He took some pride in what he had created from nothing and it was a useful base of operations for the occasional black bag job. He kept a sniper rifle and full camo gear on-site as well.

•

The Campbelltown Relaxation Centre was almost too successful. The brothel in the Old Post Office went bust – partly due to mismanagement and partly because of competition from Lindsey's attractive uni students – and they learned that their own senior girl, Raylene, was intending to buy it. If she succeeded, his business would suffer because she'd take customers. Even if someone else bought it – and managed it correctly – they'd take some of his business. It made sense for them to buy it.

> I never wanted to own a brothel, the rub'n'tug shop was sleazy enough for me, but my business head said if we don't buy it, we will suffer.

Oscar was against it. But Lindsey presented the argument and the numbers overcame Oscar's reservations. By 5 p.m. they'd pulled together ten grand and it was theirs.

The suite in the Old Post Office had three working rooms. They were small, but big enough for a massage table and they soon realised the brothel had more potential for growth. It made sense to move the brothel to the larger premises and the massage into the Old Post Office.

But the fit-out needed a spruce-up and he had to credit Kerrie, she had a good eye for it, so he asked her to pay a visit. She was flattered to be asked. They met on-site and she went from room to room and told them in no uncertain terms what they should be doing with the place.

'You've got no idea, have you?' she said to him as they walked back out.

He thanked her for the input.

New paint and carpet then one weeknight, after midnight, they rolled furniture and massage tables down Queen Street, a ghost town, and into the Old Post Office. They bought new furniture for 219 Queen, the phone lines were swapped and they named it Upstairs on Queen.

They also ran escorts so once they had more girls on board they began meeting untapped demand and they were turning a profit and making inroads into their start-up costs.

•

CM: So even then you were still on at least civil terms with Kerrie. What happened?

LR: It all started with the Staff Borrowing Incident. I didn't want any trouble, I was trying to run a good business. We looked after the girls and when the jacks from the vice squad visited they even complimented me on the quality of our record-keeping – legitimate accounts, proper staff files and showing the monthly medical checks for all the girls . . .

. . . so staff turnover was much lower than it had been under Mark's management but there'd always be some and one day a girl from the relaxation centre left suddenly for personal reasons. Having girls available at peak times was crucial; he didn't want to leave a gap and couldn't find an immediate replacement so he went looking for a loaner.

It was common practice to borrow staff from other businesses – especially if they were not in competition – as long as they went back afterwards. He phoned Mark first. Mark didn't have anyone to spare and suggested he call Kerrie.

There was a girl, Kerrie said, but she lived in the Cross and didn't have a car. How would she get home from Campbelltown after midnight? No problem, said Lindsey; he would make arrangements for her transport.

Kerrie gave him the phone number and he rang this girl, Alice, and she came around to his place the following night. As soon as she walked in the door, he knew she was top-shelf for a massage girl – well dressed, well spoken; another uni student paying her way through. The meeting went well and she was happy to start the next day. She would catch the train to Campbelltown in the morning and either Lindsey or Oscar would drop her home.

At the end of each day he handed her an envelope with her earnings and she was wary at first but by Friday he handed her the envelope and she smiled at him.

Two weeks later and a new permanent was ready to start and Lindsey let Alice know on Saturday morning that Sunday would be her last shift and then she'd be going back to Gladesville. Her face gave her away and he wasn't surprised that she was disappointed – Kerrie could be hard to work for.

The next morning Alice arrived early and her eyes were red and she asked if she could have a word.

'What is it, Alice?'

'Lindsey, I don't want to go back. I hate working there,' she said. 'Can't I keep working here instead?'

'Sorry, it doesn't work that way. I'd be stealing a loaner and you just can't do that,' he said. Finding good staff, developing and keeping them, was hard work so keeping a loaner was outright theft. More importantly, experienced girls built up a clientele of regulars and you'd lose a lot of those clients whenever a girl left. 'You know that, don't you?'

'Yeah, I know, I know, but maybe you could ask her . . . ?' she said.

'Sorry, sweetheart, if there was a way I could help you I would. If you don't like it you could quit Kerrie's but you can't work here. If you turn up working for me – even if it's months later – it'll still look like I've broken the golden rule.'

Alice opened her mouth to reply but she couldn't look him in the eye and turned to go back to work. He rubbed his brow and went about his day, but he had a niggling feeling that something more was amiss.

He soon discovered what it was. An hour later the phone rang and it was Kerrie.

'Rosie, if that bitch doesn't turn up for work next week you are going to be in the shit, big time,' she began and her voice was pitched higher than her normal contralto, so he knew how angry she was.

He explained that he'd ask the girl to return but Kerrie wasn't for listening and hung up on him.

That afternoon he took Alice out for a coffee. She explained that Kerrie had previously threatened to phone her parents at their house in Port Macquarie and tell them what she was doing for a living and that's the only reason that she hadn't left before.

'What exactly did you tell Kerrie?' he asked.

'I woke up this morning and thought about going back and I just couldn't hack it. She yells, she finds excuses for taking bogus fees out of my wage – like, every week – and she just orders me around like I'm her slave. If I say anything she picks up the phone like she's going to ring my dad. It sucks.'

'Yeah, but what did you tell her?' more insistent this time.

'Well . . . I told her I didn't want to work for her anymore and that I wanted to work for you instead.'

Lindsey tried to rub the knot out of his temple.

He explained that Kerrie would blame him if she didn't return, but she'd have to make up her mind. Either way, she couldn't work here.

Alice nodded in misery and Lindsey paid for the coffees and when Alice finished her shift he drove her home for the last time and wished her all the best.

Two days later she rang him in tears. Her father had called. Told her that he knew she was working as a prostitute. She'd only been doing happy endings but her father wouldn't know the difference, or care, and sure enough he had gone off the deep end and had said terrible things to his daughter and she felt like her life might as well be over. He made sure she had a friend with her then he told her that he was sorry for what had happened and urged her to focus on her studies and carry on with her life.

Then he rang Kerrie. Why did she have to out the girl to her father?

Kerrie said the girl had it coming then turned the blame to Lindsey. If Lindsey hadn't borrowed her then she'd never have left so it was all his fault.

It was too ludicrous to argue so there was nothing to be done. In his mind the matter was closed and he resolved, once again, to have nothing more to do with Kerrie Pang.

42

These episodes with Kerrie Pang he doesn't tell me all at once. Dribs and drabs arrive in letters and in conversations over the years and they're all liberally sprinkled with his hatred of this woman. When I eventually piece together his recollections into a semi-cohesive narrative, I have a crisis of conscience. I have no practical means of verifying any of the things he blames on Kerrie Pang. Other evidence, statements from her family, show her to have been a devoted mother loved by her grieving children. So how can I write these terrible things of her – things her children may one day read – without any corroboration? But how can I leave them out when they are the entirety of his motive?

I'm in a funk for days. I seek counsel.

In the end I arrive upon a compromise that leaves me feeling not entirely clean of hand. The compromise is to remind you here and now that many of these pages, including those alleging the poor qualities of Kerrie Pang, are informed *solely* by the words of Lindsey Rose. Believe of them what you will.

43

It dawned on him slowly. There was always some prank calling but this one day he couldn't use the phone for more than an hour and that's when one of his staff told him it had been getting worse, far worse, than usual. She'd answer the phone and there'd be no-one there. And sometimes the phone would ring and the caller would leave the handset off the hook and tie up the line for hours at a time.

He had a second line installed but soon that one was being tied up as well and while they could work around many things with mobile phones it went on for weeks so he had no doubt he was losing customers.

Every day he raged internally but he kept himself in check and went about his business and despite everything he was still getting at least as many customers in the door as Mark had.

Eventually he rang Telecom. It ended up with the police Telecom unit and eventually they put a stop to the harassing phone calls. They wouldn't tell him who'd been behind it and Choppie couldn't get an answer either – said the warrant was sealed.

Then the harassment escalated. Graffiti across signage and then a brick through one of their windows.

CM: What made you think it was Kerrie?
LR: Ah. Well, first of all it was typical of her modus operandi: destroyer. But I found out it was her because I had a spy.

One of the girls was confronted in the car park by a couple of rough-nuts and told that she'd better not come back to work for Lindsey Rose anymore or she'd be bashed. She saw them ride away on Harleys. Lindsey started escorting girls home but he couldn't do it for all of them so he rang Gary. Gary had done a lot of security work for Mark Lewis and he was happy to help and by the end of the week Gary was working security on-site as well as helping to get the girls home safely.

•

One morning Lindsey noticed a puddle under his Commodore and found a hole in his radiator, a stone strike. He fetched a water bottle and topped it up. The leak was slow enough that he'd make it from Burwood to Campbelltown. He arrived at noon and went straight to the office and Upstairs on Queen was closed – it should have been open for half an hour already. Down on the street he looked around in bewilderment. Raylene got out of her car and walked up to him sheepishly.

'Sorry, Rosie,' she said. 'Wasn't keen on being in there alone after all the hassles.'

'What now?' he asked, trying to keep it light.

'Some bikies followed Lucia home last night. Gary was with her, but still ... And when I got here this morning they were riding past and revving their engines 'n'that.'

The bikies were running a standard intimidation so of course they'd be making themselves known, slowing down, gunning their choppers. Raylene had seen their colours – it was the Grave Robbers.

The premises seemed secure but he asked Raylene to wait outside while he opened up and checked inside. All clear.

This could not continue. He began making enquiries.

•

Buzzard had friends in the Grave Robbers. He was a concreter, but he was on the smack and usually unemployed and he sold a bit of hooch to help ends meet. He'd often have a drink with Lindsey at the Burwood so they talked about what was going on and Buzzard kept his ears open and eventually he came back to Lindsey with news.

He told me the Grave Robbers were being paid to put me out of business. And it was Kerrie Pang who was paying.

He didn't want Betty getting caught up in it and despite all the anti-surveillance he was doing he didn't want to take the chance of being followed home, so he moved out of the Park Avenue unit. When he was on shift he stayed in Campbelltown and on the off weeks he stayed in the motel at Enfield. He parked his Commodore in a guest space at the back of a mate's flat on George Street, Burwood – out of view – then he'd walk to the motel. He had an arrangement there with the owner and borrowed a little Toyota to run around in.

It was all an incredible inconvenience and Lindsey wondered again, what was it with her and her persistence and the arrogance?

> One day I rang her in Gladesville and organised to meet her. I drove that afternoon from Campbelltown to Gladesville.

He wired up and arrived early. He drove past the house first, checking for familiar cars or movement inside. Nothing was out of place, but he parked around the corner anyway and approached on foot.

Kerrie opened the door and smiled, waved him inside and put the 'Closed' sign on the door. It was unusual for Kerrie to shut up shop in the middle of the afternoon. Maybe she didn't want customers turning up while he was being beaten up by heavies. He walked in, kept her in view, and peeked over the reception counter on the way past.

'Take a seat,' Kerrie said and nodded to one of the waiting room lounge chairs.

He stayed standing, looked at her, said nothing. He blinked, squinted and pushed his glasses up the wrinkling bridge of his nose and walked into each of the other four rooms of the converted suburban house. No-one.

He sat, perching on the arm of the lounge chair, facing Kerrie.

'Okay, how can I help you, Lindsey?'

He resisted the urge to snap – she might have a recorder going as well and he didn't want to be on tape making threats. They both knew what was going on and that all the pleasantries were for show.

'Okay, Kerrie, I'm here to sort this matter out. What is it going to take for you to drop off?'

'Drop off? What do you mean?'

He smiled. 'You know what I mean. What is it going to take for you to call off your hoodlums?'

'Yeah, I heard you've had a few problems. Maybe you're not cut out for this business. You can't even find your own girls without stealing someone—'

'Hey,' he interrupted. 'I told you before. That girl, Alice, didn't want to work for you anymore and she never worked for me once the loan was up. What did you expect me to do about it?'

'You stole her from me, Lindsey. What did you expect *me* to do? Your problems are your own fault. I'll tell you what, give me your business or go out of business. Which is it?'

> I actually looked on the situation with some humour because I was in control of the situation. Total control. I was calm and I was armed. This two-bit skank thought I was going to sit there and cop her shit. But she had no fucking idea who she was standing over.

She had no intention of relenting. The meeting was a bust.

He stood, slowly. 'Kerrie, okay, look, I'll—'

'Where do you think you're going?' Kerrie asked. 'I haven't finished speaking to you yet.'

He chortled. He remembered a meeting in Mark Lewis's office years before when Mark and Kerrie had first got together. She'd made some smart-arse comment and Lindsey had told her to shut the fuck up and threatened to deck her (and then Mark) if she spoke to him that way again. Back then he'd needed to set ground rules: he couldn't get his work done if the boss's wife was standing over him. But this time was different. There was no longer any need to maintain this relationship.

'Kerrie, I've got to go,' Lindsey said and started towards the exit. And suddenly she punched him. Punched him hard, full in the face. Later he thought it was a pretty good punch for a woman, but now he was briefly stunned and then he was laughing and grappling with Kerrie as she continued with the attack. He pushed her away, up against the reception desk. She adopted a karate stance and came at him again, kicking. This time he was ready and caught her flush on the cheekbone. She flew across the reception desk and landed, barely conscious, tangled up in a pot plant and a chair.

'Get up. That was just a love tap. If you ever hit me again I'm gonna drive you into next month,' he said.

All the fight had gone out of her and she was hurt. Instinct kicked in and he went over to make sure she was alright.

'Piss off, Rosie. Get away from me,' she said.

On the long drive back to Campbelltown he tried to make sense of what had happened.

> I still could not believe it! I knew Kerrie did karate; she had been doing it for years. Her ex-husband was an instructor at Dan level, but I did not expect a physical attack from her. She had bikies and crims to do her dirty work. I believe she was so arrogant, she believed her own abilities as a karate expert were far greater than they were. No wonder there were no heavies there to beat me up – she intended to 'do it herself'. That was narcissism at its best.

He'd taken the normal precautions to ensure he wasn't followed and sat in the car park behind Upstairs on Queen considering the day ahead. He had to check that taxis were booked for his staff and escorts were ready for those that needed them. All this hassle because of Kerrie trying to ruin his business as retribution for an alleged slight. He stared into space and memory: body parts, blood, stab wounds and car wrecks; two schoolgirls dead in a train carriage with their heads off; Bill Cavanagh's girlfriend, lifeless. The police wouldn't do anything, Mark couldn't control her and she was this loose cannon. He realised that the decision was already made.

> She had signed her death warrant when she demanded my businesses. In fact the weeks and weeks of phone harassment had already done it, she just gave me a resolve. I am a Taurean – when I make up my mind, that's it.

•

Then they got Oscar. He regained consciousness in Campbelltown Hospital with little memory of having been coshed outside the massage parlour the previous night.

'Gary, I need to get these fucking bikies off my back. I need a serious weapon.'

'I've got a mate. I'll see what I can do.'

They met in the executive lounge of Gary's local. He walked in and placed a sports bag under the table beside Lindsey's feet.

'I've borrowed an item,' he said. 'That should do the job.'

They stayed for a couple of beers and when Lindsey got home he opened the bag and inside was a Ruger Mini-14 assault rifle. It had a folding stock and polymer grips and it was the AC-556 variant with the fully automatic mode. Good old Gary had even supplied some ammunition. The next day, on his way into the office, he found a paddock near the industrial area at Campbelltown, checked the action and the folding stock and blew a few out of the pipe. Smooth. Not much pull.

When he arrived at Upstairs on Queen he stashed it in the locker just inside the office door.

•

'What's that on Biggles' head?'

'That, Rosie, would be a fedora hat,' said Denis.

'He's not even forty years old. What's the go?'

'Well, it's very practical, you know. All-purpose. He can wear it to the pub *and* to sign on for the dole.'

'Ha!' But as he leaned back laughing his eye caught a man coming in the door from Burwood Road and he looked familiar.

'Oh, shit,' he said and ducked his head. It was the drunk driver he'd belted in the Park Avenue elevator.

'What's wrong?' asked Denis.

'Jeez, I just don't need that guy to see me.' But the man sat facing them two tables away and he was already looking towards them. He might as well front up.

'In case you were wondering, it was me,' he said.

'You're the guy that beat me up?' said the man. It didn't look like he was going to start swinging.

'Yep. You deserved it. You drove into the car park too quickly. You nearly ran me over.'

'Yeah, well, I got a concussion and forty stitches out of it. And blurry vision for months after.'

'Shit, really? You should've got a punch in the mouth for it, but you shouldn't have got that much of a beating. Let me buy you a beer.'

They chatted a little longer and his name was Anton. It didn't seem like he was going to dob him in. He had reported the assault to the police, he said, but they never seemed too interested in following it up and nothing ever came of it.

Over the following few months he saw Anton at the Burwood three or four more times. Lindsey always bought him a drink and one night he gave him his business card and promised him a free night at Upstairs on Queen. Anton never took up the offer and it seemed like each time Lindsey saw him he disappeared soon after.

•

Then it was on.

He was in the office at Upstairs on Queen. The window looked out over the street and if he heard a chopper coming past he'd look out the window and check it out. But they must have parked locally and walked up because he'd heard nothing and there were two filthy goatees standing outside his office. They looked like bikers, though not in colours. One was a man-mountain – his belly was so big he couldn't zip up his jacket – and his mate looked like Catweazle, the old derro from the kids' TV show.

'I believe you'll be clearing out of here for good if you know what's good for you,' said Catweazle. Man-Mountain nodded and it wasn't at all clear that he possessed the power of speech.

The locker door was open and they were two metres away at the doorway so he calmly reached across and pulled out the Ruger.

'I don't think so, mate. If it's a war you want, you can have it,' and he racked the action on the Ruger and gestured towards the stairs.

Catweazle was very quiet but he was struggling with himself and he was probably speeding. He started back-pedalling. Man-Mountain hadn't moved and his bloodshot eyeballs were fixed on Lindsey's.

He lifted the end of the muzzle, tracing a path up Man-Mountain's body and Lindsey's face was flushed with anger. As he'd picked up the gun, as the stock slid into his palm, he'd thought he could do it . . . *Two short bursts, head shots, and they'd slide down the stairs to the landing, limp.*

He didn't know what stopped him. It wasn't self-preservation; that had gone out the window years ago. He eased the tension on the trigger a little.

So they backed down past the landing. Man-Mountain watched his feet while Catweazle's eyes were glued to the barrel of the machine gun all the way down the stairs and then they were at the door.

'Next time I'll be shooting. Got it?'

Man-Mountain just turned and shambled away. Catweazle had developed a facial twitch and broke into a trot as he looked back at Lindsey standing in the doorway with the Ruger leaning up against his shoulder.

•

Oscar was running late for the weekly handover. After two hours the phone finally rang.

'Where the fuck are you?'

'Outside the police station. There was a bomb in my car. I had to make a statement.'

'Jesus, what happened?'

'The car was running rough and I pulled over at Lakemba, and there was a two-litre plastic bottle of petrol under the bonnet with a spark lead going in. The bomb squad disarmed it.'

'What did you tell them?'

'Nothing. Nothing. No enemies, don't know why anyone would do such a thing, blah, blah, blah.'

They agreed Oscar would take the rest of the day off and Oscar's car made the six o'clock news. Lindsey's resolve firmed. Now they were trying to kill his partner and he'd be putting a stop to that.

•

So now he asked Gary to watch Oscar's back; he was on high alert, but his precautions weren't quite enough. Lindsey closed up for the night and walked to his car in the rear yard and someone came out of the shadows. He was too slow and woke up on the ground with a king-sized headache. His wallet and car keys were untouched.

•

'I can't believe they caught me out,' he said to Gary. He'd found a new motel and he'd also started carrying a gun – two guns. He didn't usually go around armed unless it was for a specific job, but now he always had a Beretta 9 mm and a five-shot Smith & Wesson in an ankle holster for back-up. 'It wasn't even my week on. I just went out for the night because Oscar had to be somewhere.'

'Were you followed out there?' said Gary.

'No. No. Definitely not, I was being careful and I did the full counter-surveillance. No chance was I followed.'

'So who else knew you were heading out there?'

'The only one I can think of is Buzzard.'

'Makes sense.'

'I suppose. I thought he was a mate but I guess the bikie code is more important to the bloke.'

'So what are you going to do about them?'

'I've got some ideas but I need help doing some surveillance first. Are you in?'

'Shouldn't be a problem, Rosie. Tracking devices or tails?'

'Just tails. I just need a couple of addresses to start with and then I can get some record searches done and go from there.'

'What about Buzzard?'

'Leave Buzzard to me,' he said.

•

'Oh, shit, you alright?' said Buzzard.

'Yeah, yeah. Got mugged two nights ago; a minor concussion and a haematoma, that's all. Lucky I was taking the Commodore home. If they'd caught me with the Volvo I'd have lost a shitload of cash. And there's no insurance that'll cover a cash loss in this business.'

'That was lucky.'

'Well, not all luck, also by design. I haven't got a safe on the premises so I keep the spare cash in this shitbox that's not worth stealing.'

He looked out the window as he said it and Buzzard changed the subject and Lindsey was sure he'd taken the bait.

The Volvo belonged to the late-shift receptionist at the after-hours medical clinic, half a block from Upstairs on Queen. He'd figured it wouldn't take long and on the second night they went for it and he was watching.

They weren't the sharpest tools in the shed. Rather than pop the door locks they took to the boot with a crowbar and made a real mess of it and when they couldn't find the non-existent cash box they kicked in a couple of panels and took off with the lug wrench. Lindsey felt bad for the receptionist, though she'd obviously be insured, but still he pissed himself laughing watching those clowns carry on.

One thing was for sure: Buzzard was working both sides.

•

Upstairs on Queen was between a dress shop and a discount variety store and at 10.30 at night he walked up the road to the Old Post Office to collect the massage takings, see the girls out and lock up.

Then he walked back down to the brothel which didn't close until midnight. He was decked out in pressed slacks, white shirt and a dark sports jacket and a passer-by might have raised an eyebrow as he walked along the strip of small diners and low-rent shops. The Ruger hung from a sling across one shoulder, under the jacket, out of sight. He'd removed the lining from the jacket pockets so he could walk with his right hand in his pocket and have a finger on the trigger guard and a thumb on the safety. All he had to do was lift his arm and squeeze the trigger.

He kept an eye on the traffic and there was a car crawling the kerb as he approached. It could have been a nervous punter but when he drew level he saw it was Catweazle in the passenger seat. Lindsey stopped and turned to face him, finger on the trigger. He wasn't going to shoot unless he had to, but Catweazle just grinned, spat out the window and they burned rubber and were away.

He went back inside and stayed put. The last customer left and they were finished with the clean-up and arranging the laundry and out the door by 1 a.m.

The car park was at the back of the premises, down a wooden staircase from the back verandah. He put his briefcase on the passenger seat then walked to the boot to get the water bottle and top up the leaking radiator. He'd only need the oxy torch and a couple of hours to fix it but he just hadn't found the time and if he topped it up each time it could wait.

He popped the bonnet, held it up with his hand – an old habit by now – opened the cap and poured the water in the dim light cast by the single bulb above the back door of the dress shop. He noticed a loose wire across the rocker cover. He moved to the side to get more light and it was definitely an extra wire but still he couldn't work it out.

He set the bonnet with the strut and fetched his Maglite from the glove box. The torchlight confirmed that someone had been at his engine. Hardly a surprise after Oscar's little episode. He checked every inch of the engine bay and found a cylinder-shaped object wrapped in brown paper on top of the starter motor. He didn't need to read the wrapping to know it was a stick of gelignite and it was linked in series with wires to the battery.

He stood back and looked around. Raylene had already driven off and there was no-one in sight. He looked skywards. Just black beyond the cone of light radiated by the dress-shop bulb. If he'd forgotten to top up the radiator . . .

He checked for secondary wires or for a circuit through the ignition but found nothing else. He disconnected the car battery, removed the detonator from the end of the gelignite then took them both into the cabin of his car. 'Danger – Blasting Gelignite' the wrapper said. A basic set-up but rigged to blow if he'd started up the engine. The old Commodore's leaky radiator had saved his life.

•

After a month of surveillance he thought they had enough. He'd been stood over enough in his life to know that an overwhelming show of force was the only way to get over the top of heavies. He rang Nick and Noel, two old mates from his childhood.

They'd gone on to the military while Lindsey was doing his apprenticeship and they'd caught up a few times over the years, even sharing a couple of black bag jobs.

They'd trained together and were currently attached to a regiment based in Brisbane. They were tight with three other like-minded fellows and they were all instructors now. Lindsey had been drinking with the five of them and the other three guys got to trust Lindsey enough to open up. It was always a rowdy night and they knew no-one was going to mess with them.

So he called up Nick and told him about this hurdle and arrangements were made for the five of them to lend a hand but it would take a few days for them to get ready and drive down – too much gear to get on a plane.

Lindsey booked them rooms at a motel in Camden. He met them there and he'd organised a car for each of them – two legit and three hot ones that he'd pinched himself.

They met Buzzard at a bar on Queen Street, Campbelltown, and he was introduced to Nick, Noel and the crew and they got on the piss together and were soon all best of mates. The plan was to kick on and Buzzard didn't need much encouragement and it was separate cars to one of the motel rooms in Camden. Nick arrived last and he brought in the kit bags.

They drank bourbon and Coke and told the sorts of war stories that appealed to Buzzard and then they brought out some of the gear. Buzzard was impressed by Lindsey's stash – rifles, pistols, silencers and the Mini-14 – but his eyes really opened up when they brought out more rifles then grenades, explosives and, the *pièce de résistance*, a rocket launcher.

'That rocket launcher would come in handy,' said Buzzard.

'Oh, yeah,' said Lindsey. 'Do you think your mates would keep it at the club house or out at the speed lab at Appin?'

'Dunno about that, Rosie,' said Buzzard, looking at Lindsey with his jaw clenched.

'Yeah, you know, the lab down off Macquariedale Road. Or you could ask Skull. Drop in to his place near the shops at Yagoona. Or maybe you could catch his wife Jenny when she picks up his kids from school.'

'Rosie . . .'

'Or the sergeant at arms, Aids, might want to keep it at his workshop at Revesby. I hear his wife Sharon fancies a big rocket – what do you reckon?' Lindsey roared with laughter and the others joined in.

Buzzard didn't reply. Poured himself another bourbon. Not so much Coke.

•

'They've lost interest in your brothel,' said Buzzard. It was two days later and they were back at the Burwood.

'Is that a fact?' said Lindsey. 'And how's that speed lab going?'

'There is no speed lab, Rosie.'

'Sure about that?' He waited.

'I'm telling you, there is no speed lab.' Lindsey's eyes drilled into Buzzard's head. 'But if there was one it's been moved to a different location, alright fuck ya. Jesus. I hope you know what you're doing, mate. You could do a lot of damage with all that gear you and your mates brought out the other night.'

'You got that right, Buzzy. Your shout.'

•

So the bikies were off, but the damage had been done and Oscar wanted out. Too much money had bled away and too many customers had been scared off forever. He'd spent a fortune catering for Nick, Noel and friends – the alcohol bill alone was in the hundreds. They sold Upstairs on Queen on the open market and the massage parlour to Raylene. He and Oscar recouped fifteen grand each, which was a pittance after everything they'd put in.

At least he got to move back into the Park Avenue flat with Betty.

•

CM: So, this was all before you murdered Kerrie?

LR: Yep.

CM: I thought you said your family was in danger and that's why you killed her – to protect them.

LR: She was a destroyer. Everything she touched, she destroyed. And she would have kept going.

44

Mark Lewis was complaining.

'Kerrie and I have split up. She won't let me see the boy. I've had to go to court to try to get access.' Mark and Kerrie's son was six months old now.

'Oh yeah, what happened this time?' Lindsey asked.

'One of the girls told Kerrie that I'd felt her up and Kerrie just hit the roof. She starts throwing things, smashing glasses and whatnot and I told her to get out or I'd call the police. Two nights later she comes over to pack up her things and she starts taking paintings off the walls, things that I paid for, and when I tried to stand in her way she attacked me.

'I called the police and she went berko and I've taken out an AVO on her.'

Lindsey smirked. Mark and Kerrie had had plenty of bust-ups over the years. The first separation had been about three years earlier. Mark got angry and Kerrie got scared and she was the one who'd called the cops. Mark had moved out, but they'd been back together within months. A year later she'd called the cops again because Mark had touched up a seventeen-year-old employee.

'She's going to ruin me,' Mark continued. 'Lorraine has left the beauty parlour because she got sick of Kerrie shouting at her and she's taken her clients with her. I'm going to have to sell it. I can't afford to be, you know, building that one back up again.'

Lindsey almost felt sorry for him. He'd been cleaned up by his first divorce and one of his two adult daughters had never spoken to him again. But he'd managed to build back up to seven relaxation centres, a coffee shop, two beauty parlours and the print shop. And he'd been one of the first Australian franchise holders for Bartercard. But he was losing businesses hand over fist now and the Bartercard hadn't gone so well and he'd had to sell out of that as well.

'Join the club, Mark. I had to sell two businesses in Campbelltown thanks to her and her bikie mates.'

'It gets worse. I've gone to the Tribunal to get access to the boy and when I went to serve the papers she threw them out her car window at me. Just like that. Twice!'

He could see it in his mind's eye. Totally predictable. Lindsey laughed.

'I miss the boy, Lindsey. She's killing me. To be honest, I'd give ten grand for someone to shoot her.'

'Mark . . .' he paused. 'Mark.'

'I'm serious. She's got to go. After what she's put me through. Do you know anyone who'll get rid of her for me?'

'I'll see what I can do,' said Lindsey.

45

Thursday 1241 HRS. Anti-social personality disorder. I believe it does relate to right v. wrong. The forensic psychiatrist who interviewed me spoke to me for about 13 minutes. I can only assume that the multi-page report he produced was somewhat a proforma and he gleaned a lot of his information from police reports which have never been close to the mark – appreciate that the powers that be believe me to be a hit man, a gun for hire, which is far from the truth. So, no, I do not agree with the diagnosis. If sociopathic disorder relates to right from wrong, then tell me why, when on the run I did not do the wrong thing. My first time in anger was 1984, second time 1994, both times me or mine were under threat. Why did I live a normal life in between, working, helping people, assisting at car accidents etc.?

I grew up normal, I think: did all the things young lads do, studied, decided on a career (paramedic), pursued that career, got married, did extra education etc. etc. Then I went out armed to do harm, then reverted back to my normal life, wife, child, 9-5 job etc. In between this time and the next time I went out armed, I was hassled by corrupt police, had my PI licence pulled wrongfully, and then when under threat of and actual assault, took the ultimate decision again. If I were a sociopath, surely I would have a continuous string of murders until I got caught.

Sunday afternoon
It's a given that someone who is labelled a sociopath is going to deny it, refute it, it's human nature. I refute it. Paedophiles, serial killers, a person who snatches people off the streets, they have problems. Rapists who prey on women, there are many people who come under the heading sociopath.

•

I have read two forensic psychiatrists' reports concerning Lindsey and neither mention psychopathy or sociopathy. One diagnosed 'antisocial personality disorder' (ASPD) and the other that he had an 'adult antisocial personality' (the main difference between the two being that the former may be 'treatable' whereas the latter is likely to be permanent).

My reading of Eysenck tells me that ASPD is common among criminals (it's a risk factor for development of criminal tendencies) but he breezes past psychopathy without really explaining the distinction.

I feel like I have skated to the middle of the lake, barely marking the ice, and having only the barest inklings of the depths below. In an unlikely coincidence, just as I am torturing that metaphor I hear the cuckoo-cuckoo chiming of our novelty doorbell. It's a courier with the timely delivery of a book that I could only find on Amazon.

Perhaps Lindsey isn't a psychopath after all (if two psychiatrists failed to mention it). And what of the sociopath – a word that Lindsey has used in relation to himself – where does he fit in? Perhaps my new book will help me: *Without Conscience: The Disturbing World of the Psychopaths Among Us.*[17]

46

'Rosie, have you thought of anyone for that job?' said Mark. 'I keep asking and you keep hedging around it.'

'Mark, it's not a good idea. With your history you'll be the first suspect, even if you got someone else to do it for you. Isn't she granting you access to the boy now?'

'Yeah, yeah. I see him three hours every Wednesday and every second Sunday – she gave in to avoid court. But you don't know what it's like. She's still trying to run the rest of my businesses, making my life hell and she's back with the threats again – if I ever leave her then she'll take me to the cleaners.'

'Bitch.'

'Why don't you do it, Lindsey? You can do it. You'll do a good job and no-one will know. I'll give you ten grand.'

'Mark, it's really not a good idea.'

•

A week later.

'Rosie, pop in here, would you?' said Mark. 'I've got something for you.'

Lindsey was typing out reports in the muster room, nearly finished. He stuck his head around the door frame.

'Yep?'

'Don't say I never do anything for you. Take a look at this.' Mark was holding out a large green garbage bag wrapped around something long and bulky. Lindsey walked in, opened the bag and looked at the canvas rifle pouch inside. Weight. There was obviously a weapon inside it. He closed the door behind him.

'What's this for?' he said.

'This ought to get the job done. It's not licensed and not traceable. Now you've got no excuse not to look after Kerrie for me.'

He looked up at Mark in some surprise. He'd always known Mark to wear a licensed five-shot revolver and he had a collection of rifles at home. But Lindsey hadn't pegged him to supply a weapon for a murder.

Mark grinned at the reaction. 'It's just another job, Rosie. I'll make it twenty grand if you do it in a hurry.'

'Mark, look. I'll take a look. I've got to head off. I'll see you tomorrow.'

Later he took the gun up to his flat and it was a .222 high-powered rifle. *Great, he wants me to start shooting high-velocity rounds in the middle of suburban fucking Gladesville.* It did demonstrate that he was serious, though, and Lindsey realised he'd already made the decision: he'd be taking Mark Lewis's money.

'The gun's no good,' he told Mark. 'Can't silence it. Have you got a .22?'

'Oh. Well, I do but they're all licensed to me. No good?'

'No good. I'll have to make other arrangements.'

•

It was a busy night at the Burwood, but few of the locals were in. A pair of young blokes were sitting at the corner table – his office – and he politely asked if he could sit with them. He sat and ignored them and they moved away.

He felt comfortable here. He'd lived in many different houses – not to mention motel rooms – but this pub was a constant; he could relax here. Of course, he did have some business he wanted to discuss with an old mate.

He bought a beer and sat at his corner table and watched the near pool table. One of the young locals, Campbell, was playing and they chatted between shots. Campbell and another young one were playing a massive, drunk Samoan and his girlfriend and she had to go fetch him from his wanderings every time it was his shot. It was a long, slow game. He didn't mind talking to Campbell. He worked in banking or something – a straighty-180 like most of the locals, but green as all fuck. Lindsey decided he'd stay and keep an eye on things in case there were problems with the Samoan.

It was January and, when the sun finally fell, the darkness behind the windows reflected the room back into itself. They were in a brightly lit fishbowl. He watched the punters. The jukebox was playing INXS, but the din of the crowd was louder. Milling about, happy people for the most part, relaxed back into their bar stools. Lindsey collected empty glasses on his way to the gents' and left them on the bar.

The door to the gents' had a glass panel so before he even opened it he could see the Samoan standing at the sink and pissing into it.

'I think you've got the wrong bowl there, big fella,' he said, slapping him on the back. The Samoan swayed back a little and looked at him with bleary red eyes. Some of the piss went on the floor. Good Christ. Lindsey continued through the next swing door to the urinals.

He was halfway through his next beer when his mate turned up.

Lindsey could tell he'd been on the piss all afternoon. But he was the kind of seasoned alcoholic who could still keep it together.

'VB?' offered Lindsey.

'That would be grand,' he said.

Lindsey returned with the extra beer and lit another smoke. He leaned back and threw the first plume back up over his head. His mate's eyes narrowed.

'What's on your mind, Rosie?'

'Nothing gets past you,' Lindsey said, grinning. He leaned in. 'Mark's been at me for months to find someone to knock off his missus. I don't reckon he's got the money, but jeez, I'd love to top that bitch.'

The smile dropped from his mate's face and, he couldn't help it, he looked sideways to make sure no-one was listening, caught himself, then took a cigarette from Lindsey's packet and arched his back with the first drag.

His eyes were creasing as he leaned back. Smoking. Calculating.

'Was it a firm commitment?'

'Oh yeah, he's really had it with her this time.'

'Alright. What do you need to get it done?' Nice that he'd invited himself along.

'You're keen. Broke again, are you?' Lindsey asked.

'Well, mate, now that you mention it, I do happen to have some debts that are about to fall due. Now that you fucking mention it and all.'

'I need back-up. Someone she doesn't know to get me in the door, or in case there's trouble. Up for it? We'll split whatever we can get out of Mark.'

His mate paused, squinting.

'Rosie, would love to help you with that one, but afraid I'm going to be washing my hair that night. You know how it is.'

'Smart bastard. Come on, the two of us . . . Can't go wrong.'

'I'm not saying no, but try and find someone else,' he said. 'What else?'

He wouldn't do it. Move on.

'I need a gun. I'm going to have problems getting the gun for this one.'

'The gun? Don't worry about the gun, Rosie. If you've got to you can use mine.'

Lindsey looked at him over his glasses and suddenly he could make out every distinct sound – the music, individual voices – colours brightened and it was like he'd taken a trip. He was on the ceiling looking down at two blokes having a chat over a beer, and he wondered what the hell that fellow sitting across from him was thinking.

'Well thanks, *mate*,' he said, dragging in smoke to create the pause. 'Thanks for that. We'll keep that one in mind. But seeing as we both know that weapon is licensed to you, I might as well use my own bloody gun. Are you a pie short of a picnic basket, or what?'

'Well, yeah. I just meant . . . Let me make some enquiries.'

'Okay, make your enquiries. Then get me a gun. It needs to be a .22 so I can silence it.'

'Copy that.'

'Copy tha—. Yeah, mate. Over and fucking out.'

•

A week later his mate dropped over. Lindsey followed him down to his car. Inside the boot was a brown paper shopping bag with string handles. Inside, a cloth wrapper and a box of cartridges. No-one was in the vicinity so Lindsey took out the cloth and unwrapped the pistol on the floor of the boot. It had an eight-inch barrel. The barrel and mechanism looked black in the darkness of the car boot; black and shiny from the WD-40 that his mate used to protect the metal and obliterate fingerprints. It had a large timber grip with finger-grip indentations and a small cocking handle on the right-hand side. It was a .22 semi-automatic target pistol. He picked up the box of cartridges and read the side of the box. Low-velocity .22 rounds. Perfect for indoor work.

'Okay, Rosie, now we're all set. Now, when are we going to—'

'Hold your horses, Mark. Let's talk first about how we're going to get her, before we worry about when. You reckon she's cagey 'cause there's some angry Lebs after her as well. So how are you going to get me at her?'

'Alright, alright. Look, it's easy. She's at the Oasis just about every night. It's on a quiet street. And I still talk to her every day so I know her movements. I'll pick a day and a time when I know she'll be there. You go around and do her.'

'Oh yeah, a piece of piss. Look, give me some time to get organised and I'll let you know, okay?'

'Organised? You've got the gun, I'll give you a date and time – what else do you need to organise?'

'Mark . . .' Lindsey turned his head away, trying to hide the flash of anger. 'Mark, there's other matters to be seen to. For example, I still need to test this weapon and I haven't silenced it yet either.' He also needed some time to recruit an assistant, but Mark didn't need to know about that.

The assistant would get him in the door – standard procedure at the massage parlour was to check out the punter through a peephole before unlocking the door and he didn't think Kerrie would be letting him in if he arrived unexpectedly at night. He'd been considering candidates and one night he decided Donnie R. (not his real name) would be the one. Donnie was a tattoo artist, didn't get much work; Kerrie had never met him and he'd be up for it. Donnie would be keen for the cash. Donnie would be solid.

'G'day, Rosie. Good to see you, mate.'

Conversations with Donnie had a certain rhythm to them so he knew this one would eventually turn to money. And so it did.

'Speaking of which,' said Lindsey, 'I need help with a job. Pays well – five hundred. Interested?'

'Are you serious? What do you fucken reckon?'

'Okay, okay. Look, this is a serious job and I need a back-up guy I can trust. Okay?'

'Yeah, yeah, okay, what is it?'

'I need to talk to this girl. I just need you to knock on a door so they'll see your face instead of mine so they'll let me in to talk to her.'

'That's it?'

'That's it.'

Donnie stubbed out his cigarette and looked back up at Lindsey's deadpan.

'Okay, Rosie. Alright, I'm in,' said Donnie.[18]

•

It had been ten years and two weeks since he'd shot Bill Cavanagh, he reflected as he made similar preparations. This time he used his workshop at Wentworthville to manufacture a silencer and it was a different paddock for the test firing. But otherwise it was all quite familiar. One shot to test the weapon and two more with the silencer on and it wasn't making too much noise so the weapon was ready to go.

Then, as before, it was time for a dry run. He picked up Donnie and they drove to Gladesville. They drove past Kerrie's Oasis, checking out the vehicles, and the white Fairmont Mark had described wasn't there.

There was a large car park across the road, backing the Victoria Road shops, and they parked up the top and watched, got a feel for the traffic, the pedestrians. Donnie got bored and walked up to the shops. He came back with a packet of smokes and a Coke.

'You'll need to shave that beard off, Donnie,' Lindsey said. 'You should look neat and tidy to make sure she lets you in the door.'

He rang Mark Lewis, trying to work out where Kerrie was and when it would be safe. No answer. It was after 7.30 p.m. when they left. The car park was empty and it was starting to get dark and there was little passing traffic. It would be a good time of day.

He drove them back to the Burwood and they joined in the throng. Mark hadn't called back so he tried him a couple more times and his phone just rang out and it started to give him the shits.

Mark Lewis didn't call back for two days. Then he did.

•

He'd finished restoring the 1960 Holden and it had come up nice – light blue with a dark blue flash. Donnie rode shotgun and they were quiet as he drove. He switched on the radio to hear the news. UN talks to resolve the Siege of Sarajevo, which was in its twenty-second month. Gang leader and owner of the Lansdowne Hotel Barry McCann to give evidence at the Coroner's Court about the disappearance of Christopher Dale Flannery. Mr Rent-A-Kill himself. Why bother with an inquest when he'd obviously been taken for a swim off the heads by some of New South Wales's finest – tied to a stove. And someone had stolen a famous painting from the National Gallery of Norway: Edvard Munch's *The Scream*.

After the news the DJs came back on and started talking about Valentine's Day and he realised it was today, 14 February. It was Valentine's Day and he was on his way to shoot a former lover.

It was approaching 6 p.m. and twenty-five degrees with a breeze from the east and the sun beat down hard so he kept the window down and his right elbow pointed out over the window frame. Crossing Ryde Bridge towards Rhodes he glanced at the view down the Parramatta River towards the city. The air was clear and the landscape here on the river plain was flat and the mangroves were mostly intact. So the waterfront was dark green, little bays fronted by the reflecting white hulls of moored leisure craft. Millions of dollars worth of steel, wood and fibreglass. On balance, at least a couple of those boats would be overleveraged and need to be repossessed or sold under duress.

He remembered confiscating, years earlier, a Halvorsen Cruiser on which a finance company was owed arrears of several months. It had been used as a floating brothel so he'd taken three armed agents with him. Once they'd taken possession, they rang a few mates – agents and cops included – and they motored around the harbour picking up passengers and cases of beer, moored in a bay and partied through the night. The next morning they cleaned up the cruiser and returned it to the owner – another successful repossession.

The only thing he'd be repossessing today was a human life.

•

They parked where they could see the front of Kerrie's Oasis diagonally across the car park.

'All set? You ring the bell and I'll wait out of sight until the door's open,' he said.

'Yep. Okay,' said Donnie.

Lindsey carried the .22 in the same brown paper shopping bag that his mate had given it to him in. The silencer was attached and he'd included a long-bladed kitchen knife.

The front door was on the left side of the house down a short path. Lindsey stood with his back against the dark red brick. Donnie stood facing the front door, got the nod, took a deep breath and rang the bell.

Within seconds he heard the key turn in the deadlock and the door opened. His hand was already in the bag and he walked through the doorway behind Donnie and pulled out the gun. He pointed it at . . . and then he realised it wasn't Kerrie who had opened the door. A small, dark chick was standing there staring at the gun, sick in the face.

Mark had told him Kerrie would be here and no-one else.

'Where's Kerrie? Where is she? Where the fuck is she?' he yelled at the girl. He could feel his face burning, about to burst.

'Don't hurt me, please . . . What . . . what do you want? Do you—'

He cut her off. 'We're here to see Kerrie. Just tell me where she is. *Where is she?*' he said.

'Don' . . . don't hurt me. Kerrie's gone to the doctor . . . she's at the doctor's, with her husband. She's got the key to the safe,' she said, cringing at the sight of the gun, starting to cry. 'Please.'

He had to put this girl somewhere so he could work out what to do, calm her down.

'Look, we're just here for Kerrie. We won't hurt you. Just keep walking and turn right,' he directed her. He knew that room looked out into the street so he'd be able to keep an eye on things.

The girl went where she was told. The room contained a massage table, pot plants, a two-seater lounge. He waved at her to sit on the lounge. She flinched at the gun.

The girl was wearing a short white sundress with crossover straps at the back. White sneakers, no socks, nice legs. Young. He looked back out the window and adjusted the venetian blinds. The girl had said Kerrie was at the doctor's. With her husband. So Mark knew she was there and he hadn't called it off so they must be good – he'd stay put. Perhaps the doctor's appointment had just run late.

It didn't occur to him until later that he'd focussed on the wrong thing. Yes, she was at the doctor's, but she was at the doctor's *with Mark*.

'How long will she be?' he asked.

'I don't know, she said she'd call when she was on her way,' the girl said. 'Unless I am with a customer, then I leave the phone off the hook.'

He walked out to reception, tipped the phone out of its cradle and went back to her.

'Just sit there and do what you're told. You're doing okay. You'll be okay.' He didn't go for wog chicks as a general rule and this one . . . He didn't look back at her, but at Donnie hovering outside the doorway. She'd seen them both, and with the gun. Donnie's eyes flicked between Lindsey and the girl. Lindsey turned away from his gaze.

'We'll wait until Kerrie gets here,' he said. He leaned against the wall where he could keep watch out the window. He didn't want to be caught by surprise when Kerrie, or someone else, arrived. The girl was in front of him. He kept the .22 in his hand.

47

The first time Donna visited she walked into the Long Bay visits room and he stood up as she swept up to him and wrapped her arms around him. Donna's arms were around him and he stood there with his arms by his sides at first and stayed strong.

'That's from my mum,' she said. Then she let him go and looked him up and down at arm's length.

'Hello, Lindsey. How are you?' she said. He could see she was trying to keep the mood up, bring some lightness to the meeting.

'Donna . . .' he began. 'Donna, not bad considering, thanks. A lot better for seeing you.' He broke off; there was nothing else he could say and he gestured for them to sit. They looked at each other in silence and he tried to read her then looked down at his feet. Donna began.

'Lindsey, did you hurt Max?'

'No,' he said, 'of course not.' She was relieved.

'And what about those other people they say . . . you didn't hurt those other people, did you?'

'Yes, Donna, I did,' he said. Even though she knew it was coming her heart ran cold. Again. Like it did the first time she'd seen his face on the television, the first time she'd had any inkling that he might be anything other than the favourite uncle who she'd grown up with. Of course her body hadn't wanted it to be true. He'd replied to her first letter, writing how he might have helped her recover from her mother's death (had he not been in prison), and she'd considered what he was accused of and thought, no way, he couldn't have done those things. But now she had confirmation and it was like the loss of another family member, another added to the long list.

But she'd followed his advice, taught herself how to compartmentalise. This was the only way she was able to deal with the stress of her mother's illness – the first time around – and complete her studies at the same time. Put the bad thing in a little box in your mind and put that box aside while you deal with other things, so you can get on with your life, he'd told her. And so it was when she visited Lindsey – what he had done was too painful to bear so she put it away in a box and focussed on the man she'd known and loved.

She told him about her life and some of the things she hadn't wanted to put into her letters.

She'd spent a lot of time with her mum before she died and seeing her sick like that again had made her think more about Lindsey. She'd seen the news report and she told him how shocked she'd been; when more information came out in the papers she talked to her mum about it and it broke her heart too.

And she told him that her father had been right about Donna's husband – the one who he'd offered to 'take care of' – and Donna had left him. 'You should have called me,' Lindsey said to her. 'I would've—' Donna looked mortified and he stopped, almost regretted saying it. Despite how the man had apparently behaved, Donna didn't wish harm upon anyone.

Visiting became a habit and for two years she went to Long Bay nearly every week. She'd bring him cigarettes and they'd mainly talk about people they both knew. If it was a Sunday she'd bring her two kids along and the visitors' centre had all these wooden toys made by prisoners and the kids would play with them. Up to ten prisoners received visitors at a time and one day Lindsey pointed out a long-serving crim with a media profile. Donna looked over and there he was, lying on the floor with kids jumping all over him.

'He looks like a proud and happy grandfather,' she said.

'Don't be fooled,' said Lindsey. 'The man is a thug.'

After he was moved to Goulburn she visited a couple more times. But the trips to Goulburn took their toll and became further apart and then she'd had her own medical problems to worry about. There was one last visit and she was agitated because her father had a new girlfriend and it was disrespectful to the memory of her mother, she said.

Lindsey tried to talk her down. His stepfather, his Pa, had taken a new girlfriend after Glenda died and he was glad because of it – rather that than the old man be alone. Get over it, he told Donna. She was upset when she left and later he wondered if that might be the end of it with Donna.

48

Q415 ... When you travelled to Kerrie's Oasis, did you have the .22 target pistol with you?

A   On the 14th?

Q416 Yes.

A   Yes.

Q417 Now was that loaded at that time?

A   Yeah it would have been.

Q418 Do you remember loading it?

A   Not particularly, no.

Q419 Alright. What was the reason you loaded it?

A   So I could shoot bullets out of it.[19]

Ten minutes, twenty minutes or was it thirty minutes – he couldn't be sure how long passed before he saw Kerrie's white Fairmont pulling in. His entire focus had been inwards, on this room, the girl. There'd been no conversation during the stagnant passing of time.

Q219 What did she do when she pulled up?

A   Well I just saw the car pull up and then I went into another room.

Q220 What happened then?

A   Oh prior to going into the other room, I shot the other girl.

...

Q230 Why did you shoot her?

A   So she wouldn't cause any trouble.

Q231 Did you realise when you shot her you could kill her?

A   Yes.

Q232 Did that cause you any problems?

A   Yes.

Q233 Why?

A   Because she shouldn't have been there. Mark Lewis had totally
         buggered it up.

'It's her,' Lindsey said quietly. Donnie was breathing hard. Lindsey looked
over the top of his spectacles at him – the doctor look – met his eyes.
'Go into the other room,' Lindsey said and shook a thumbs-up in front
of Donnie to boost him up. Donnie nodded back. He'd be okay. 'You
wait in there until she walks past you.'

Donnie moved into the room to the left of the front door and waited.
Lindsey selected another room further down the hall. While he waited
he held up the pistol and checked that the silencer was still secured. He'd
used three bullets and the smell and heat of the firings were strong on
him in the small room.

> The body is that of a well-developed, well-nourished adult Caucasoid
> female who weighs 50 kg, is 150 cm in height and appears compatible
> with stated age of 26 years.
> The body is received clad in a short white dress, blue underpants
> and white track shoes.
> There are multiple pearl studs in both the right and left ears.
> There is a yellow metal chain around the neck with a half moon
> pendant.
> There is a brown cord around the neck which contains numerous
> pendants including an opal, a green and white stone and a Chinese
> medallion.
> At the time of autopsy, the body was cold to touch.[20]

They heard the key in the lock and Kerrie walked past the door in
front of them.

'Fiona, why aren't you at the . . .' and then she saw Lindsey step out.
He stepped out with the gun poised and then everything speeds up. Two
steps out of cover and suddenly there is another person right behind
Kerrie. It's bloody Mark.

Kerrie sees the gun and talks, high-pitched, vocal cords constricting:
Wait, Mark and I . . . we're all sorted now. You don't need to . . .

Mark gives her a shove up the hallway.

It's too late, Lindsey hears himself say, the other girl's dead, I've got to do you too. A plastic shopping bag drops: milk, bread, tins of tuna . . . He aims. Two shots, both missed and Mark ducks out of the way into the room at the front.

Kerrie runs at him and he tries to push her back but then Mark walks back out and he has his rifle in his hands and in a moment of clarity Lindsey can see it is a Winchester .22. Why is he . . . Donnie runs out and punches Mark, knocks him down, knocks down the rifle. Don't hurt him, he's the guy paying, Lindsey yells. And Kerrie grabs at Lindsey's pistol and they both have two hands on it, wrestling, and Donnie, give us a hand or we're both going to get thirty years for this. Donnie lets go of Mark and punches Kerrie in the face. Then she falls back and releases her grip on the gun. Panicked and confused bodies grabbing, pushing and hitting each other. What is Mark doing, has he changed his mind or does he want to shoot her himself? Kerrie runs. Finish it, Rosie, you've done it now, do it quick, do it quick, Mark is yelling. Get it done, for God's sake . . .

The blur. Discombobulation. Fragments of colour and motion. His glasses are off. Down the hall and he is outside the room with the massage table and the dead girl. He gets another shot away and it snaps through the quagmire like a shockwave – the silencer is off. The shot misses and there is running, the hallway turns left and Kerrie is nearly at the bend and the silencer is back on and she turns to look and the next shot hits her in the eye, and she falls. But she's back up, running, left and down to the back room. No, Lindsey, no, Lindsey. You got me already. Don't kill me. Don't . . .

Behind him Lindsey hears a round being chambered and he turns and Mark has his rifle out, loaded. Grab him, Donnie. Get him out of here, he's not supposed to be here. Mark, get that . . . get that bloody rifle out of here and clear the area. And Mark is yelling, She's not dead! She's not dead! Jesus, put her— Two more shots miss – no bullets left – and she is trapped in the back room and then the knife is out and he is plunging it . . . then cutting . . . Shut up. Die. Get it done. Quickly. That's it, the carotids.

Then he is slashing at cushions in the back room, pushing combustibles up against the wall, yelling at Mark to get out. Mark is walking up and down the hallway ranting, raving, with his dirty great rifle. Get out, Mark, you're not the boss here now, get off the premises. Why are you . . . Just go, quick, while I . . .

Gets out his lighter, gets the fire started, opens a window. He turns and for a second he can't tell if it is Mark or Donnie down the hall, his vision is blurry at that distance. He feels the heat of the fire on his buttocks and he starts walking.

Donnie smells smoke, looks back over his shoulder and time slows. A demon is walking down the hallway towards him. The back room is crackling and Lindsey is sweeping towards him trailing a cloak of black smoke, thick, and Donnie feels his fingertips sting as the old guy with the rifle reefs his polyester shirt out of Donnie's weakening grip. The taste of burning rubber. Lindsey is upon him and leans over . . .

. . . Finds his glasses on the floor, puts them on but one of the lenses is broken so he takes them off and gets the paper shopping bag and puts the gun, knife and glasses in there, bits from the broken glasses. He walks out to reception and Mark is still there and he puts his hand on Mark's shoulder and guides him towards the door. Mark, listen, you'll have powder residue on you. Get rid of those clothes. The paper bag is dripping. Lindsey points Donnie out the door then follows with Mark, talks him out. Leave the door ajar, let the fire take hold. When the cops come to tell you what's happened, fake a heart attack or something, get yourself taken to a hospital so you can settle yourself down, get yourself organised. And they are hot-footing it across the road and through the car park to his car. You've got to drive, Donnie, my glasses . . . And suddenly he is sitting in the car, in the passenger seat, and Donnie was there next to him. 'Fuck, Rosie. Fuck, man,' said Donnie.

Mark's white Tarago, with the ML-001 personalised plates, was parked near Kerrie's car and how had he missed it? Donnie started the engine and Lindsey saw Mark open the back door and put the leather rifle bag on the floor – somehow he'd got the rifle back in the bag. Mark got in and drove off – wobbly, nearly took out the post at the side of the car park gate on the way out.

It was darkening, but not dark enough yet for headlights. The street was silent, no-one in sight. He raised his hand in front of him as Donnie engaged first and stalled it. 'Easy, fella,' he said, looking at his hand. Steady as a rock. Bloody. He wiped it on a spare shirt from the back seat as Donnie put it in first again and bunny-hopped away from the kerb. He graunched the gears changing into second and Lindsey told him to pull over.

'Mate, I can drive blind better than you can with two eyes,' he said.

'Not used to a manual, Rosie, that's all.'

'Get out, I'll drive, you look ahead and tell me what's coming.'

They drove back to Burwood, slowly. When they got to Lindsey's place Donnie went to the boot to remove the bag with the weapons but as he lifted the paper bag it fell apart. The blood had wet through the bottom of the bag so it separated as he lifted, and the knife and the gun fell through the bag and into the boot. Lindsey's glasses were in there too with the broken lens. Donnie gathered them up with the remnants of the bag and the clothes and Lindsey was already up the driveway with the door open so Donnie slammed the boot and ran inside.

Donnie showered and Lindsey went through the contents of the bag and tried to piece his glasses back together. There was some glass missing and one of the plastic nose pads. They could get DNA off the nose pad. 'Donnie, did you see the nose pad off these glasses?'

'Nuh.'

'Fuck, Donnie, this could do us. Let's hope the fire took care of it.' Donnie looked downcast and Lindsey gave him a clean shirt.

'I'm meeting the guy tomorrow to get the money,' he said. 'You never saw me today and don't say a word to fucking anyone or you'll need fixing too, understand?' he said. His forefinger was aimed like a gun-sight between Donnie's eyes.

'Okay,' was all Donnie could muster in reply. He walked home.

•

An hour later Lindsey walked into the Burwood RSL in fresh clothes. He'd bagged up all the clothes he'd worn to Kerrie's along with Donnie's shirt and buried the bag in a skip bin at an industrial site in one of the backstreets of Burwood. No-one was in sight and he'd rewrapped the .22 and hidden it underneath a similar bin – it would be safe there for at least two days until he could dispose of it properly.

He walked through to the poker machines and Alan was playing his favourite machine: Jewel of the Nile. It was a ten-cent machine and he had a little over a thousand credits. But he was dropping a hundred per spin – the maximum.

'Not going to last you long at that rate, Choppie,' he said.

'No shit, Sherlock. Always thought you should have been a detective, Rosie,' he replied, without looking up. 'Grab yourself a beer, I'll have a New while you're at it.'

By the time he returned with the beers, Alan was feeding another twenty dollars into the machine.

Spin. Dacka-dacka-dacka-dacka-dacka.

'How long you been here, Choppie?'

'Since six o'clock,' he said, still looking at the spinning reels of the poker machine.

Spin. Dacka-dacka-dacka-dacka-dacka.

'I was already here when you arrived. Okay with that?'

Choppie froze, for barely a second, his poker machine finger hanging in mid-air. It was the only sign he gave before the reels resumed their hypnotic whirring clatter.

Dacka-dacka-dacka-dacka-dacka.

'No worries, Rosie,' he replied.

49

There are two responses to bullying. The victim acquiesces or the victim resists. The bully must either intensify his attacks or desist, but the bully won't desist as that's a sign of weakness especially if done in front of others and if the victim resists then the bully isn't exercising their power over them and so there is no pay-off for the bully. I was a resister.

This he has written in a letter and I raise it the next time I visit.

'I'm not sure if *bully* is a helpful term,' I say. 'Aren't you really talking about two people trying to exercise power over each other? And using violence to get your way – in a way doesn't that make you a bully too?'

'The psychs in here have been trying to tell me the same thing. Maybe I was twenty or thirty per cent bully but the rest was standing up for people.'

'Alright, then. What I'm trying to get at is that most people – outside of prison anyway – don't use violence to solve their problems.'

'Look, most people are weak. They acquiesce to the bully. So there's all these people in the world living miserable cunts of lives because of bullies standing over them or whatever and not having the balls to do anything about it. That's what really makes me mad. That's why I went after Pang and Cavanagh – all the lives they ruined. It was bad enough all the stuff Pang did to me and Oscar – but imagine all the other lives she affected.

'The psychs asked me: why do I feel the need to do something about it? Because most of the time everyone else will stand around and do nothing, I told them. I do something about it because no-one else is going to. One night I was on a harbour cruise – I always went out of my way to accept when a cruise was on offer – and one of the patrons fell overboard. He was floating twenty metres out the back before he knew what had happened. Someone threw a life buoy but the man overboard couldn't swim so it did no good. I handed my phone and wallet to the woman I was with. I can't remember which woman it was. If it was Lydia she would have figured it was par for the course; if it was a first date the girl must have thought, "Who does this bloke think he is?" So I jumped in to rescue this non-swimmer and I was only in it for about six minutes but when I got out I was absolutely frozen.'

Is this the act of a psychopath, to rescue a drowning man? I recall the story of the free TV he wrangled for an old lady early in his career as a PI, and the stories from his ambulance days suggest a genuine care for the patients he treated. Good deeds, evil deeds; they still seem irreconcilable.

50

The next morning, he lay staring as two flies chased each other around a static point in the space above his bed. He was supposed to meet Mark at 10 a.m. at his office in West Ryde to collect the money. But would he show? Probably not. Mark and Kerrie must have been at the West Ryde massage parlour before driving to Gladesville. The cops would question the staff at West Ryde so Mark must be under suspicion. He might even be in custody already. It wasn't safe to phone him – the only way to find out was to drive out to the meet.

On the drive he assessed the odds that cops would be waiting for him. No chance. Firstly, Mark was many things but he wasn't a dog. Secondly, if Mark put him in it would only be to save his own skin. The cops wouldn't have evidence to charge him yet. And there's no way Mark would put Lindsey in for the murders because he knew he'd be implicating himself. And if they wanted to arrest him they could've just come to his unit – Mark knew the address.

But there was no harm in playing it safe so he parked a block north of Victoria Road, walked to the corner and checked out all the nearby vehicles and pedestrians. Nothing. He walked up to the office. It was empty. He hung around until 10.30 to be sure. Mark never showed.

He drove back to Burwood. He'd better stay away from Mark until things cooled down.

•

Three days later he went for a walk down Burwood Road. He had a canvas carry bag. At St Vincent de Paul he browsed to the back of the shop then made sure no-one was watching. He took out the kitchen knife that he'd used to cut Kerrie Pang's throat and put it on a shelf with some other knives for sale. On the way out he bought a cheap glass ashtray.

Next stop was Donovan and Moore's Optometry, on Burwood Road near Westfields. His Alfa Romeos were missing the right lens and the nose pad. He ordered soft contact lenses while he was at it; wearing glasses in a melee was clearly not a good idea.

Then he went to the Burwood. Oscar was there.

'What the fuck is going on at Gladesville?' said Oscar. The double murder had been in the news.

'Buggered if I know,' he said.

•

'I've got to get rid of a gun,' Lindsey said. 'I've got it stashed, but I need to get rid of it permanently.'

'Ah . . .' said Alan. He thought about it for a second. 'Give it to me. A friend of mine collects guns, lives in Castle Hill. Should be able to get some money for it.'

'Is this bloke . . . I mean, is it safe with him?' asked Lindsey, then took a mouthful from the schooner glass. He'd pictured the gun being melted down for scrap metal somehow. He was a bit wary of leaving it in circulation.

'Well, if he wants it, it's perfect. He's a collector, he's not a crim. He just looks at them – it'll never get used for anything.'

He thought about it. Having the gun in a collection – hiding in plain sight, like the knife – might not be such a bad idea.

'Okay, Choppie. Give it a go. Thanks for that,' he said.

•

They parked their cars together in the car park of the Burwood RSL – up the back and behind a pillar. Lindsey had cleaned the gun and used his mate's trick with the WD-40. Alan came and picked up the white plastic shopping bag from Lindsey's car and looked inside. It contained the pistol, silencer and a dozen unfired cartridges. He put it into his own boot.

'I'll let you know how I go. How about a few beers?'

'No, mate, I'm going to head out. Might be a good idea if we aren't seen together for a bit.'

'Okay. I'll call you on your mobile if I've got some cash for you.'

•

'Rosie, here's the money I got for that item,' said Alan Thomas. He tapped Lindsey on the knee and passed the folded notes to him right up against the bottom of the table so no-one would even see their hands. Lindsey trousered the cash immediately.

'How much'd you get for it?'

'Five hundred.'

'How much did you keep for yourself?'

'Nuh. It's all yours,' said Alan. Lindsey looked at him. 'Sure? I know you've been a bit short lately. Let me give you half.'

'I'm alright for now,' he said and made a fuss of lighting another cigarette. Lindsey was surprised to get as much as five hundred for the pistol and within a week – Choppie must have got at least a grand for it. He let it slide.

'Thanks, Choppie, much appreciated.' But he was still on edge because even though Mark was a canny old lizard, he still might slip up, and it wouldn't be too much of a leap for them to widen their enquiries and come for him. And now he was worried about the gun again. If his name came up the .22 target pistol was one of the few things that could connect him to the murders.

'Choppie, we should have changed the ballistics on that gun. Even if your mate's never going to use it, if someone gets hold of it and tests it . . . Bingo.'

'Rosie, the man is straight and he has no idea where it came from. And no-one else knows I got it from you. It'll be alright.'

It didn't feel right. He persisted.

'Do you think you can borrow the gun back so I can fix it?' he asked.

Alan looked at his coaster and put his hands out, thumbs pointing at the sky, ten fingers stretched out. 'Mate,' he said. 'How can I just . . .' he exhaled in exasperation. 'How the fuck would you *fix* the thing anyway?'

> Q360: Okay and you also said that you'd explained to Alan Thomas how to change the ballistics of a pistol. How do you do that?
>
> A: You remove the firing pin and fold the end of the pin so it leaves a different witness mark on the percussion cap. You pull out the ejector pin and file the ejector pin and the surrounding area where the shell is picked up by the reloading mechanism and . . . and chambered. And then you

. . . put the weapon in a vice and put a ball bearing slightly bigger than the calibre in the end of the barrel and hit it with a hammer. And that changes the three marks that the shell leaves.

'Jesus Christ,' said Alan.

•

A week since the murders and he'd been drinking at the Burwood every night. This night he was with Choppie, Zane, Donnie and Shane.

Choppie was in the dumps because he'd been brawling with his wife again and Zane, out of nowhere, asked what everyone had been doing on Valentine's Day.

'Ah, Valentine's Day,' said Lindsey, winking at Donnie, 'a day to remember.'

Donnie looked downcast and Choppie shook his head. 'We were doing a job for an Englishman, me and my offsider here,' he continued, nudging Donnie. Choppie downed his beer and left and the conversation moved on.

It was getting late and the crowd was thin; they started talking about continuing on at Shane's flat. Someone finally said 'Let's go, then' so it was straight out the door and right up Burwood Road and halfway down Belmore Street Zane asked, 'Where's Donnie?'

'He lives the other way, probably went home.'

They got to Shane's place and the boys started pulling cones but Lindsey stuck to beer and soon he was doing most of the talking. And he was still worried about the gun with the unaltered ballistics and Choppie had seemed edgy and now he was wondering if Donnie wasn't going to give up the ghost. What do you reckon about Donnie, he started saying. I don't know if I can trust him, you know. The type of work we're doing, if you can't trust your apprentice you're fucked. Or he's fucked, more like it. That type of work . . . if your offsider becomes a lagger they're liable to get shot.

He was saying it to no-one in particular. The couch was right next to the doorway to the kitchen and Zane yelled out, 'Donnie's here.'

Oh fuck, what gives, and he stormed across the living room and the front door slammed and he followed Donnie out to the street and he was waiting for him in the street lights.

'Where did you bunk off to just now?'

'Nowhere, I just went to the dunny and when I come out youse were all gone. I wasn't sure which unit was Shane's so I just walked up looking. What did you say you were going to shoot me for?'

'It's okay, Donnie boy, it's just talk. You're not going to talk to any cops now, are you?'

'Of course bloody not,' said Donnie.

'Well, you've got no need to worry then. Because if you keep your mouth shut there'll be no need for me to come over to your place and give you the Gladesville treatment and then your mum for good measure. Is there?'

'No, Rosie, course not.'

'And don't forget, even if I'm locked up I've got contacts. If they don't get you on the outside, they'll get you on the inside.'

'That's fucked, man. There's no need for that, I'm with ya,' said Donnie.

'Alright, alright, keep your hair on. Is there anything you need?'

'Have you got twenty bucks? I'm flat broke,' said Donnie.

Lindsey walked upstairs and borrowed twenty dollars from Zane then handed it to Donnie, who turned and walked off down the road towards home.

'Fuck the little prick,' said Lindsey when he got back inside the flat, but no-one seemed to notice. Everyone was dopey and staring at the tinny music videos on the television. 'Let's go, Zane.'

They walked out; his restored FB Holden was a block up the road and the night was warm and still and the starlight lifted the weight from his shoulders.

'Watch out, Zane,' he said, 'enemy ahead,' and he pulled the pistol from the back of his trousers and rolled across the footpath into the gap between two parked cars. He was a commando. Zane wasn't reacting.

'I've got you covered,' he said, pointing the pistol at imaginary foes up ahead. He walked out from behind the car, keeping the pistol at arm's length, sweeping it from side to side and darting between parked cars on both sides of the road. When they got to his car he shoved the pistol under the driver's seat and drove Zane home.

•

CM: I asked Lindsey about that night. He told me the commando story is bullshit. He would never misuse a weapon that way.

Z: Well, that's right. He generally wouldn't. I was in the army for three years and spoke to guys who'd served with Lindsey in the reserves and they all said he was a good soldier. A real good soldier. He was security conscious. It was out of character for him to misuse a weapon.

CM: How do you explain it then?

Z: I'd never seen him acting silly like that before. He must have been under some sort of enormous pressure. It was like a spring had broken in his head.

•

The next day, sober, Lindsey realised things couldn't continue like this. Donnie hanging around and drinking with them and young as he was. 'You're too hot,' he said. 'You need to get out of the state for a few months until things cool down. I've arranged transport.' He didn't give Donnie much of a say and the next day he was in the back of a truck on his way to South Australia.

•

At 7 p.m. there was an announcement over the PA system of the Burwood RSL. 'Phone call for Lindsey Rose. Please come to the bar, Rosie.'

It was Donnie: 'I'm stuck in Mount Gambier. It's a fucken shithole and I've run out of money. Can you put some money in me account so I can get out of here?'

'I still haven't been paid, but I'll see what I can do. Everything else alright?'

'No problem there, Rosie.' Hung up.

Zane asked who had called.

'It's your mate, Donnie.'

'He's not my mate,' said Zane and Lindsey laughed.

'I'll be needing a new apprentice now that Donnie's off the scene,' he said.

'I don't know what you blokes get up to,' said Zane, 'but you can leave me out of it.'

51

'I'm on the bones of me arse, Choppie. I can't work for Mark anymore – and he owes me money. I'm just getting pocket money from the workshop and I've got no hooch ready to sell,' Lindsey said.

'I'm much the same. What about the money Mark Lewis owes you?'

'He's cleared out. I don't want to outlay cost to track him down 'cause he's probably broke anyway.'

'After all those businesses he owned? He must have it stashed somewhere. I wouldn't give up so soon,' said Choppie. 'Anyway, I might have another earn coming up. Someone I know needs an alibi. And they've got money.'

'Oh, yeah?'

'You'll probably just need to tell the cops you were having a beer with this bloke. I can get you four grand upfront if you agree to do it.'

It was tempting. They'd been mates for ten years – best mates, he supposed. But he'd seen Choppie fuck over mates before and a bent cop could be in a precarious position from time to time. And the last thing he needed in his current situation was to be bringing himself to the attention of the authorities.

'I'll think about it,' he said.

•

Eventually another crop finished drying. The standard deal now was a larger fifty-dollar bag instead of twenty, so the margin was a bit smaller but he had to make fewer deals. He tried the Pine Inn for a change; a couple of Nomads used to score from him by the ounce.

As soon as he sat at a bar table, a hand clapped him on the back. It was Gary, the bodyguard who'd helped him with the bikies at Campbelltown. Gary bought him a beer, bought a bag of hooch as well and they sat. They'd both worked for Mark Lewis so, naturally, he came up in conversation and Gary had heard through the grapevine that Mark had moved back to Carlingford to be closer to his daughter. He didn't have the address but was pretty sure it was close to Carlingford Road.

'I wouldn't mind catching up with the old fella,' Lindsey said. 'How's your contact list these days?'

'Okay. Not flash, but okay.'

'Telecom?'

'Yeah, probably,' said Gary.

They agreed to meet the following day and Gary's contact had turned up an unlisted number for a Mark Lewis in the right part of Carlingford.

'You're a good man, Gaz. Here, take another bag for your trouble.'

•

He made sure the pistol was loaded and he strapped on his ankle holster. There was an old, yellow Mitsubishi L300 van in the driveway of Mark Lewis's house. Lindsey parked against the kerb right outside the house. If the cops were watching there was no point looking devious. Just visiting an old friend.

He rang the bell and thought he heard a shuffle behind the door but it didn't open for another full minute. Mark opened the door and he was holding the boy, his son; Kerrie's son. He was nearly two years old now and pointed at Lindsey with a smile on his face. He pointed at Lindsey and said, 'Dadda.'

Lindsey smiled. 'You're a cute little fella, aren't you? But I'm almost certainly not your Dadda.' He nodded towards Mark, who was looking fraught.

'Rosie, I'm under surveillance, mate. You probably need to make yourself scarce,' Mark said, leaning around and looking out the door behind Lindsey, never one to shy away from the melodramatic.

'Mark, I'm just here to collect that cash you owe me. Remember?'

Mark obviously knew this was coming and he tried to deliver a prepared answer.

'Look, I'll get you the money, but I'm . . . I've just got cash-flow issues right now. Look,' he said. And he reached around to get his wallet and with the boy still in his arms he pulled out a card and held it out. It was a pension card. 'That's all I'm living on right now. All I've got is some charity furniture and the van – and I can't even afford the rego for that.'

'Well, that's fine, but that's your problem, not mine. I need the money because I've got to pay the other bloke,' said Lindsey. He kept his voice civil but hard.

'Who the bloody hell was that other bloke, anyway?' asked Mark.

'Just a bloke, you don't need to know who it was,' said Lindsey.

'Yeah, but he could give us up, you know. Is he strong? Why didn't you tell me you were bringing someone else?' Mark had that whiny tone in his voice he got when he was nagging, grasping at something he could hold over Lindsey.

'Mark, if you hadn't shown up when you weren't supposed to be there you wouldn't have even known about him and you wouldn't have to worry about it. I can subcontract in help, just like any other job. What the f— . . . hell did you turn up for anyway?' If it hadn't been for the toddler he'd have been yelling. It was an effort to suppress the anger. Mark was answering his question, but Lindsey was looking into the eyes of the small boy, hanging from his father's forearm, staring at him with wide eyes and open mouth. Mark's waffling reply was blowing straight past him.

'Mark,' he cut him off. 'Enough. I just want the money.'

'Okay, okay, you'll get it. I just need to get myself organised. Give me a few weeks and I'll have it together for you. Okay?'

Lindsey looked at Mark, at his cute little boy. They were still standing there at the front door of Mark's house. Lindsey was armed and Mark probably was too. The suburban street yawned behind him and he knew it was probably going to be a lost cause.

'Alright, Mark,' he said. 'Alright. Take my phone number and call me when you're sorted.'

He said goodbye to Mark and his boy, turned and walked back to his car. He U-turned, smiled and waved out the window and beeped his horn twice as he drove away.

That night he caught up with Choppie. He'd take the four grand and give this bloke his alibi.

•

The meeting was set for the Burwood Hotel and Lindsey was introduced to an intermediary.

They sat around a bar table to talk business.

They agreed that on the day in question Lindsey had met Choppie's mate here at the Burwood and they'd stayed for several hours. To add some realism to the alibi they'd admit that they'd met to talk about selling pot around Burwood.

They talked about when they'd be paid and when they'd be available to give their statements. The trial was scheduled to start in three months and they needed to get their statements down soon or it would be too late.

While Choppie was asking for favours Lindsey asked him to find out what he could about the Gladesville investigation. He wanted to know if Mark Lewis was the major suspect. Alan agreed to make enquiries at the North Region Major Crime Squad and a few days later he told Lindsey that the inquiry was stalled and had been scaled back after the Mark Lewis lead ran cold.

Lindsey was relieved at first, but later he thought back to Choppie's demeanour and then to the times he'd taken money from people and delivered nothing. He'd probably just fed him this line to make himself look like a big man. Lindsey would have to tread warily.

52

Six months had passed since he'd visited Mark Lewis and still he hadn't heard boo. Hardly surprising. He couldn't get him on the telephone so he drove back out to the house in Carlingford to have a word. A woman in a sloppy joe and tracksuit pants opened the door. Never heard of a Mark Lewis. He'd bailed.

He rang the Telecom Service Department and pretended to be one of their technicians who'd been sent to the wrong address. First some small talk and then he gave Mark Lewis's Carlingford details and asked for his new address. He'd used this trick sparingly over the years and it worked more often than not. But not on this occasion – Mark Lewis had not connected a new service after leaving Carlingford.

In May Lindsey turned forty and Choppie and a friend of his, a woman named Amber, took him out to dinner at the Philip Lodge Motel at Ashfield. Betty decided to stay home when she found out who was going.

Lindsey told Choppie he needed a favour. The Mark Lewis trail had gone cold and could he help? Choppie said he'd be happy to oblige and wrote the details on the back of a coaster.

Choppie had a room already booked at the motel and at the end of the night Amber said she was going to take a room and stay the night too.

'You can't leave yet, Rosie. I've got something for you,' Choppie said. He led Lindsey back to his motel room and handed him a green canvas bag. 'Don't mind the gift wrapping.'

Inside was a .22 Mark I Ruger, a box of Winchester hollow-points and the bayonet from an M16 in a metal scabbard.

'Happy birthday, old fella,' said Choppie.

53

The date of Lindsey and Alan Thomas's court appearance was fast approaching. They were slated to give their evidence the next day.

'I've made a statement to the solicitor, but I'm not going to court,' said Choppie. 'My position is compromised.'

'Well, fuck that, I'm not going either,' said Lindsey. 'I was already thinking it looks too dodgy. When I gave the statement to the cops, they kept hassling me about why it took more than a year for this alibi to turn up. They're not buying it.'

'It's not the cops you need to convince, just the numbnuts jury. I thought I told you not to give the police a statement. They can pin you on it under questioning, catch you out,' Alan said.

'Mate, what do you take me for? After all the witness statements I've taken over the years – even when I was an ambo – I think I know what I'm doing. Read it.'

Choppie had to admit that it wasn't too bad. 'Nice touch,' he said. 'You remembered the date because it was the day of the Newcastle Newmarket.'

'Yeah, Sir Bernard won at twenty to one and I didn't back it, the bastard.'

'You've got to do it,' said Choppie. 'It'll be fine.'

•

The next morning Lindsey fronted up to the court house and gave his evidence: that he'd been drinking with Choppie's mate at the Burwood Hotel to discuss the sale of cannabis.

Seven days later the jury returned a not guilty verdict.

That night they were back at the Burwood Hotel and the intermediary turned up and the agreed sums of cash were handed out. *What a day.*

'Did you see those suits up the back of the gallery?' Choppie asked.

'What about them?' Lindsey said.

'I know one of them. Works for Professional Integrity. The fucking toe-cutters.' Choppie and his mates, he'd recently told Lindsey, were already on edge because the Royal Commission into the New South Wales Police Service (Wood Royal Commission) had been on the news and showing all this hidden camera tape of bent cops taking bribes.

'Do you reckon they're on to you?'

'What do you think?' said Choppie. 'Why else would they be there if they weren't investigating us?'

Later, Donnie walked in, nodded to Lindsey and bought a beer. Then he went and sat by himself on the other side of the room.

'What are you talking to him for?' asked Donnie when Lindsey walked over.

'He's alright, he watches out for me,' said Lindsey.

'Yeah, well, I need to talk to you about somethink. But I don't want to talk about it in here.'

Lindsey returned to Choppie.

'What's his problem? Why didn't he come over to our table?' said Choppie.

'He's not happy that I'm talking to you. He wants to see me at the Vauxhall Inn and told me not to bring you.'

'Well, fuck him, then,' said Choppie.

•

The next day Lindsey stuffed a thousand dollars in cash in an envelope and mailed it to Lydia in Perth. He'd ring to talk to Penny every few weeks and Lydia never missed a chance to remind him about the child support she expected him to be paying. Maybe that would shut her up for a bit.

That night he met Donnie at the Vauxhall. Donnie was worried about his safety and he was stressing about being busted for murder and seeing Lindsey talking to a cop had not improved his state of mind. Lindsey told Donnie just be cool and stay strong. Donnie just needed the reassuring and that calmed him down.

54

I am a flawed person.

Flawed because I lost patience, had enough. I have seen friends have mental breakdowns over lesser matters. Different people deal with matters (stress) differently. I had enough of standover and extortion, but did not go postal, though at times I was tempted. Instead, I attacked the attackers.

Was it a proportionate response? With Cavanagh it was the only way. He was a criminal and heavily into the underworld. Pang – same level. She stepped up attacks, took it to new levels, ramped up continually. It was always 'what's next?' It went on for over a year.

There are different types of killers: going postal (e.g.: crazed gunman, Wade Frankum, Bryant, etc.); serial killings (Milat); ritualised killing (Van Krevel).

Wade Frankum, for example, had separated from his partner shortly before and planned to kill her in revenge. Sitting in that Strathfield coffee shop a young girl had shot her mouth off and Frankum had evil intentions and so he'd started on her then and there even though that hadn't been his plan. He used a knife on the girl because it was up close – personal. All the other killings were random targets he shot using the M1 carbine he pulled from his bag. And finally as he heard police approaching, he'd apologised to the lady whose car he was trying to hijack, stepped from the car, knelt and shot himself in the head – the one part that did go according to plan.

The narcissist in me substantiates my actions.

The realist in me realises I am flawed.

The rationalist in me realises I assumed an 'I don't care' attitude.

The fatalist in me realises due to 'I don't care' that my reasoning faculty went out the window.

The moralist in me can't believe my actions. I have lost faith. A big catalyst was my unfaithful wife.

The egotist in me: 'how dare they do this to me!'

So it comes down to Antimony. The principle: don't be unfaithful; treat people with respect; don't bully; don't stand-over or extort; don't attempt to kill.

Normal precepts go out the window. If there is no recourse because police and the law are corrupt then principles must take precedence over law. Be pragmatic.

I felt aggrieved.

As a PI I was altruistic.

There is no mitigation. I am flawed.

55

Alan Thomas was right to be worried about the Professional Integrity Branch (PIB). The NSW Drug Enforcement Agency had been tapping phone calls as part of an operation against drug dealers. The intercepts picked up conversations which appeared to be discussing the planning of a false alibi. Lindsey Rose was named, as were two police officers, including Alan Thomas.

The PIB attempted to gather more evidence of the conspiracy, but the persons of interest had grown cagey and the PIB didn't have the resources for a full-scale investigation. In December 1995 Task Force Yandee was established by the NSW Crime Commission to investigate a number of drug-related murders. The apparent conspiracy to provide a false alibi was included in its terms of reference.

Task Force Yandee would be led by Detective Chief Inspector Darryl Wilson and the lead investigator was Detective Sergeant Rod Baker.

The Yandee investigators spent weeks trawling through intercepts and found nothing helpful so they prepared themselves to go out into the field and interview some of the players.

PART 3

Psychopaths are social predators who charm, manipulate, and
ruthlessly plow their way through life, leaving a broad trail
of broken hearts, shattered expectations, and empty wallets.
Completely lacking in conscience and in feelings for others,
they selfishly take what they want and do as they please,
violating social norms and expectations without the slightest
sense of guilt or regret.

ROBERT D. HARE, *WITHOUT CONSCIENCE: THE DISTURBING WORLD OF THE
PSYCHOPATHS AMONG US*[21]

56

I read Hare's book on psychopathy inside twenty-four hours and it clears a few things up. He explains that sociopathy and psychopathy are used by different people to describe essentially the same condition – sociopathy is more likely to be used by one who favours the sociological origins of the condition, or seeks to avoid confusion with the psychotic (who is quite different).

And, according to Hare, antisocial personality disorder (ASPD), as described in the DSM, was 'supposed to have much the same meaning as "psychopath"'. The psychopath, however, displays personality traits such as egocentricity and lack of empathy which are excluded from the DSM criteria because 'the average clinician could not reliably assess [them].'[22]

Even though the majority of prison inmates would have antisocial personality disorder, only about twenty per cent would also be psychopathic.

The issue of responsibility is raised and again no excuses are provided for the subject. Psychopaths know the difference between right and wrong, understand the rules of society and are capable of exercising self-control. They understand the consequences of their actions but perform them anyway.

So now I realise that just because two clinical psychiatrists did not use the word 'psychopath', it does not mean Lindsey is not psychopathic – it's just that psychiatrists don't use the word; it's not a category listed in the DSM.

57

As things cooled off, Lindsey was living back with Betty and they had grown close again. He thought living away from Burwood for a while might be wise so in the spring of 1995 they were living a hundred metres from Botany Bay in a unit at Brighton-Le-Sands. He liked the sea change.

He still visited Burwood but usually only if he'd arranged to meet someone, and so it was when he met Choppie for the Mark Lewis update. Choppie held up the print-out from COPS, the police computer system, and read aloud Mark's new address: Shepherd Street, St Marys.

Choppie wouldn't give Lindsey the print-out because he didn't want it found in anyone else's hands and have that come back to him. Lindsey rolled his eyes at Choppie's sudden propriety. When Alan turned away, Lindsey sneaked a peek and memorised the phone number too.

Parramatta Road, M4, he only had to check the street directory once and in forty minutes he was outside Mark's house. It was small, housing commission, blond brick with no front fence or footpath and patchy lawn right up to the front door. Mark's yellow van was parked in front of the roll-up garage doors and there were kids playing on the lawn. One of the kids looked like Kerrie's boy – less baby-like, definitely a big toddler now. Nine months since the visit to Carlingford – must be him. He took all this in, barely slowing down, and he kept driving. He wasn't going to put the hard word on Mark when there were others around.

•

Two weeks passed and he had considered giving it away as a lost cause but then Choppie was on the phone.

'I'll pick you up in an hour. We need to collect on that debt,' Choppie said.

He must be even more desperate than usual.

Choppie picked him up from the workshop at Wentworthville in a second-hand red Cortina; his old Escort had packed it in. They drove to

Mark Lewis's. The backyard had high fences on all sides. 'Dobermans, that's what the fences are for,' he told Choppie.

There was no answer at the door and no sign of Mark's yellow van.

'He's probably at the shops,' Lindsey said. They drove the twenty minutes to Blacktown then through a few car parks and down the main street and sure enough there was the shitty yellow van.

They parked across the street from the van where they could watch for Mark. They smoked Lindsey's cigarettes and discussed some of Alan's recent near misses on the punt. He'd landed many good bets over the years and Lindsey had seen him back winner after winner some days. But hearing about some of the near misses, usually the fault of the jockey, it was no surprise that Alan was always short of money. He didn't talk as much about his big losses as he did about his wins.

Alan started asking questions about the murders. Why did Mark want her dead, anyway? Well, she was a bitch and there was going to be a custody dispute and he wanted custody of his son. What happened? Mark drove her there and I killed her; she was crying on the floor and I told her 'Look at me, look at me' and when she did I just shot her. What did Mark do? He was hysterical. I tried to calm him down. I made one mistake, I put my hand on the back of his shoulder and left a palm print there in blood. I can't believe they haven't interviewed me, thought they would have identified my palm print off the shirt.

They waited. Every so often Alan would ask, do you really reckon that's his van? He was edgy and his colitis was particularly bad and Lindsey at one point got out of the car and walked to the corner and back to let Choppie's emissions clear from his nostrils.

Eventually Mark returned to the van, but with him were his daughter and her husband. 'That bloke's already suspicious about the murder, I can't let him see me with Mark.' They aborted the mission again and Choppie dropped Lindsey back at the workshop for another day of repairing cars.

•

He gave Mark a call. He'd wanted to avoid using the phone – the Wood Royal Commission was still on the news so he was paranoid about phone taps. But he couldn't be forever driving out to the boonies for no result. Mark answered.

'Do you know my voice?' Lindsey asked.

'Yes,' he heard Mark say, and if he was surprised there was no tell. Mark would know not to say anything incriminating or identify him on the phone. The cops wouldn't have given up this soon when they had Mark in their sights for the murders. Lindsey wondered why they hadn't just loaded up Mark in the first place. He supposed it was a bit harder to fix someone up for murder without the murder weapon to plant. Unless you had the forensics team on-side: you'd have to swap the ballistics in evidence for the ballistics of your proxy weapon. A lot of ducks to line up.

'I need to talk to you,' he said to Mark.

They agreed to meet at the local McDonald's. They drank the crappy all-you-can-drink coffee and Mark's tale of woe unfolded. He'd lost all his businesses and still owed thousands; Kerrie's other kids had all moved to Adelaide to be with her parents and they'd got the money from Kerrie's estate and he wasn't going to get anything. He'd put in an application for victims of crime compensation for Kerrie's death and promised to share some of the cash if it came through. He had nothing much left but the old Mitsubishi van, which he was still driving around unregistered and now unlicensed as well.

Lindsey remembered when he'd first met Mark – he'd had a small business empire of sorts and he'd always had nice cars so it was a long way that he'd fallen. Giving him a hard time now was going to be fruitless. And with a murder investigation in progress there was another, more pragmatic, reason for keeping him on-side.

In the end he lent Mark a fifty and promised to keep in touch.

58

Members of Task Force Yandee interview Detective Alan 'Choppie' Thomas and another police officer about the suspected false alibi mentioned in phone taps. They both deny any wrongdoing and decline to be interviewed further.

Next cab off the rank is Lindsey Rose. Thomas has told them that Rose drinks at the Burwood Hotel just about every night of the week.

•

Two detectives from Yandee catch up with Rose at the Burwood Hotel two nights later. Rose won't admit to anything, but the detectives think he might respond to further pressure.

That night Detective Chief Inspector Wilson, commander of Yandee, works with Legal Services to get approval to take an induced statement from Rose.

The next day Detective Senior Constable Kelly and Detective Sergeant Sommerville drive to the workshop at Wentworthville to serve Rose with the summons. He'll be required to attend a hearing at the Crime Commission that evening.

Kelly explains that anything he says at the Crime Commission can't be used in evidence against him. It was the corrupt police they were after.

Rose agrees to talk to Alan Thomas about it.

•

Lindsey paged Choppie and he rang straight back and they agreed to meet at the Plumpton Inn, four minutes from Choppie's house at Hassall Grove, his local.

Lindsey sat in the back seat of the unmarked police car as Detective Kelly drove them to the Plumpton Inn. The detectives waited in the furthest car park while Lindsey walked into the lounge bar to meet Choppie.

'They've already been to see me, Rosie. We're all denying it.'

'But do you know what they've got on you?'

'Ahh, someone was caught on a phone tap blabbing about it. It's bullshit. Where do you stand on this?'

'Where do I stand? Well, it sounds like you've fucked this up, is where I stand. You got me into this and now look at this mess. If they've got a recording then we're fucked. We plead to the charges. We'll get a lagging but it's still better than doing the lot.'

'Mate, I'm a cop, I can't go to prison,' said Choppie.

'Choppie, they've got us. We need to just wear it,' Lindsey said.

'No fucken way,' said Choppie.

'Think about it. If we plead guilty we'll be out in under five years. Do some courses inside, come out and make a fresh start. Never have to worry about it again.'

'Rosie. I can't . . . I can't do time, fuck ya.'

If the detectives weren't out in the car park he might have thumped him for his stubbornness, but Choppie wouldn't budge so he gave up.

'Alright, Choppie, we'll do it your way. We'll say nothing, try to get off it.'

•

Detective Kelly sees them walking out together and he pulls Thomas to the side. Thomas maintains he had nothing to do with a false alibi, but he'll go on the record and tell them the little that he'd heard about it if that's what they really want.

At the Sydney Police Centre, Alan Thomas keeps to his story until Yandee's lead investigator, Detective Sergeant Rod Baker, plays him some of the tape from the intercepted phone calls. Then his aspect shifts. Yeah, okay, he had been speaking with someone about the case but he'd done nothing wrong: his mate was being set up and he knew he was innocent so he'd helped with the alibi because he was otherwise going to be stitched up unfairly. All he'd really done was introduce a few people, he tells them.

They charge Alan Thomas that night with intent to pervert the course of justice and Rose with conspiracy to pervert the course of justice. They both make bail and Rose is required to report to the task force every Monday, Wednesday and Friday.

59

Peter at the NSW Retired Police Association is happy to pass on my contact details. It's my first attempt to contact anyone involved with the police investigation so it's a pleasant surprise when retired detective Rod Baker rings me back later that same day and is perfectly willing to meet and assist.

It takes six months to overcome constraints of geography and diaries. There is no answer at his front door and finally I poke my head inside the flyscreen and he calls me inside. I had assumed a retired policeman would be wary of vengeful criminals and here I am, a stranger, welcomed into an unlocked house.

It is morning and I've brought pastries but Rod won't partake. One day a week he fasts on the recommendation of his doctor. I'd seen him interviewed on an episode of the TV program *Forensic Investigators*[23] ('The Valentine's Day Murders') – it had been first broadcast five years prior but I wouldn't have recognised him. He's bigger, has glasses and his hair is grey now and long, in a ponytail. He wears a loose, flowing tie-dyed shirt and he invites me to sit at his dining table.

He tells me about the formation of the task force and his role in it and a little about the Wood Royal Commission. Yes, it was obvious from the outset that Alan Thomas was dodgy and from there the investigation branched out. I have a long list of questions. Rod's blue eyes are watery behind his spectacles and at first, with his gentle manner, he seems dreamy, absentminded even. But the illusion is quickly dispelled as he answers my questions with an economy of expression that betrays the sharpness of his mind. No gazing skywards to recollect a detail: he provides an immediate, succinct answer or says if he doesn't recall and I imagine this is a skill of the successful detective.

His wife Lynn passes through and we are introduced and she asks after Lindsey as if he were an old friend, though of course she can't have ever met him. I got on okay with Lindsey, says Rod, no personal animosity towards him at all. He came across as the type of bloke you'd like to have a beer with. But he was typical of the professional criminal. Thought he was bulletproof. Mark Lewis? He was a nasty piece of work.

He tells me about the investigation and he has made arrangements for me to have access to some documents. They are public record documents produced for trial. Later I realise it's a gold mine, hundreds of pages: forensic reports, intelligence reports, charge sheets, fact sheets, copies of police duty books, faxes between agencies, warrant applications and statements and transcripts of interviews with suspects and witnesses.

I ask him about the stresses in Task Force Yandee and he is modest – it was no more than the normal stress of major strike force work, which is always there. But there was job satisfaction too. The reward for a successful murder investigation came from providing a degree of resolution to the family of the victim.

I ask about his life after the force. He and Lynn run a bed and breakfast, he says, but they also do church work. They have recently joined a new church and help them with the six hundred free meals they provide to the local community each week. And Rod does mission work so he's on the road a lot, travelling the country. His giving in this way seems to be a natural extension of his time in the Police Force, serving those in need.

We meet a few more times and I send questions by email and he is always willing to clarify details for me around his busy schedule. He signs off his emails with 'God bless' and I have no religion but feel blessed all the same.

60

The Wood Royal Commission releases its First Interim Report in February 1996, concluding that 'a state of systemic or entrenched corruption had provisionally been shown to exist'.[24]

Detective Rod Baker and Detective Chief Inspector Darryl Wilson meet with the Wood investigators and it is agreed that the Yandee task force will run as an adjunct to the Royal Commission. Rod Baker and his team are now working for the most significant internal investigation in the history of the NSW Police Force.

They suspect Thomas is more deeply corrupt than he makes out and they aren't making much headway until a Leo W. comes forward. Leo is known to police as he'd been busted in Bowral with a substantial cannabis plantation in January 1995. He tells them he'd discussed his charges with a Lindsey Rose at the Burwood Hotel and had then been introduced to Alan Thomas, who said he could get him off if he paid $15 000. They'd taken the money and done nothing to help him and Leo had served time. He can identify Rose and Thomas, knows the dates that they'd met and is willing to give evidence.

Rod Baker rings Thomas and they get together for a chat about Mr W. and his $15 000. Thomas's head sinks and he already has the grey look of a defeated man. He has a wife and two young daughters and a son from his previous marriage and now he is facing prison unless he can cut a deal.

•

On 24 April 1996 Baker takes a call from Thomas, who says he has further information. Baker and Wilson drive out to his house at Hassall Grove. He tells them Rose may have committed two murders at Gladesville, that he'd mentioned it several times and at first he hadn't believed him.

'When was the first time he mentioned it?' asks Baker.

'Well, years ago he asked me for advice on a massage parlour and he had these dealings with a fellow named Mark Lewis and his girlfriend . . . or whatever . . . named Kerrie Pang. And I saw on the news this Pang woman was murdered, with another girl, at a massage parlour so I mentioned it to Lindsey at the RSL and he told me he'd done it. "It was me," he said.

'I didn't believe him. We used to drink together a lot and a couple of times, when we were really pissed, he told me he was a hitman, called himself "The Mechanic" after the Charles Bronson movie. "I am a mechanic in the true sense of the word," he'd say. I thought he was living in a dream world.'

'If you didn't believe him, why are you telling me now?'

'Well, a couple of weeks later he gave me a pistol and asked me to get rid of it for him. Even then I still thought he was full of shit. But he . . . a few more weeks later, he asked me to look up the address for Mark Lewis. I didn't bother, but he kept hassling me and in October I did, I looked up Mark Lewis's address on COPS – he was living in St Marys – and gave Lindsey the address, just to get him off my back.

'But then a couple more weeks later I was around at his workshop and he asked me to drive him out to St Marys to collect $20 000 from this Mark Lewis for murdering his girlfriend for him. The coin dropped – he was going to all the trouble to drive out there to confront the man – it seemed that maybe Lindsey had done these two murders after all. I asked him about it and he told me some of the details, how Lewis had hassled him to do it – offered him extra money to do it quick – how he'd shot the second girl because she would have been a witness and how he set fire to the place to get rid of the forensics.'

They talk to Thomas for nearly two hours and he tells them about the dinners and the drinking and the stories told by Rose.

'What happened to the pistol?' Baker asks.

'Oh, that went to a friend of mine named Jacob,' he says.

Baker tells him that they'll ask him to formalise the statement at a later date but first they need to do some research.

•

They contact Ryde detectives and the next day a Detective Sergeant Gary Williams brings over the case files from the murders of Kerrie Pang and Fatma Ozonal at Kerrie's Oasis in 1994. Williams had worked on the original investigation and he gives them a briefing.

On face value, what Thomas had told them is consistent with the facts of the case. But everything he told them had been released to the press, including the alleged involvement of Mark Lewis, who, as prime suspect, had been interviewed extensively.

Rose's name appears once in the case files, but only as a passing mention by one of the people interviewed – there'd been nothing at the time to indicate Rose as a suspect.

Winchester cartridge casings, .22 calibre, had been found at the murder scene and there were more cartridges and a .22 calibre rifle in Mark Lewis's Tarago. Police were still at the scene at 9.15 p.m. when Mark Lewis returned to Kerrie's Oasis on Flagstaff Street. He collapsed on the road and was taken by ambulance to Ryde Hospital. He was released shortly before midnight then conveyed by detectives to Gladesville police station, Flagstaff Street, VIP Massage in West Ryde, Kerrie Pang's house in Cherrybrook and then Lewis's address in North Rocks, where four rifles were confiscated. Then he was taken to the Major Crime Squad offices in Chatswood, where the recorded interview went for an hour and concluded at 5.57 a.m.

There was a bloody handprint on the back of Mark Lewis's shirt and he was the de facto husband of one of the victims. Numerous statements from acquaintances and employees attested to the tempestuous nature of their relationship.

Lewis claimed to have left Pang at Kerrie's Oasis around 6.15 p.m. and returned to the West Ryde massage parlour at 7 p.m. But phone records and witness statements all indicated otherwise.

The receptionist at the West Ryde parlour remembered Mark Lewis returning: it was 8 p.m., she said. The timeline Mark Lewis had claimed differed by an hour from all other evidence.

Even though Lewis was the obvious suspect, the original investigators had been thorough, looking at the background of both victims. Pang had minor convictions for possession of Indian hemp and unlawful possession. Ozonal had no criminal record but interviewees stated that there had been threats from a former boyfriend (a former employer from a different massage parlour). Ozonal had apparently flown back to Turkey, in fear of the boyfriend, to have an abortion. She had returned to Australia only three weeks before being murdered. She'd spent the first week working for Terry McIndoe at a massage parlour in Lakemba, then left without notice. McIndoe and Pang had been lovers years before and McIndoe spoke to Pang on the phone in the two hours before her death. Among other things they were arguing over Ozonal, as McIndoe wanted her back.

But none of these other leads produced any evidence. McIndoe and his business partner both had strong alibis and there was simply no evidence to link them to the murders. And it was the same for Ozonal's former boyfriend.

Lewis remained the strong suspect, but they hadn't turned up enough evidence to charge him. DNA testing of the stain on Lewis's shirt was inconclusive. Specks of blood were found on Lewis's shorts and the inside of the burgundy rifle case that had been in the back of his Tarago. DNA testing showed it to be Pang's blood but that was no proof of guilt: they were in a relationship together so there may have been an innocent explanation. And ballistics showed that the Miroku rifle from Lewis's Tarago, and the four other rifles at his house, could not have fired the rounds found at the crime scene.

The investigation had stalled but there was a more recent update in the file. In May 1995 Mark Lewis had submitted a claim with the Victims Compensation Tribunal – for himself and his son – arising from the murder of his de facto wife, Kerrie Pang. His submission outlined a dire financial situation: no remaining assets, government assistance his only income and tens of thousands of dollars in outstanding debts. And he was trying to raise a small child in this situation. Detective Mayger had been in contact with the tribunal informing them that any payment should be withheld pending completion of the investigation and that neither Mark Lewis nor his solicitor should be informed of this fact.

Detective Sergeant Gary Williams finishes the briefing and Rod Baker nods in approval. Williams's familiarity with the case is a great advantage so Baker makes arrangements for him to be attached to Yandee and he starts the legwork.

The team proceeds on several fronts.

So far they only have Thomas's second-hand hearsay as evidence. They want to get Rose on tape admitting to the murders. Thomas agrees to help.

Next cab off the rank is Alan Thomas's claim that the murder weapon had been given to a friend named Jacob. They discover that Jacob's house had been raided in August the previous year on other matters and a single-shot .22 calibre rifle had been seized. The task force's technical specialist reviews the records at the Forensic Ballistics Unit and the weapon had been test fired. The projectile was still in storage at the Ballistics Unit. Williams asks him to run a comparison against projectiles recovered from the Gladesville murder scene.

•

Baker hopes to create, at the very least, a compelling circumstantial case against Rose. And if they end up having to rely at court on Alan Thomas's evidence, the chain of evidence needs to support his statements. So they start fact-checking. On 26 April a member of the PIB runs the audit log of Alan Thomas's access to the COPS computer system. It shows that on 23 October 1995 he accessed several records including that of Mark Lewis, DOB 17/10/37. That part of the story stacks up and they take a formal statement from the PIB member to attach to the audit report.

They look to the forensic evidence collected by the original investigators. It takes them a day to get through it all. There was blood and DNA taken from the scene that was never matched and might belong to the offender. Strands of hair had been found in both of Kerrie Pang's hands. But they don't have any hair from Rose to check for a match so Baker orders a tail for Rose. It only takes a day. They follow his car into the city and he leaves it parked on Goulburn Street; the team takes some hair off a hairbrush he has in a toiletries bag and it's off to the lab.

Meanwhile, Detective Williams is running Alan Thomas and they are talking almost every day. To get Rose's admission on tape Thomas has an idea: they will book a room at the Manly Seaview Hotel and go drinking and he'll get Rose back in the hotel room talking about the murders.

The team applies for the warrants to install devices at the hotel, 19 Pacific Street, Manly. Only a Supreme Court Justice has the power to approve those warrants. The Justice gives them a hard time. First they have to demonstrate the evidence against Rose and then he won't sign because the warrant doesn't specify the room numbers. But the Seaview can't allocate the room numbers yet and the Justice eventually relents and the warrants are granted on Friday, 26 April 1996.

The next day, Saturday, Baker gets the bad news. The Seaview says that the only rooms available are across the road and known as a different address. The warrants are no good. They find another Justice on Sunday and he grants new warrants for the correct address, 46 Malvern Street. The STIB[25] is running the surveillance gear and they're installed by lunchtime: a camera in the television and a listening device secreted in the frame of the couch.

But the warrants are set to expire on Monday afternoon and Thomas can't get Rose there on the Sunday night so on Monday morning Baker's team are back in front of another Justice, the third one, and after another grilling an extension to the warrants is granted.

Monday afternoon, the 29th, Rose and Thomas check in and the devices are working but nothing of consequence is said. Then they're off to the bar.

That night Baker gets a message from the STIB. 'LDs were located by Rose. Monitoring terminated.'

The next morning Baker goes in and watches the tape. Rose and Thomas walk into the room and Rose walks straight up to the camera and says 'How dumb are they, hey, Choppie?' Then blackness and then silence.

Rose couldn't have found them that easily. Thomas must have told him they were there.

•

Their forensics specialist reports back. He's completed a comparison of the projectiles from the Jacob exhibit and from the Gladesville crime scene. In his opinion they were fired by different weapons. In any event, eight shots had been fired at Gladesville so he believes a semi-automatic weapon was probably used. Jacob's single-shot .22 can be eliminated.

And the forensic biologist has compared the hairs from Rose's hairbrush with hairs that had been recovered from Gladesville, clutched in Kerrie Pang's left and right hands. There are similarities, she says, but it's also possible that the recovered hairs belonged to the deceased. Another dead end.

•

'Has Mark Lewis paid you that twenty grand yet?' Alan asked. They were drinking at Uncle Buck's in Mount Druitt.

'Choppie, the old bloke's fucked,' he said. 'He's in a bad way, we're not going to get any money out of him. He reckons he's got nothing unless he gets this compo claim. It's a dead end.'

'You're a soft touch, Rosie. Leave it with me. I'll flash my badge at him and apply the hard word. I'll sort it out.'

Lindsey had seen various versions of Choppie 'sorting things out' and he didn't figure this was going to be one of the better ones. It turned out he was right – Alan Thomas never recovered a cent.

61

It used to be that two prisoners at a time were allowed in the basketball court and the library, but now it's only the 'non'-computer room (where the computers were before they were confiscated) and the exercise yard – and then, only by special arrangement. Both prisoners have to sign an application for 'association' and have it approved by the security manager. The palaver is all the fault of Carl Williams, Lindsey tells me. Carl Williams, the so-called baby-faced killer of Melbourne's gangland wars, has recently been beaten to death with the stem from an exercise bike in Barwon Prison, so Goulburn has tightened up its rules.

I ask him, as usual, about prison life. Some of the troublemakers have been moved out so things have been more quiet, he says. I ask who he spends time with.

Until recently Mark van Krevel used to walk laps while Lindsey did his gardening but now Phuong Ngo is his usual garden associate.

Phuong Ngo keeps himself neat and tidy and he has a support group outside the prison still trying to secure his release. Phuong is serving life, found guilty of ordering the murder of Cabramatta MP John Newman – generally regarded as Australia's first political assassination. In 2008 Phuong told Lindsey that he would be challenging his conviction at the Supreme Court. It had taken the cops only twenty minutes to locate the alleged murder weapon – a pistol – which had been thrown into the Georges River from a footbridge at Voyager Point, he said. And at his third trial an expert had assessed that the corrosion of the weapon was older than the crime.

Phuong's theory was that the cops had planted it there. Lindsey was already aware of Operation Florida, an investigation by the Police Integrity Commission that had caught corrupt police in Chatswood taxing drug dealers, and more. One of the cops had turned informer and put them all in for maintaining a 'future evidence' locker. They'd had a locked cabinet full of weapons to load up suspects, but when they got wind of the Wood Royal Commission one of the senior officers had taken his cabin cruiser for a spin with a colleague and they'd dumped all the weapons in the Hawkesbury River.[26] That's where they'd conjured Newman's murder weapon from, according to Phuong. Lindsey gives the story considerable credence, given his experience with bent cops. However, the judicial inquiry, which was finalised in April 2009, found no error with Phuong Ngo's conviction. That was probably rigged as well, said Lindsey. He had no specific knowledge of the inquiry, it was just his natural scepticism of everything judicial.

In 2010, if they are in the garden together, Phuong Ngo waters while Lindsey does the weeding. Lindsey teases him relentlessly.

62

Detective Gary Williams and Alan Thomas discuss the next steps. Thomas says that Rose has money problems and maybe he can convince Rose to move in with him.

A week later they have found a suitable property at Old Toongabbie and Thomas tells Williams that he can get Rose to move in. They brief the STIB, who are ready to install the listening devices, but the next day Thomas rings them back. 'Lindsey's too cagey,' he says. 'He's paranoid about bugs and he won't move in with me.'

Two days later Thomas rings Williams early in the morning. Rose wants to meet him that night at the Austral Bowling Club to 'talk business'. They can't bug the whole club. The only way it can work is with Thomas wearing a wire and he agrees to it. Williams scrambles and they get the warrant by early afternoon. The STIB are on standby and go to Thomas's place at Hassall Grove to wire him up. It's cool enough to wear a jacket – below ten degrees Celsius overnight – so they install the wire under his armpit.

It's 9 May, a Thursday night. Thomas tells them they will meet at the Wentworthville Hotel first and go to the Austral afterwards. At 8 p.m. the listening post monitors see Thomas's car pull in to the car park at the Austral Bowling Club and then they pick up the live audio. For an hour they listen to inconsequential banter that gets rowdier, laughing and then scuffling as Rose apparently grabs at Thomas, pretending to tackle him.

The noise recedes and the monitors can tell that Alan is in the toilet. 'He knows I'm wearing it,' they hear and then rasping, a muffled thud and silence tells them that he's removed the device.

The lead monitor reports back to his senior and he tells him to recover it. They are all plain-clothes and a senior constable walks in and retrieves the device. Thomas had wrapped it in toilet paper and left it on the windowsill in the toilet.

CM: Do you remember drinking with Alan Thomas at the Austral Bowling Club?

LR: Oh yeah, I do. Alan was so pissed he crashed his car. I yelled out to him to watch out but he crashed straight into a brick wall and smashed up his car.

CM: Were you aware he was wearing a wire that night?

LR: I could always tell when someone was wired. You can always tell because they will keep trying to turn the conversation to a particular subject.

•

Every week Baker attends an operations meeting with the Crime Commission, including the chairman (later commissioner) Phillip Bradley. At the next meeting they discuss the gathering of evidence against Rose – it seems likely that Thomas is playing both sides and that Rose knows what they are up to. They agree to redirect their efforts away from secretly recording an admission. As a matter of course they should get a formal statement from Alan Thomas. While his allegations of Rose's admissions are insufficient to lay charges, they do fill in some of the missing pieces in the chain of evidence. Baker's job is to find the rest.

•

13 May 1996. Detective Williams spends the morning with Thomas to take the statement.

Thomas tells Williams how he first met Rose in 1984 and how their drinking-based friendship had developed over the years. They'd grown much closer from 1991 and Rose had sought his advice about a massage parlour he'd purchased at Campbelltown. He described several conversations he'd had with Rose where murders had been mentioned.

Rose had given him a .22 calibre target pistol that he claimed to have used for the Gladesville murders. Didn't know where Rose got it from. Rose gave it to him in the car park of the Burwood RSL and he left it in the boot of his car.

A few days later Alan Thomas booked into the Log Cabin Hotel at Penrith. The next morning, before dawn, he took out the pistol and examined it. It had a wooden handle with finger grips and a curved lever jutting out one side which he took to be a cocking handle for a semi-automatic. He pushed the four-inch silencer onto the end of the barrel and it was a snug fit.

The hotel fronts the river and a scenic pathway runs along the waterfront and under the bridge for the Great Western Highway as it continues west. Alan Thomas walked the pathway in the pre-dawn light to throw the pistol into the river. He had it in the same plastic bag it came with, along with the silencer and spare rounds. But there were people under the bridge so he walked back to his car and returned the plastic bag with the gun and accoutrements to the boot of his car.

Then his friend wanted a gun for protection, Thomas says, so he gave him the target pistol from Rose. They discussed Rose's claim that it was a murder weapon. 'He's not the type,' said Jacob. 'It takes a special type of person to kill someone and he's full of bullshit.'

Thomas tells Williams how they'd celebrated Rose's fortieth at the Philip Lodge Motel at Ashfield. This was the night Rose first asked him to find Mark Lewis's address for him. It wasn't until five months later that he'd looked up the address on COPS and accompanied Rose on an abortive mission to confront Mark Lewis.

Only a week ago he'd been drinking with Rose at Uncle Buck's Hotel at Mount Druitt. Mark Lewis was mentioned and he asked Rose if he'd been paid yet. 'He's waiting for some money from a compensation claim,' he said. 'Then he'll fix me up.'

Williams gets the statement typed up and Alan Thomas signs it the same day.

•

The next morning Williams briefs Rod Baker: Thomas has firmed up the allegation that the murder weapon went to Jacob. Baker wants to wait before they question him. Wants to collect more evidence before they tip their hand. Inspector Wilson and Chairman Bradley of the Crime Commission agree.

•

16 May. They get Thomas in to the Forensic Ballistics Unit of the Sydney Police Centre in an attempt to identify the type of weapon from their

collection. A Senior Constable (Technical) takes him through the firearms library. There is no match. Thomas's recollection is of a weapon similar in appearance to a Crosman Arms .22 air pistol but with a wooden handle and similar in colour – light grey, metallic – to a Smith & Wesson self-loading .22. The bullets looked like Winchester Winners but with a darker-coloured lead head.

20 May. A soft plastic nose pad from a pair of spectacles had been found at the Gladesville scene and was still in evidence. A detective takes the nose pad to a privately run lab at Lindfield to check for DNA.

23 May. Williams is at Windsor, taking a statement from Oscar, Rose's Campbelltown business partner. He tells them there was a dispute with Kerrie Pang over an employee who had been 'borrowed' from her, but cannot provide any other useful information. He has never seen anyone in the industry with a firearm, he says, and while the murder of Kerrie Pang had been discussed (Oscar had met her once or twice), Rose told him he had no idea what happened.

27 May. The lab results come back on the nose pad. No DNA was detected. Williams takes it to a metallurgist – they want to see if it can be determined that the nose pad had been removed by force. The metallurgist reports that there is no fracture in the nose pad – it could have just as easily slipped off as been forced.

30 May. Another detective has been chasing up the Health Insurance Commission to look for any medical treatment received by Rose in the four years from 1990 to 1994. They have a eureka moment when records turn up showing Rose had attended an optometrist in Burwood only two weeks after the Gladesville murders. Williams drops in – it's on Burwood Road, only two blocks from the Burwood Hotel – and speaks to one of the two owners, who looks up his files and finds the card and there it is, Lindsey Rose. His partner had attended to Rose on 1 March 1994 and he'd ordered a replacement lens for Alfa Romeo spectacles and a pair of soft contact lenses. They'd checked the prescription by testing the left lens and the left eye, meaning there was almost certainly a missing right lens.

•

Betty had only been getting partial shifts as a receptionist and he'd hit a flat patch as well so they were struggling to keep up with basic expenses. The car was overdue for maintenance and she'd been at him for weeks now to get a proper job or at least come up with his share of the rent. And he wanted to build up a reserve in case he needed to skip town.

He'd already offloaded the last of his pot and Detective Kelly had been ringing him up and hassling him every week about phone records and dates so he decided to stay away from the dope business for now. He was chasing people daily – people that owed him money – for little reward and he started trying to sell goods.

He'd been using the workshop to clean up and retack some wooden furniture he'd bought cheap. He planned to go to the markets on Sunday but it wouldn't all fit in his box trailer so he asked Mark Lewis if he could borrow the yellow L300 for the weekend. Sure. It was the least he could do.

But first, on Saturday, Zane was getting married.

Betty didn't want to go so he drove himself to the house in Greenacre for the ceremony and then on to the reception, which was at Zane's house in Bankstown. It was a low-key affair, about a dozen people, not much was happening and Lindsey was getting bored. So he started organising speeches and before long he'd made himself the de facto MC. Zane's mum was a sweetheart, so he spent most of the evening chatting her up and having a laugh and at the end of the night he decided the flat at Brighton-Le-Sands was too far to drive pissed, so he slept at the workshop instead.

•

Sunday he hit the Blacktown Trash and Treasure markets in Mark Lewis's yellow Mitsubishi. The refurbished furniture sold slowly.

Late in the day he had to drop the prices to get rid of the last few items so his profit was hardly worth the effort. He left with nearly five hundred dollars but that wouldn't go far.

When he returned the van to Mark it was obvious that he hadn't left the house.

'See you later, Mark. Look after yourself and let me know if you get hold of that extra money,' he said.

'Yeah, Rosie, ta ta,' he said, his pallor now wraith-like. Mark didn't rise from the lounge and Lindsey walked out and closed the door behind him. It was like closing a chapter of his life.

He stopped for a few drinks at the Burwood on the way home, repaid a loan, and when he got back to the flat at Brighton-Le-Sands, Betty was waiting and she was unimpressed. He was not in the mood to take any shit and the argument turned ugly. He slept on the couch.

•

The next morning, things were no better with Betty. He wasn't apologising and she told him, well, he'd better sleep elsewhere.

Choppie would help him out. He sent a message to his pager and Choppie called straight back. He was at the Chinese restaurant on Burwood Road so Lindsey packed a bag and met him there.

Choppie waited, drinking, while Lindsey ate and they were in no hurry so it was nearly 4 p.m. by the time they finished. They walked the block down to the Burwood and they bought more drinks and Lindsey told him how badly he needed cash and Choppie could only sympathise as he was skint too.

Lindsey did the rounds and chatted to people he knew at the various tables and the only new gossip was that Chinese Phil had pulled up stumps and moved to Melbourne.

Then he was back talking to Choppie, who complained that his charges had been upgraded to conspiracy to pervert the course of justice and asked if Lindsey would take the fall – confess and say that Alan hadn't been involved.

Lindsey was already facing his own charge of conspiracy and there was a good chance it would stick. He kicked himself again for getting involved, going along with Alan Thomas even though he'd known from the start that it was a bad idea. He was in limbo again – waiting for a court date and reporting to those Yandee pricks three days a week – trying to get by on the pittance from the workshop, and he'd be needing to find new digs if things with Betty stayed on the current path.

And now Choppie sat there and asked if he'd take the fall for *him*.

Lindsey nearly hit the roof. Alan Thomas took it all without a blink, waited till Lindsey was finished then drained his glass. 'My colitis is killing me, I'm off,' he said.

Lindsey stayed, playing pool – paired up with one of the other locals and they held the table for an hour. He slept at the workshop that night.

•

6 June. Detective Sergeant Williams has made an appointment with Peter Moore, the optometrist who had repaired Rose's glasses, and meets him that morning at his shop on Burwood Road. Moore has no recollection of Rose, so he has no recollection of replacing the nose pad of his spectacles when he fitted the new lens. It was normal practice, he said, to replace a nose pad free of charge and no record kept. Williams gets all this in a signed statement – another small link in the chain of evidence.

The phone number written on Rose's customer card doesn't match any of the numbers they have on file so they refer it to the Telecom unit to obtain the subscriber details.

Tracing the nose pad back to a model of glasses might help tie Rose to the scene so Williams has one of the team members visit the local distributor of Alfa Romeo spectacles. No result; none of the models on hand has a nose pad matching the one from the crime scene.

•

At the weekly meeting with the Crime Commission they decide it is time to interview Lewis and Rose. Once they've been interviewed there is a good chance they'll talk to each other about it. They apply for phone intercepts on two phones registered to Mark Lewis.

They talk to Alan Thomas to see if he has any other information that might help. Thomas drops a bombshell: Rose had mentioned other murders but Thomas hadn't believed him. He recalls a newspaper clipping that Lindsey pulled out of his shirt pocket one day at the Burwood – a list of unsolved murders.

'Lindsey said: "I wonder why Kerrie's picture isn't here, because that's unsolved." I said: "Maybe it's been solved." He said, "Well, no-one spoke to me about it, how could it be solved? But anyway, the other two are in here. The two drug couriers, the husband and wife."'

Thomas can't remember any other details, but he thinks one of the names started with a 'K' and that one was a truck driver. 'I hope they enjoyed the oysters,' Rose had told him.

There is no central database of unsolved murders so one of the team hits the newspaper archives. They find an article that lists a number of unsolved murders and the double murder of Edward 'Bill' Cavanagh and Carmelita Lee warrants a closer look. They were found murdered at their home in Hoxton Park in 1984 – Cavanagh had run a trucking business.

One of the Yandee detectives, Detective Sergeant Matt Appleton, retrieves a box of files from the Homicide Squad of the CIB and there it is, in the third photograph of the crime scene: a jar of oysters smashed at the front door. This detail had never been released to the media. 'Hoxton Park definitely sounds familiar,' says Thomas. 'I reckon that's them.'

'Any other murders spring to mind?' asks Baker.

'Well . . .' starts Thomas. 'A couple of times he told me he'd done five murders in all. I used to think it was crap. But if he did those four, maybe there was another one. But he definitely told me nothing about the fifth. If there was one.'

The Management Committee of the Crime Commission meets later that day and – on the recommendation of the Yandee commander, Darryl Wilson – agrees to formally extend Yandee's brief to include investigation of the four murders. Rod Baker will remain as chief investigator. He delegates a team leader for each double murder. Detective Sergeant Matt Appleton runs the Cavanagh/Lee investigation, code name 'Coal', and Detective Sergeant Gary Williams has Pang/Ozonal, code name 'Aintree'.

•

Around noon Choppie dropped by the workshop and invited him for lunch.

> Sometimes Choppie's lunch invitations were to discuss a job, usually it was just social. Today it seemed like there was something on his mind.

The car repair could wait so he changed out of his overalls and into clean jeans, shirt and jacket.

They went in Alan's red Cortina. He needed to visit the Police Credit Union in Parramatta, which wasn't far, to collect a new Visa card and some cash. It was on George Street and there were plenty of restaurants nearby so they walked a block and into a quiet Japanese joint they'd not tried before.

Choppie ordered half a dozen dishes for them to share. Lindsey gave him the look and leaned in close.

'What's up, Choppie?'

'Hmm. The conspiracy charges are getting to me. And the missus is none too pleased, doesn't want me around anymore. I've got a lot of pressure on me and I need to relax and make sure I keep my head clear.'

'What are you going to do, then?' Lindsey asked.

'I've been reading some books on gold prospecting and I'm thinking about going back to the bush again and doing a bit of pig shooting. I used to do that all the time with an old mate. The only trouble is I'll let my mate kill the pigs because I made a real mess of the first one I killed. We brought a pig back alive, fed it up and I'll never forget that fat pig when I slaughtered it. You're supposed to put the knife straight down the centre of the throat and twist it so the blood comes straight out of the aorta.'

Lindsey fiddled with chopsticks: 'I had the same trouble with Kerrie, you know, when I used the knife on her.'

Alan filled Lindsey's glass with more sake.

'Did you know I took an apprentice with me on that job?' Lindsey continued.

'No, mate, you never mentioned that before.'

'Well, I did, he's a young bloke at Burwood. He's a tattoo artist.'

'What, the Lebanese guy that got arrested?'

'No, mate, no. The bloke's Australian, you've met him. He's very much into karate and martial arts.'

'What about Gladesville?'

'Yeah, he helped me get in the door. That's how I ended up putting my bloodstained hand on Lewis's shirt. Lewis walked in and my mate decked him. I yelled at him, "Don't do that, he's paying the bill." Then I picked Lewis up and that's how my palm print got on his shirt. After I got Lewis up I shot Kerrie.'

'Oh yeah, I heard you were a shit shot,' said Alan and he did deadpan pretty well.

'Very fucking funny,' said Lindsey. 'See that guy there?' He was looking at a man at a table on the other side of the restaurant. 'That guy's about the same distance as the guy I shot at Hoxton Park. I told him to get on the floor, he took one and a half seconds too long, so I shot him right in the centre of the forehead. How's that for a shot, eh? Twenty-five feet away, right in the centre of the forehead.'

'Oh yeah, did he go down?'

'He went straight down. Then I walked over and put another one in his head. You've got to put two in their head to make sure they're dead.'

'Okay, Rosie, whatever you reckon, mate.'

Choppie paid the bill then they walked down the road to the Albion and Lindsey bought the drinks. A friend of Alan's turned up and joined the shout. Neil had just had some charges heard down the road at Parramatta Local Court and he brought Alan up to speed on how it had gone over.

Alan was off to the dunny every ten minutes to clear his tricky bowels so Lindsey – four sakes and eight bourbons in – talked Neil around to their common interests, which (apart from bourbon and Coke) included speculating on the ultimate armed robbery (an inside job and a million-dollar payday) and, less dramatically, the easy money that could be made at trash and treasure markets. Lindsey put two and two together and he needed the cash so he told Neil there was a certain item that he could make available, if the price was right.

Lindsey's phone rang so he stepped outside so he could hear and it was Betty. They'd both cooled down a bit and it was time they talked things over. She agreed to meet him at the Albion when she finished work.

When he got back inside, Neil had disappeared. He and Choppie went two more shouts each before Betty arrived. She'd barely made it to their table when Choppie, nodding his greeting, passed her on his way to the door.

'That guy gives me the creeps,' she said.

•

24 June. Monday. Alan Thomas comes in again and tells them about a lunch he'd had with Rose the Friday before. Rose talked about both double murders but, more importantly, he has told Thomas for the first time that he had an accomplice at the Gladesville shooting. They have to try to get the accomplice. Thomas says he's another local drinker in Burwood and he can provide a rough description but no name.

25 June. Intercepts for Lewis's phones are signed by a Justice of the Family Law Court and Baker prepares operational orders for Operation Coal, which includes interviews with Rose, Thomas and Jacob.

Baker also compiles a thirty-page summary of the investigation to date. The only clear evidence against Rose is Thomas's statement alleging that Rose admitted the murders to him. Even though many of the details provided have been corroborated, it is not enough. And the evidence against Lewis is only circumstantial, so, Baker concludes, there is insufficient evidence to charge either Lewis or Rose with the murders. Unless they make admissions.

•

Detective Williams has been running an informant, a friend of Alan Thomas's named Neil who also knows Rose. 'The informant says Lindsey offered to sell him an unlicensed handgun. He probably still has it,' he tells Baker.

'Let's pick him up and charge him for the firearm. See if he wants to talk to us about the murders.'

•

Lindsey woke at dawn and it was a cold June morning. Betty was still asleep so he let himself out and wandered down the road to buy the Saturday paper. When he returned she was awake and they shared the newspaper over breakfast.

'I've got to go. Are we still on for tonight?' he said.

'Yeah, Rosie, take care, okay, and I'll see you later.'

They embraced and he kissed her on the mouth then smiled goodbye and walked out with his travel bag – it still contained the gun he'd tried to sell the day before, the .22 Ruger Choppie had given him as his fortieth birthday present.

The battery on his Commodore was nearly gone and this morning it wouldn't start so he moved Betty's car so he could jump-start his. While his head was under the bonnet a white plumber's van suddenly stopped beside him and someone jumped out of the passenger side and pointed a gun at his chest. He froze, considered his options, but the guy had him covered. And he looked like a cop.

Sure enough, 'Step away please and place your hands on the roof of the vehicle.' The voice was loud and insistent. He did as he was told as two other vehicles pulled up and four other plain-clothes piled out.

There were a few passers-by on their way to work and another cop diverted them to the other side of the road as he stood, handcuffed, being frisked.

It didn't take them long to find the Ruger in his carry bag and a small bag of dope under the front seat of his car. He was calm and relaxed. He could take whatever they dished out.

On the drive to Kogarah police station they asked him about the gun and he thought he'd have a bit of a laugh. He'd bought it off some bloke called Wayne at the Burwood Hotel for a grand, he told them. They gave him a hard time about it – 'Are you sure that's the story you want to stick with?' – and they seemed confident, and he realised they must have known he had the gun with him. Choppie must have turned.

'Okay, that was bullshit. I was trying to protect a mate. It was a birthday present from a mate of mine: Alan Thomas of Earlwood detectives,' he said. And just for good measure: 'Actually I've also got a .303 rifle belonging to Alan at my place in Wentworthville if you'd like to return it to him.' Choppie could bloody well go down with him.

They took me to the workshop and I told them where to find the rifle. The rifle was a .303/25 camouflaged with a 4x40 scope, tripod – a sniper rifle. They also found face paint, webbing and a gillie [sic] suit.

He was charged for possessing a weapon without a licence and for the dope. By noon he was in front of the Central Local Court, refused bail and sent down to the Metropolitan Remand Centre at Long Bay.

•

In the afternoon two detectives visited him and took him from Long Bay to the Police Centre on Goulburn Street, Surry Hills. Down one hallway he saw a noticeboard showing Task Force Air. This was the Milat task force: Ivan Milat's trial was drawing to a close and it had been in the news for weeks.

Then he faced what felt like a room full of detectives asking him about the murders of Kerrie Pang and Fatma Ozonal. A detective sergeant of police had told them he'd heard you admitting to these murders, they said. Just as he thought: Choppie had put him in. He just had to make bail so he could get out of Sydney. He made sure he wasn't being recorded and told them he knew who did the murders. He'd been there when they occurred. But he wouldn't agree to be formally interviewed. He'd talk about the murders, but not if it was going to incriminate him.

He quickly worked out that Rod Baker was the lead investigator and he seemed like a straight shooter so on a coffee break he had a quiet word. 'You're a good bloke, can we have a chat alone?'

Baker said there were no free interview rooms and Lindsey suggested one of the empty offices he could see across the hall and Baker agreed.

So Lindsey sat in an office chair while Baker sat on the edge of the desk and he told him: 'Look, Alan Thomas is the boss. He's running the show. I've been running with him for years. No-one does anything without his say so.'

That got them interested and that evening he was taken to the NSW Crime Commission on Kent Street in the city and into one of the hearing rooms. Baker took him in and introduced him to Chairman Bradley and the chief solicitor, Giorgiutti.

He told them Alan Thomas had committed the murders and he had ridden shotgun. It was the best kind of lie, grounded in truth. He simply substituted himself for Donnie and Choppie for himself then told it like it was. They asked him details of the murder, even about the nose pad for a pair of spectacles found at the scene, and he said yes, it was probably his. They asked about the workshop at Wentworthville, what he was doing when he was arrested and about the car theft racket he'd been busted for in Queensland. They were particularly interested in police misconduct and he laid it on thick and at the end of the hearing they asked if he would be willing to assist with gathering further evidence against corrupt police. He wouldn't make bail if the Crime Commission locked him up for being uncooperative so he told them what they wanted to hear.

•

Nothing else they've seen places Thomas at the scene of the Gladesville murders. Detective Baker doesn't give it much credence but Thomas is no cleanskin and it will need to be investigated, so they pick him up and he goes straight into protective custody at Long Bay.

Rose's admission to being present at two murders can't be used in court, nor to hold him. He'll make bail on the firearms charge so they need to get something else, quickly. Their best chance is to get hold of the murder weapon and hope for a quick result on the forensics. Baker doesn't think they have enough time, but it's worth a shot. He asks Detective Matt Appleton to contact Jacob for a chat.

•

At Long Bay Lindsey was taken from his dank cell for the mandatory induction course and while they were rallying all the new prisoners he was shown into a caged holding yard. There was a wire fence between him and an adjacent yard and he couldn't believe it, Choppie was in there. He came over to the fence. They shrugged at first, shared a few smokes and had a long conversation.

Lindsey squatted down and talked under his breath through the wire.

'Why did you put me in for Gladesville?' he asked Choppie.

'I thought I'd get a deal. Y'know, witness protection and immunity.'

'You've killed me, Choppie. I'll get two life sentences for this. I'll have to neck m'self. If you'd just confessed to the false alibi like I said and left it at that we probably would have both got five years. Instead, I'm up for life, and just to save you a couple of years.'

Alan Thomas looked hurt. 'Jesus, Rosie. They had me and I guess I panicked. Now I'm in here anyway. If I had my time again I'd do it different. You don't know how close I came to telling you that I was wearing a wire.' Lindsey shook his head. An apology wasn't going to do him the slightest bit of good but this was probably as close as he was going to get.

'Why did you say I did those murders for?' asked Alan.

'It's a furphy. They told me that you couldn't have got all the details of the murders from police records. It's just a furphy so I can get bail. I pretended that I'd wear a wire and set up Mark Lewis. I know I'll be under surveillance but once I'm out I can lose them and piss off. They think I'm a minor player and I can get Lewis and you. I'm going to Kogarah Court on Tuesday and I know they'll give me bail even if I plead guilty to possessing the pistol. I'll have to get out and then I can piss off to Queensland.'

•

Detective Sergeant Matt Appleton can't get hold of Jacob on Sunday or Monday. Rose's bail hearing is on Tuesday. They aren't going to make it. Baker calls the PIB again to book a surveillance team to follow Rose as soon as he is released the following day.

On Tuesday, Jacob calls back and he's working at a site out west. Appleton drives straight out there with another detective. They meet in a side street and serve Jacob with a summons to appear before the Crime Commission that evening.

Jacob arrives at the Commission with his solicitor and tells them the weapon is stashed at a mate's place. They all drive out together, collect the weapon then return to the Crime Commission for a formal interview.

They ask Jacob how he came by the pistol. He said Alan Thomas was trying to sell this pistol that Lindsey Rose had given him and said he'd used in a double murder. They both thought he was full of shit. Jacob agreed to get rid of it for him. They met in the car park of the

Burwood RSL and Jacob collected the gun, silencer and ammunition from the boot of Alan's car.

Yes, he knew Rose, knew he was good friends with Alan Thomas. Rose never knew that Jacob had the gun so it was never discussed with him. He never liked Rose anyway. He knew nothing of the Gladesville murders. No useful information.

•

Lindsey was taken from Long Bay back to Sydney Central Court and he made bail. He walked out the front door of the court house, onto Liverpool Street, and he was almost surprised to be out in the sunshine again – he'd thought his days of freedom might have been over already. He'd played them for fools and he was a free man.

Free to a point. He had new conditions for this bail: to report to Kogarah police station Tuesdays, Thursdays and Saturdays. He was already reporting to Yandee Mondays, Wednesdays and Fridays so now Sunday was the only day of the week that he didn't have to front up to cops and sign a form. It was time to get out of town. Quickly.

Betty came in and picked him up and took him home to the flat at Brighton-Le-Sands, and a hot shower was the first thing he needed.

63

We are, as a society, cultivating many time bombs, future Bryants, future Frankums. We sit in surprise at the amount of massacres in the US: Colombine, Postal Workers, and many others. Why do they do it? Because people feel aggrieved.

A couple of times Lindsey has mentioned that, at various times in his life, he might have just 'gone postal'. But mass, indiscriminate shooting contradicts the value system that he lays claim to – that he targeted people who he believes 'deserved it'. I write and call him out on it and here is his reply:

If I contradicted myself, or seemed to, it's because of my inability to express myself, explain my actions, clearly.

I acted contrary to normal principles. I had a 'don't care anymore' attitude, so my own principles went out the window. However:

- not irrationality. I acted cool, calm and collected, planned, surveilled, executed my plan perfectly. Irrationality was the behaviour of Bryant and Frankum.

- my flaw was not losing patience or over-reacting. My flaw was losing care. It didn't matter anymore.

You used the word vigilante. My counsellor came up with the same word some weeks ago. I was not going to let these people get away with it, no chance. If the corrupt police would do nothing I would and I did. Someone had to stop those people.

My regret is the witnesses. It has been mentioned before so I take it as a given. They were the result of 'get a result, don't stop till target eliminated.' Once I start, no stopping, I've made the decision.

The counsellors think I am a bully. Exactly the opposite to all I have said to them. When I explained that I am the antithesis of this and why, they don't get it.

•

Is this consistent with psychopathy? Lack of empathy is a defining trait and by his own words he 'didn't care' anymore, so perhaps yes. He claims to regret the witnesses he killed but 'they were the result . . .' We've discussed it in person and it always feels like a regret of circumstance rather than a heartfelt compassion for those victims and their surviving families.

How can we know for sure? Well, we can't, but a test exists, devised by the aforementioned Robert D. Hare, called the Psychopathy Checklist – Revised (PCL-R). The results of the test may be accepted in the courtroom but only if it is conducted by a fully qualified psychologist following strict protocols. Hare specifically warns against attempting lay diagnoses. I should not attempt a lay person's diagnosis.

Well, of course I did – I read through the twenty characteristics measured in the PCL-R and took a stab. You could google PCL-R and play along at home if you wanted. The conclusion? I scored him a 30 out of 40 and that puts him on the boundary of a definitive classification.

It's hard to accept: that this amenable person I've known for so long could fit this label straight out of a horror movie. But even this dissonance is explainable: the other seminal text on psychopathy is titled *The Mask of Sanity*[27] for a reason. The other defining trait of the psychopath is an outward persona exuding confidence and charisma, a 'mask' hiding the damaged person behind.

Well, that's as close as I got to answering the psychopathy question. But it raises one more question. Not all psychopaths (if one he be) turn criminal (some become CEOs – or celebrity chefs) and for all my reading on genetic and environmental risk factors for criminality, the loop is not closed – why has Lindsey ended up this way?

64

Betty had left for work so he sat down, made a cup of coffee and considered his options. He'd told them he was involved in two murders but it was inadmissible so they couldn't charge him without other evidence. He hadn't seen a tail on the way over but they must have him under surveillance. They'd stick with it until they had him or they'd load him up and he'd go down anyway.

He didn't have time to build a new identity so he went through his papers until he found the birth certificate in his birth name, Lindsey Lehman. The cops probably had it down as an alias but it was better than nothing.

Betty got home that night and he told her he'd be going on an overseas holiday – tomorrow.

•

First thing Wednesday Lindsey drove to Liverpool Street and signed on at Yandee then he went over to Burwood and found Denis at the salon. Would he give Lindsey a dye and a haircut, he asked? Of course. Not the salon – can you get to Dawn's place? Sure, call me later.

He stopped by the ATM on Burwood Road and withdrew $500 – the daily maximum. Then he drove to the Sawdust at Gladesville to see Robbo, his old mate the ex-screw.

'G'day, Rosie.'

'I need a favour.'

'Sure, what's up?'

'Take my ATM card. And here's the PIN. There's about $300 left in the account. It's yours. Wait one week, take out the money, then destroy the card.'

'What's going on?'

'You don't want to know. For your own protection, I promise, you Do Not Want To Know.'

•

298

Late afternoon he rang Denis from the Burwood Plaza payphone and he was ready so they met at Dawn's house on Oxford Street. Sharon, another Burwood local, was there too and the girls chatted over drinks while Denis went to work.

He cut Lindsey's hair short, so the curls didn't show, then dyed it black.

'Thanks, Denis, I owe you one,' he said.

'What's with the new look, anyway?' asked Denis.

'Denis, mate. Let's just say . . .' but Denis saw the look in his eye and the tension in his shoulders and his smile fell. 'Say no more, Rosie.'

'See you soon,' said Denis when the taxi beeped from the street.

'I don't know about that, mate,' Lindsey said.

Denis gave him a hug at the doorway.

'Okay, Rosie, love. Take care,' said Denis.

They broke apart and Lindsey pulled out a baseball cap to cover his hair in case the dog squad was watching, opened the door and walked.

•

Lindsey went home to Betty. This would be their last night together.

'Some people will come over and ask about me. Just remember that I'm on my way to a meeting with my solicitor. That's all you know.'

'Okay, Rosie.'

•

CM: Did you do anything special together for your last night?

LR: Nope.

CM: But you'd been together all that time. *Years.* How did you feel?

LR: Easy come, easy go.

It's tempting to accept that's how he really felt. For one thing, he's spurned just about everyone else in his life by now. But on the other hand, to this day he is protective of her. He won't tell me anything about her, never has. She's got her own life, he said; the people who knew us together will recognise her in your book, even with the alias, so I won't tell you anything that might otherwise identify her.

I don't try so hard to track down Betty. I am happy for her to remain as this will-o'-the-wisp figure, shadowing Lindsey through his last few years of freedom, who was probably the love of his life.

•

Early Thursday morning he walked out the door with Betty and a single carry bag. The bag was full and he wore a beanie against the winter cold and to keep his hair hidden.

The bag contained clothes, papers, some tools and whatever spare cash he'd been able to get his hands on, including two thousand US dollars that Betty had given him. Betty drove and Lindsey turned the wing mirror so he could look behind them. The followers were professionals but he knew what to look for and when they crossed Canterbury Road the nondescript Commodore turned off and a grey Alfetta took up the chase. A good choice – he'd used an Alfa once himself – small enough to park and manoeuvre easily but with a powerful engine. And a fairly bland-looking car so it didn't draw much attention. Grey was a good colour for blending in.

He didn't want to give the game away so he didn't tell Betty they were being followed, but he told her which turns to take and took them a slightly longer way so he could confirm the tails. And then they were going up Coronation Parade and across the Hume Highway at Enfield and they passed the howitzer he and Max used to play on and wondered if that fat sergeant who had warned them off was as crooked as all these other bent pricks who had landed him in his current predicament.

The third car picked them up on Parramatta Road. He figured three cars would be the most they'd use.

They pulled up outside Peter Wynn's sports store on Church Street, Parramatta. He picked up his bag and got out. No kiss goodbye, just a casual wave and he crossed the road behind Betty's car and walked into the Greenway Arcade without looking back. Straight down, turn left and into the public toilets. He removed his beanie and glasses, inserted contact lenses and then changed from his jeans and sports coat into dark slacks and a pale blue sloppy joe. He put his carry bag into a plastic shopping bag. The arcade had a back entrance but the dog squad would be all over it so he walked back out the front of the arcade. He crossed back over

Church Street and there were a few browsing shoppers. He paused and in the reflection of Peter Wynn's front window he could see one of the followers on foot to his left so he turned right and walked slowly up the road, same pace as the other punters.

Right at George Street and the taxi rank was only fifty metres further and there were cabs ready to go. If they were any good they'd check the taxi ranks and the bus stops first, but he was sure they'd missed him and it would take them a while to realise he'd left the arcade so it was worth the risk of getting a cab for the pay-off of being out of the area before they twigged.

'Ashfield, thanks,' he said to the cabbie.

He took a room at the Philip Lodge Motel on Parramatta Road where he'd celebrated his fortieth. He paid cash.

•

Rod Baker gets a phone call from the surveillance team. 'We lost him.'

'You've got to be kidding me,' says Baker.

It's obvious that Rose had deliberately evaded the tail so Baker sends people out looking.

Detective Kelly goes to the workshop at Wentworthville. An elderly lady shows him around and she hasn't seen Rose. He wants to ask her son Malcolm, but he is off driving trucks, she says.

Rod Baker phones the Kogarah police station and they confirm that Rose has not signed on for the day.

Other team members are sent out to his regular haunts: the pubs and clubs in Burwood, the RSL at Enfield. No-one has seen him.

That night they visit Alan Thomas at Long Bay. He had spoken to Rose in the yard, he tells them.

'Lindsey said he was going to make bail then piss off to Queensland,' he says. 'I thought he was full of shit.'

•

The next morning, nine o'clock, Lindsey walked into the Traveland in Liverpool and asked for a hire car. They rang Hertz and booked a red Pulsar for him to pick up at 11 a.m. He used his own name for the booking; he knew they'd track it down eventually and then they'd find the car parked at Adelaide airport and think he could be anywhere.

He drove through the day, only stopping for petrol, and when it got dark at 6 p.m. he'd been on the road for seven hours. He found a low-rent motel at Hay and they didn't need to see ID.

When he stopped for petrol he bought pies, chips and Cokes, smiled vaguely and said as little as possible. Just like a regular square-head.

Another seven hours and he was in Adelaide; he remembered to turn right at South Road and then the signs took him onto Sir Donald Bradman Drive and he was there. He parked in the long-term car park, walked to the arrivals gate and hailed a taxi. Glenelg was the obvious choice. Close to the airport and multiple accommodation options. The taxi dropped him there and he bought a copy of the Adelaide *Advertiser* and wandered into a hotel that he liked the look of – it was cheap and it had a separate block of motel rooms that could be accessed without having to go through the hotel's foyer.

It was cheap for a hotel, but he'd need something cheaper still. That night he sat down in his small hotel room and started reading the *Advertiser*'s 'to let' pages.

•

Baker rings Kogarah again and Rose still hasn't been in – as expected – so the paperwork for breach of bail is prepared.

They visit Betty at Brighton-Le-Sands. He has left his mobile phone behind. Said he had a solicitor's appointment but never came home. Took US currency from her bedside table, she tells them.

The solicitor confirms that Rose had made an appointment but never turned up.

'He's gone,' says Baker, back at the office. 'Probably left New South Wales already.'

They order alerts on his bank account and passport. They prepare a brief and send it around the state and also to Victoria, South Australia and Queensland.

65

Boarding houses were the go. Cheap and anonymous. Didn't need to sign a lease and you had your own room with a lock on it – more privacy than a share house.

He found a place on Taylor Street in Brompton – close to North Adelaide. He liked it because it had multiple exits and there was an industrial site over the back fence. Also he could walk into Adelaide city, though it took nearly an hour. The first night he walked in and found the Salvation Army halfway house, round the corner from their head office on Pirie Street. It provided a free hot meal and bread rolls. He still had cash in reserve but it would only cover a few weeks of rent so he had to economise. He availed himself of the Salvos' generosity almost every night.

He scoped out the other boarders, made friendly chat where possible. This young bloke, Cody, had the room at the back corner that had a separate door out to the driveway and he seemed decent enough.

Cody was on the dole, like most of them at the boarding house, and for a bit of extra cash he'd scavenge empty bottles and cans and take them to the recycling depot.

The next day Lindsey joined him and at the end of the day he'd made $30. It would do for now. He went out with Cody again and by the end of the week he'd covered his rent and knew Cody well enough to ask him a favour.

'How would you feel about swapping rooms?' asked Lindsey.

Cody smiled at first, not getting it. Then: 'Oh. Right. How come?'

'I owe some guys money. Your back door might come in handy one day,' he said.

'Well . . .'

'Look, I know you're a top bloke, I can tell. Do me this favour and I'll look out for you. Help me out and then I'll owe you one. Okay?'

Cody wasn't left with much of a choice and the next day Lindsey skipped the bottle-collecting and swapped the rooms. Neither of them had much property so it didn't take long. Disinfecting Cody's room took longer than the move.

In the afternoon he went for a check-up at the local GP and got the name Lindsey Lehman on file. After twelve months the GP would be able to sign the back of a passport photo for him.

He watched the TV news every night. The five o'clock bulletin if he could. If they broadcast his mug shot he'd have to run again. *Australia's Most Wanted* was broadcast at 7.30 p.m. local time, so every Monday night he'd ring Robbo in Sydney and ask if he'd been on and because of the time difference he'd have half an hour head start.

He had a bag packed and he'd head north. Stand beside the Princes Highway and hold up his truck driver's log book. It was part of the truckie code to help another driver and he'd say he needed to get to Katherine to pick up a truck. He'd stay a night then go on to Darwin. Darwin was still like a frontier town. He could disappear in Darwin just fine.

•

'Rose used to be married. They had a daughter,' says Appleton.

'Found the wife?' asks Baker.

'Yep. Perth.'

'You'll have to go see her. What's her name? Can you call her and tee it up?'

'Lydia. Okay.'

•

'She says we've got the wrong guy. It's all bullshit.'

'What's she like?'

'Well . . . it was a vigorous conversation. She can talk. Someone had told her about the media release already and she reckons it was a bolt from the blue. She'll talk to us, but she isn't happy about it.'

•

Rod Baker is recorded as the contact against Lindsey Rose's extensive record in the COPS database. Five days after he disappeared Baker gets a call from Liverpool police station. The local Hertz had reported that

Lindsey Rose had hired a red Pulsar for one day and it had not been returned.

Detective Williams takes it and starts on the phone. Hertz has the rental agreement and the manager provides a phone number for the sales assistant who'd booked out the car to Rose. She remembers him – mid-forties, stocky build. She recalls that he had on shorts similar to Stubbies and muscly legs. He'd paid a deposit of $100 cash but the hire fee had already been paid – he'd pre-booked the car through a travel agent.

The manager at Traveland had made the booking herself and also remembered Rose. He was wearing blue jeans, sneakers and a blue and white tracksuit top zippered up the front, she said. Rose had told her he needed a hire car because his own car, a Commodore, had been stolen from Liverpool train station. He was carrying a white plastic shopping bag and he was alone.

•

They hear from the St George Bank. It's been eight days since Rose skipped and his bank account has been accessed at an ATM at the Criterion Hotel, Carrington – near Newcastle. Two detectives drive up and ask around. There is no camera on the ATM or in the hotel. They show Rose's photo around but no-one recognises the face. He must know they'd be monitoring his bank account, says Baker, so why would he do it? Arrogance? Forgetfulness? Or maybe deliberate misdirection. They stay in Newcastle for a day but it looks like a dead end, so they leave.

•

Detective Appleton flies to Perth and meets Lydia.

They'd still been together in January 1984 (when Cavanagh and Lee were murdered), she answers, but they separated later that year. The divorce wasn't finalised until 1986. No idea about any criminal activity, she says. Knew he was a bit naughty, was familiar with guns, but he was licensed for his security work.

He'd recently made a small dent in the child support he owed but the last contact was a few weeks before when he rang to chat with Penny. There was no mention of any of this funny business. He had family in Sydney and Queensland but she had no other ideas where he might have gone.

'Do you believe her? Seems unlikely,' says Baker back down the phone.

'Hard to read her. She's a real live wire. She may have actually said "outrageous, darling" to me. But like you say, you'd have to think—'

'What did she say about witness protection?'

'Not interested. Still says she finds it hard to believe he could have done it. Anyway, she's sticking to her guns that she never knew anything about his offending. Wouldn't even sign a statement.'

•

Telstra have come back with subscriber details for the phone number Rose gave to the optometrist. It's registered to a Zane S., residing in Bankstown. Williams calls the number and asks for him by name and Zane confirms that he knows Lindsey Rose and he seems surprised, but he'll answer questions if necessary.

•

Detective Williams drives over the next day and Zane tells them he is a close friend of Rose, the closest thing to a brother, but he knows nothing of any criminal behaviour. They'd spent time together socially in Burwood in 1994 and Rose had borrowed his phone for a few weeks for 'work-related matters'. When Williams provides Thomas's description of the accomplice, Zane thinks he might know the guy. Rose referred to him as his 'apprentice' and called him Don, or Donnie. Zane doesn't know his last name. He remembers mention of a fist fight on Valentine's Day in 1994.

•

They need Alan Thomas to identify the murder weapon, the .22 Browning they'd recovered from Jacob's mate. Williams takes Thomas back into the Ballistics Section of the Sydney Police Centre and they show him.

'That's not it,' says Thomas.

'What do you mean?' asks Williams.

'That's not the gun that Rosie . . . that Lindsey gave me. This silencer is twice as long and half as fat as the one I got from Lindsey and it's black instead of silver.'

'What about the gun?'

'That's definitely not the same gun. Lindsey's pistol was heavier, two or three inches longer and had finger grips on the handle. And this one's the wrong colour: black instead of metallic. Also, I'd have remembered if it had a gold-coloured trigger like this one does.'

One of them must be lying – Jacob or Thomas – and Baker has his money on Alan Thomas. He hides his disappointment. They have no other leads on the location of the murder weapon.

•

Three weeks in Adelaide and his beard had filled out. He bought a cheap kit and dyed his hair blond. Once it was long enough it would naturally bunch into tight curls and he'd be a poor match to any photograph the police might bandy about.

He was getting by on the Salvos' free meals and the bottle-collecting. The manager at the recycling depot bemoaned the poor reliability of his staff and when he was short-staffed one day due to no-shows Lindsey offered to fill in. It took minutes to be trained as a sorter and he worked a full shift, into the evening.

It was mind-numbing work but he began working casual shifts there, often three days a week, and when one of the machines jammed he helped fix it so he was a casual sorter who did some maintenance fitting on the side. He should have been earning $35 per hour, but without any usable trade papers he was paid off the books, in cash, a pittance. But $80 a day was still more than double what he'd made collecting bottles and cans.

It gave him enough for beer money. The Gaslight Tavern was only a five-minute walk from the boarding house and Friday nights became the routine. The Gaslight had a dart board and as he'd left his precision darts in Sydney he bought a new set. He went easy on the locals to start with.

Cody showed him the Brickworks markets, two kilometres from the boarding house, and he invested in a cheap pushbike. Now he could get in to Pirie Street for his free hot meal in fifteen minutes instead of an hour. Most Sundays he rode to the markets – it was free to enter and often had a live band and he kept his eye on the kinds of cheap gear on offer. It was something to do to speed the passing of time, bring him closer to the day when he'd skip the country. And he'd been talking to Robbo, who had some overseas contacts who might come in handy, and soon, he thought, he'd have a plan that was going to fly.

66

He was working on a painting when three screws and a suit arrived outside his cell.

'Mr Rose, you'll need to come with us. We've got some questions to ask you,' said one of the screws.

'Not a good time, fellas,' he said. 'Just touching up the bus in this painting before me paint dries. Maybe check with my secretary and I might be able to squeeze you in tomorrow.' He turned back to the canvas and made out like he was going to apply some more brushwork, though in reality he wasn't going to risk messing it up trying to paint with these palookas distracting him.

They unlocked the cell door and no-one, apparently, was laughing. Manacles. Down the hall and through to an interview room.

A plastic key had been found in the main gaol. They could tell it was one of Lindsey's and they immediately asked him how he'd got it out of HRMU. Lindsey laughed when he realised what was happening.

'Exactly,' he said. 'How would I get it out of HRMU if I wanted to get a key into the main gaol? That is a very good question.'

They didn't take to his attitude, especially the suit, who was, it turned out, the regional head of prisons – effectively the warden's boss.

The tactics were pretty obvious: ask him questions phrased in such a way that his guilt was already assumed. They had nothing on him, they were just fishing. He played along for a while, but the whole thing began to give him the shits, and the manacles were beginning to rub, so eventually he just told them he had nothing to do with it and he wouldn't be answering any more questions. They huffed and puffed for a while and eventually he was taken back to his cell.

He sat down and his heart and mind were racing, his temples were throbbing and he felt like punching the walls. It took him an hour – an hour of standing there in his cell fuming – to realise what the problem was. He'd been locked up for so long that a sudden departure from the long ingrained routine was a shock to the system, like a body blow. That was it for painting for the day; the next day the paints he'd mixed had dried and the resentment boiled over again and even though he knew it was irrational he was bent out of shape for days.

A month later a letter came in addressed to him and inside was a brochure and an enrolment form for a locksmithing course. One of the other inmates had sent away for it in his name and it had made it through all the security checks. It was pretty funny.

•

I ask Lindsey about this key-making business. He's mentioned it a couple of times – it's the reason (one of the reasons) he gave for being moved to Supermax. He wants to think about it first, consider the risks, but eventually he tells me about it. When he was still in Long Bay . . .

•

. . . his cell door had a tumbler lock with a central pin so he'd need to acquire a blade and manufacture a drill to produce the hollow shank key.

Within a week he had the blade out of a Stanley knife, lifted from the workshop.

He pulled apart the aerial from the radio in his cell. Each telescoped section gave him a drill bit of a different diameter and he used the blade to cross-cut jagged edges into the ends so his drill bits had teeth. His cellmate looked on. Yeah, yeah, he'd keep his mouth shut.

An old toothbrush formed the blank. He removed the bristles then used the blade to whittle it down to the diameter of the keyhole. At night he sat in front of the TV in his cell and carefully rolled the drill bits between his hands to slowly, slowly form the hole in the end of the toothbrush. After two weeks he could slide the transformed toothbrush over the pin and into the lock.

He scavenged hard plastic from a bowl and soft plastic from a yoghurt container. He heated the soft plastic over a lit match then pushed it carefully into the lock and measured the marks left in the plastic.

He cut the hard plastic to match his measurements and now he had the teeth for his key ready to cement into the slot he'd cut into the toothbrush.

He'd purchased chewy lollies at the buy-up and once he'd chewed for long enough he used the sticky liquid to affix the teeth into the slot in the toothbrush. Once dry it was rock hard.

Then it was trial and error, small adjustments, and on the fourth night he felt the plug turning so he had a fully functioning key to the door of his cell.

He wrapped it carefully and at the right moment he knocked and passed it through the hatch to the passing sweeper and it was arranged so another prisoner, the Custodian, would hold it for safekeeping.

Meanwhile, he'd already started taking measurements for the prison gate.

●

Robbo's letter arrives and it contains the agreed code, so he knows there's a car parked outside the prison walls with the key in the exhaust pipe for him. Good old Robbo.

He'd finished the key to the gate weeks ago and the Custodian has them both and yes, yes, they were still safe. And now the car is waiting so he is good to go.

The next morning his cell door opens and at first he thinks it's the standard let-out but the squad is there and they ramp his cell. Nothing. He'd long since disposed of the tools and they come up empty and the keys are still safe. *The keys are safe.*

The screws didn't say what they were looking for and they can't have picked up the code from Robbo's letter. It was impossible, they can't have, surely.

He puts the hard word on his cellmate. Mate, tell me now if you've dogged me. Tell me now and you can make it up to me. If I find out later, then you're a dead man. I swear, Rosie, he said, it wasn't me.

The next morning they come again, ramp his cell again, and again they find nothing and after the third morning it's got around the prison that Rosie's cell is being ramped every day and after the sixth time he's had enough. He sends word. He wants his keys.

He's in a hurry and it's worth the risk and the Custodian is willing so he passes him the keys right there in the open yard and Lindsey bends to adjust his footwear and shoves the keys, still in their wrappings, down into his sock.

•

He is going tonight. *He is going tonight.* Just before lock-down three screws walk up to his cell and one of them asks him outright if he has any keys. Six ramps they've done and keys had never been mentioned and the day – the very same day – that he gets them back this screw is here asking him.

He reaches into his sock and hands them straight over. They'd have searched him anyway.

67

August 1996. Baker sends a detective to canvas the medical centres and GPs in the Burwood area again, this time armed with the description and name of the supposed accomplice. The medical centre on Burwood Road turns up a potential. On 15 February 1994 – the day after the Gladesville murders – a Donnie R. had been treated for a closed right fist injury. Could this be the person?

The address is in Burwood, so Williams and another detective pay a visit. Donnie has moved out. He was in South Australia, then Perth for a while; has family in Inverell. Williams leaves with a photo of Donnie R. The photo fits the description given by Thomas.

9 August. They show Alan Thomas the photo of Donnie. Yes, he says, that's him. Never knew his name but that's the guy he'd seen with Rose, the one he thought Rose had said was his accomplice at Gladesville.

Now they just have to find him.

•

Thomas's written statements contain a longer list of facts to be checked. Detective Sergeant Williams runs with it.

He goes to Penrith and asks to see the guest register at the Log Cabin Hotel for the night that Thomas planned to throw that pistol – the one they had thought was the murder weapon – into the river. The records show that Thomas stayed there on 27 February 1994, as he had said. Williams takes a copy of the registration slip and a statement from the manager. So far, nothing he has told them can be disproved.

•

15 August, another breakthrough. The missing rental car has turned up. It's at Adelaide airport and Baker arranges for the Adelaide CIB to check it out. The car park's records show that the red Pulsar arrived on 6 July. After seven weeks the parking attendant became suspicious and called the local police. CIB take a statement and fax it to Baker. Rose's fingerprints are in the car, as expected. No other leads. They recheck

the airlines with a narrower focus, domestic flights out of Adelaide, but nothing turns up. It wasn't so hard to fly domestic under a false name – he could be anywhere in the country.

•

Meanwhile Appleton's team has been trawling the Cavanagh/Lee files. The original investigators had plenty to deal with. Cavanagh himself had criminal activity on file as far back as 1947. He was known to transport marijuana through his trucking business and to be a receiver: a stolen VCR had been found in his house after his murder. Many witnesses reported that he always carried large amounts of cash and boasted of never paying tax. A number of former employees had cause to bear a grudge against Cavanagh and his history of relationships with women revealed even more people who might have motive to do him harm.

In 1976 he had responded to a newspaper advertisement and started writing to a woman, Bernadette, in the Philippines. The following year he proposed marriage by letter and met her for the first time when he arrived in Manila for the wedding. She moved into Bill's house in Tamworth, where they lived with two of Bill's sons, ages twelve and twenty-two, from two previous marriages.

By 1980 they had moved to Hoxton Park on Sydney's western fringe, Bernadette had a son to Bill and they became close with a local family, the Langtons. Lucy Langton had a niece in Manila, Carmelita, who'd become pregnant to a married man and it was arranged for Carmelita to have the baby in Australia to hide the birth from the family. Carmelita soon took up with a Colin Lee, an employee of Bill Cavanagh; Lee took the new baby under his wing and a year later they were married and living in the Philippines together. One of Cavanagh's sons believed Lee had left the country because he'd being caught stripping trucks. Carmelita, now Carmelita Lee, became pregnant to Colin Lee and flew back to Sydney with the new baby to find work. Colin stayed in the Philippines.

Meanwhile, Bernadette had moved out of Bill's place, complaining that he'd been beating her. Bill agreed to give Carmelita work cleaning in his house and within weeks she had moved into his bedroom. Bernadette rang Colin Lee to let him know that his wife was shacked up with Bill

Cavanagh, his former boss. Four months later Bernadette received an anonymous phone call stating that Colin Lee intended to murder Carmelita and Bill.

The relationship between Carmelita Lee and Bill Cavanagh had its tensions – it appeared that Cavanagh had found a letter addressed to Lee encouraging her to 'get as much as you can out of him'. Bill had court proceedings pending for his divorce from Bernadette and also for custody of their child together. At the time of his murder Bill Cavanagh was also having an affair with the 21-year-old daughter of the Langtons; she had been one of several people he'd been drinking with at the Stop and Rest on the night of his murder.

Despite many promising leads the original investigation had found no evidence against ex-wives, disgruntled former employees or anyone else.

Forensics also pointed to an unidentified party. Blood was found at the scene, and under Cavanagh's fingernails. DNA typing didn't exist in 1984 so the blood had been typed using PGM and Hp blood grouping systems. The blood under the nails was PGM 2+1-, Hp 2, a combination found in approximately 2 per cent of the population. It was a reasonable assumption that the blood under Bill Cavanagh's nails belonged to the perpetrator. But no-one relevant to the investigation had that blood type. It didn't match Cavanagh, Lee or fifteen other associates and family members listed as persons of interest.

Another suspect, truck driver Russell V., had complained to a witness about being bashed, almost to death, at the behest of Cavanagh. But the original investigators hadn't been able to locate him in 1984. It wasn't until 1989 that Russell V. was located in prison. His blood type was taken and it didn't match the blood from Cavanagh's nails either.

Another seven years later, Detective Matthew Appleton is reviewing the case file and he recognises the name. Russell V. is on the list of Rose's known associates. Could it be that Russell had enlisted Rose to kill Cavanagh in revenge for having been assaulted? Appleton decides they need to take a closer look.

•

A sunny Sunday afternoon and Lindsey was in the backyard of the boarding house with its dilapidated and rusting shed, scrappy lawn, discarded furniture and boxes, edged by unkempt shrubs, weeds and wooden palings.

Three weeks before, he'd started cleaning up the yard, a few hours each weekend. This day he set his cup of coffee and newspaper beside a weather-beaten deckchair and went to work. After an hour he had a pile of weeds on the go and was working in a garden bed up against the back fence when he heard his name called. It was the landlord.

'What are you up to, sport?' asked the landlord.

'Just a bit of weeding,' said Lindsey.

'There's no need for that. You're not expecting to be paid, are you?'

'Nah, just something to do in me spare time, really. Nice day, I come out here with my paper and a cuppa and take my time, improve the yard a bit as I go.'

'Just came over to collect the rent.'

'I'll grab it for you.'

The landlord seemed satisfied once he'd been paid and Lindsey went back out to the yard. He was glad the landlord hadn't taken a closer look. He might have wondered why Lindsey needed a claw hammer to remove weeds. Half an hour later he had finished loosening two fence palings. They looked like all the others but Lindsey knew which ones he could yank if he needed to make a quick escape.

He woke at 3 a.m. for a dry run. He imagined the knock at the door, looking down the hallway and getting the nod from Cody and he let himself out the side door of his room to the driveway. He saw which way the shadows fell and followed them around to the back fence. The moonlight was dim. He removed the fence palings by touch and pulled them back into place behind him. The lot next door was used as a workshop and he knew to watch out for car wrecks and debris. He still barked his shins on a discarded bumper bar; he suppressed the gasp and moved on to Gibson Street.

And here was the beautiful part. Less than a block down Gibson was a yellow Corolla in its usual spot. A dozen years earlier, when he was repossessing cars for a living, he'd kept this Toyota car key that had a knack for working on other vehicles. Over the years he'd found it worked on about one in twenty Toyotas and he'd found two that were regularly parked within range of Taylor Street.

He tried the key in the door, it took a little jiggle and he was in. He started up the engine then immediately killed it. The dry run was over. It was a pass. He locked the Corolla and walked back around to the front of the boarding house. Home.

•

October, 1996. They have a name and a date of birth and they run the usual background checks and eventually get a hit on a bank account for Donnie R. It takes a few more weeks to get the warrant and the search request fulfilled and then they have an address in Orange and a detailed list of the activity on his bank account. Williams can see that he'd made several withdrawals at the Burwood RSL three days before the Gladesville murders and one withdrawal only two days before – at a convenience store in Gladesville, a short walk from Kerrie's Oasis.

•

Part of the scant evidence they have against Rose is the hearsay from Thomas that Rose told him details of murders over lunch at a Japanese restaurant on 21 June. Baker wants it firmed up so Detective Senior Constable Perry spends the morning in Parramatta following the trail. The Police Credit Union provides a statement and a copy of the form that Alan Thomas had signed when he picked up his new credit card on his way to lunch with Rose. And the owner of the Tem Ichi Japanese restaurant provides a copy of the credit card slip and a statement to vouch for its authenticity. It's just as Thomas had told them, he'd paid for their lunch with his new Visa card: $108.40.

•

Appleton's team is reinterviewing the witness list from the 1984 investigation into the murders of Cavanagh and Lee. Detective Davies interviews the younger son of Bill Cavanagh at Campbelltown police station and he says that in 1990 he had been told the name of the man who had supposedly killed his father. The man had been in gaol in

Queensland at the time, he'd been told. He didn't recognise the name but had made a statement at Flemington police station that he believed a Lindsey Rose had murdered his father.

•

They have a strong circumstantial case against Donnie and it's time for him to be interviewed.

The drive to Orange is three and a half hours and the sun rises at their backs as Detectives Williams and Perry commence the climb through the Blue Mountains to make the 8 a.m. rendezvous at Orange police station. They don't expect trouble but they wear their sidearms and three local constables join them in their patrol car for the arrest of Donnie R.

It's a white weatherboard house on a suburban street on the far east side of town, a kilometre short of the sewerage works. Even though it's nearly summer it's only twelve degrees and Williams's breath fogs as he walks up the driveway and onto the verandah. Two constables are already in position at the back of the property in case Donnie decides to run for it. A young woman opens the door and when Donnie comes out he's wearing worn jeans and a lumberjack style fleece jacket, cigarette lit.

Donnie's eyes flick up and down and when he looks out and sees the back-ups, each with their right hand on their holster, he knows.

He is placed under arrest. He asks the young woman to bring him his wallet and his Johnny Reb boots then they drive him to Orange police station.

In the interview room they tell him they know he was involved in the Gladesville murders and would he give a recorded interview? He agrees and the interview is under way at 10.40 a.m. It has already been a long day for Williams and Perry but they stay focussed. It takes two and a half hours.

•

'I have no doubt he was telling the truth. Everything he said fits with the crime scene.' Detective Williams is talking on his mobile phone to Rod Baker while Detective Perry drives them back to Sydney.

'And his own involvement?'

'Says Rose was going to pay him just to get in the door. Knew nothing about Kerrie Pang or that any violence was intended.'

'And the description of the other bloke fits Mark Lewis exactly?'

'Yep. And he's willing to pick him out of a line-up if required.'

'Payment?'

'He said five hundred was promised but Rose never paid him. In fact he says he didn't even ask for it – something about the value of a human life. I almost feel sorry for the young bloke. When it happened, he was only twenty-one.'[28]

•

Now that he had been going about as Lindsey Lehman for a few months, his thoughts turned to the man who'd given him that name. One afternoon in the city he used a payphone to call his birth father, Ron Lehman. He was pleased to hear Lindsey's voice, he said. He'd retired now. He'd left the postal service many years before, been a driving examiner for the DMT and then driven interstate coaches for years. Now he was living on the pension in the caravan park and yes, he was still married.

They talked about Lindsey's childhood and about his mum Glenda, who'd been unwell last he heard – before he skipped town – and he asked his father why, all those years before, he'd stopped all contact – pretty much as soon as Lindsey turned sixteen.

He just wanted them to get on with their lives, Ron told him, and so that was why. Lindsey had never really held it against the man for leaving Glenda, leaving him fatherless. Who could blame him? Glenda had been a hellion at the best of times and he could only imagine what she must have been like with prenatal hormones coursing through her veins. Ron Lehman was a decent man, Lindsey realised, and good for him that he got out when he did.

•

15 November 1996. At 5.45 a.m. Detective Senior Constables Maranesi and Davies arrive at Mark Lewis's house on Shepherd Street, St Marys. The front door of the house is open and a light is on in the kitchen. Davies rings the doorbell and a man wearing only dark blue shorts comes to the doorway.

'Are you Mark Lewis?' asks Davies.

'Yes.'

Lewis leads them into the lounge room and Davies says, 'I'm here to tell you that a person was arrested and charged with the murder of your former wife, Kerrie Pang, yesterday. The person described another person fitting your description who was present at the time. Would you be prepared to take part in a police identification parade?'

'No. I want to speak to my solicitor first.'

'Yes, of course. Do you want to give him a call now?'

'No, not at six o'clock. I'll ring him at nine.'

Davies writes down names and telephone numbers and the detectives return to Liverpool Street. At 9.05 a.m. Maranesi receives the call from Mark Lewis: he has spoken with his barrister and been instructed not to take part in a police identification parade.

•

When he fled Sydney Lindsey had taken his indenture papers with him and with the aid of some liquid paper and a couple of trips to the library's photocopier he was able to produce passable trade qualifications in his name of choice, Lindsey Lehman.

A used car yard at Woodville Park – fifteen minutes by bike – was advertising for a mechanic. They were happy with his papers and he started that week.

The yard took an old Mazda 929 with a blown engine as a trade-in. He bought it off them for $275 and a towie dropped it at the front of the boarding house. He picked up a second-hand engine for $10 and with $50 worth of tools from the Brickworks markets he rebuilt the engine right there in the street.

He had it registered, installed a tow bar and bought a busted-up box trailer. The trailer he repaired using sheet metal he found discarded around industrial sites. He took his box trailer to garage sales, auction houses and charity op shops and picked up furniture or bric-a-brac that was damaged or undervalued. Then he fixed them up and took up a stall of his own at the markets.

He still took his evening meals for free at the Salvation Army. He drove in to town, parked a few blocks away and walked in.

Now he had money left over after paying for rent, beer and basics – he even bought a cheap mobile phone. He saved a little, but he wasn't too fussed. The cash would come later.

He just had to stay out of trouble for another six months. Once he had his passport he'd acquire a weapon and hold up a few drug dealers. He'd only have to do it three or four times to earn a mill. The hard part would be converting most of the cash to bearer bonds; eight or nine thousand dollars at a time to avoid ending up on an AUSTRAC report. He'd keep enough cash to walk around with and pay for transport and mail the bearer bonds to himself – care of a post office in Tennessee.

Then he'd drive up north – Cairns, or Cooktown if he had to – and pick out a light plane that wouldn't be missed for a week or two. His passport would already be stamped with outbound immigration, forged with a rubber stamp he'd manufacture himself, and he'd fly the stolen plane to Port Moresby and clear inbound customs, trusting that he hadn't been added to the PNG watch list, and gain a legit stamp in his passport.

Then he'd buy a seat on a commercial flight to the States and pay cash for a second-hand car and off he'd drive to start his new life. He'd start off working at the county lock-up and after six months he'd be deputy sheriff in a two-pub town an hour out of Nashville. He'd been talking long distance with Chuck, a mate of Robbo's, who was setting things up at the Tennessee end.

•

November 1996. The Yandee detectives are building up the motive for Mark Lewis to have murdered Kerrie Pang. In 1993 Mark Lewis had made an application to the Family Law Court, asking for access to their son, who was only seven months old at the time. A week after the notice was served Pang granted the access and the matter was withdrawn from the courts.

Detective Gary Williams gets a search warrant for the Family Law Court and they visit on 22 November 1996 and get copies of the documents, along with a statement from the registry manager.

And another witness comes forward. Someone who's known Kerrie Pang for most of her life.

Two weeks before her murder she'd rung him and asked to borrow twenty thousand dollars. He'd previously lent money to her and Mark to invest in Bartercard and Mark hadn't paid it back when promised.

He'd never liked Mark Lewis: he was twenty years older than Kerrie and he never followed through on what he said. The witness had seen the holster under Mark's jacket and Kerrie had told him about regular death threats and when he heard about Kerrie's death he assumed Mark must have had something to do with it.

The witness statement goes into the evidence locker – another link.

•

Meanwhile, Rod Baker still needs to get convictions for the false alibi conspiracy and committal proceedings will commence in January. But Rose is still at large and now Alan Thomas is refusing to plead guilty and refusing to testify at court so the chances of convictions are slim. Thomas knows this – he's trying to get a better deal for himself.

Baker thinks that giving Thomas immunity for the false alibi in exchange for his evidence against others is a worthwhile trade-off.

Only the DPP can grant immunity and Baker writes the submission. He writes that Thomas is facing other charges, including extortion – the plantation owner he'd ripped off – and accessory to murder and if convicted is likely to face a custodial sentence. The letter outlines the details of the conspiracy and the evidence against the co-accused that Thomas would be prepared to give. He spends half a day getting it right then Yandee's legal rep reviews it. On 29 November it's ready and Rod Baker walks it over himself to the DPP's offices on Liverpool Street.

68

When I next visit there's been an equipment change in the visits room. The new kettle is made from transparent perspex so one can clearly see the heating element and all the wiring.

'Yeah, this mob got a contract for the whole prison. See-through kettles and TVs for security. Shame – the TVs used to be good for hiding things in.'

The short routine of coffee making is completed and we sit. I want to talk some more on the subject of police corruption. It keeps coming up: Alan Thomas, the Royal Commission and this outrageous belief he has (which I can't leave unchallenged) that every other cop is bent and virtually every detective.

But we start with the small talk and prison gossip. Ivan Milat has cut off his pinkie finger so he can mail it to the High Court and Lindsey says he cut off the wrong one – should have given them the bird. When he roars with laughter, the yellow stubs of his ruined teeth catch my eye.

They've been ramping all the cells weekly and they've had a full week of lock-down. 'The Lebs have been fighting. Fighting each other for a change. About time.' He thought that was hilarious too. 'They've split into two groups. They smashed the round dish from the bottom of a microwave and turned the shards into shivs to stab each other with.'

I suppress the image of a gang fight prefaced by the equitable distribution of the weapons and move on to my agenda. I tell him some of what I have read in the Wood Royal Commission's report about the establishment of the NSW Police Integrity Commission (PIC) and how they can't employ anyone who has served with the NSW police.

Lindsey has previously argued that a corrupt officer won't take a 'pay cut' and so once bent, always bent. I point out that hundreds of police named by Wood resigned or were pushed out and since more than ten years have passed, many more would have left by natural attrition.

'Things have changed while you've been inside.'

'Mate, you've got your head up your arse. I know it's still happening. I do a multitude of work on people's legals and it's clear that police are still loading up evidence.'

There's no budging him and I drop it.

69

December 1996. Matt Appleton's team, the Cavanagh/Lee investigation, has been reinterviewing witnesses and asking about Russ.

'Did you know Russell V.?' Detective Davies asks a witness.

'I don't think I met him, though I may have. I'd heard of a Russell something who was involved with hot trucks. And I seem to recall Bill Cavanagh telling me he had a problem with him. Bill said he went down to Russell's place to sort it out and one of Bill's drivers sorted out Russell.'

'Do you know the driver's name?'

'Well, actually, he might have been a relative too. I don't know his name, but everyone called him Smasher.'

It doesn't take them long to identify Ross 'Smasher' Cane and he's living in Melbourne. He's the son of a distant relative of Bill Cavanagh and he'd briefly been indentured to Bill's trucking business. They speak to Smasher on the phone and he confirms he was involved in a fight with one of Cavanagh's drivers.

So Detectives Davies and Perry fly down to Melbourne. Frankston is about an hour's drive from Tullamarine Airport and they arrive at Frankston police station at 4 p.m. and check in with the station head. The interview room is ready with the audio and the VCR and Ross 'Smasher' Cane is waiting for them. After the introductions they play Cane a video of mug shots to see if he can identify anyone. He can't be sure. There are a couple of faces that look similar to the man who Cane said he fought that day. Then they press record on the tape decks.

Cane's is a tricky interview. He's cooperative enough, but he's trying too hard to give them the answers he thinks they want to hear. Williams has seen it before, in the guilty or in the paranoid. Cane has spent time in prison.

Eventually they get the story out of him. One day in maybe 1979 Cavanagh had rung ahead then picked him up to sort out this truck driver who Bill said was this arsehole who had been harassing Bill's family when he was out at work. Cavanagh had driven him to a workshop, pointed out the bloke and wrenched an iron bar out of the man's hand before Cane stepped up.

Cane was a former amateur boxer and made short work of the beating. When the man fell to the ground, Cane started in with his boots but Cavanagh intervened, castigated him for fighting dirty and threw him into the back of his car.

Williams tries to establish the extent of the man's injuries but Cane's account is muddled. He was coming around okay, just a bit groggy, but he was also incapable of speech and couldn't stand unassisted. And Cane hadn't had a decent look at him anyway; he'd been thrown into the back of Cavanagh's vehicle that quick.

Davies and Perry ask more questions about Ross Cane's background and to tie down the details of the assault. Cavanagh had told Cane that he would have done it himself except it wouldn't have been a fair fight, Cavanagh being the much older and more experienced man, or so he said. Nothing much else is forthcoming and Cane doesn't know the names Russell V. nor Lindsey Rose. Time to wrap up.[29]

Cane leaves and Davies calls Appleton to provide an update. He couldn't ID Russell for sure, he says, but the description he gave is a good fit and his account is consistent with the statements from other witnesses. At the very least they've established another motive for someone to do harm to Bill Cavanagh.

•

A week later Rod Baker flies to Queensland to visit Borallon Correctional Centre, forty-five minutes west of Brisbane, to interview Russell V. Would he attempt to identify the man who'd assaulted him back in 1979? No, he would not, said Russell. He had no recollection of any such event.

•

There has been no further sign of Rose. They will need to go public, so they prepare the strategy. On 13 December 1996 they issue a press release and the media liaison officer has been talking to the TV stations and

Rose's mug shot is shown on the lunchtime news bulletin and again on the Friday night news, along with the Crime Stoppers phone number.

The head of the task force, Detective Chief Inspector Wilson, is the designated contact and he gets a phone call from Crime Stoppers later that night. A man called Anton has phoned through, claiming to have been assaulted by Rose nearly five years earlier. He has no information about Rose's current whereabouts but is sure that it was Rose who had assaulted him: they had run into each other some time after the assault and he still has a business card with the name Lindsey Rose printed on it. Wilson thanks him for the call and says he will get back to him.

Their press release also makes the papers, as they'd hoped:

Man sought over murders

Police yesterday identified a man wanted over the brutal St Valentine's Day murders of Sydney massage parlour workers Kerrie Pang and Fatma Ozonal.

Launching a nation-wide search for Lindsey Rose, detectives said he was believed to have vital information about the 1994 slayings. Ms Pang, 40,[30] and Ms Ozonal, 26, were shot and stabbed by a customer before their Gladesville massage parlour was set alight.

Ms Pang, a divorced mother-of-five, was stabbed 18 times before the murderer cut her throat and shot her in the head.

Ms Ozonal, a divorced mother-of-one, was shot three times in the head as she sat on a lounge.

Police have arrested one man over the double murder but it is understood investigators always thought more than one person was involved in at least the planning.

Detectives yesterday refused to reveal what role Rose was thought to have played in the killings but said it was believed he could assist with inquiries.

(*Daily Telegraph*, 14 December 1996)

70

He'd been in the wind for nearly six months and Christmas was approaching. Lindsey and Cody purchased the basics: a large bird, ham, bread and beer. The yard had a long trestle table but it was rough enough to give you splinters so they also bought a Christmas-themed plastic tablecloth. Two of the charity cases received hampers from Vinnies and they were shared. Most of their fellow boarders had nowhere better to be on Christmas Day and they invited a few friends to join in.

Nine of them sat down to a feast. It was a cool day but warm enough in the sun and they had their fill and Lindsey stood and made a toast to their collective rough-headedness and they all laughed like hyenas.

•

The car yard was still only giving him three days a week and his kitty was growing, but slowly. In the new year he found another couple of days working as a truck mechanic near Parafield Airport. One afternoon he drove through for a look and it was pretty open and you could get right up close to some of the hangars with nothing but a wire fence in the way. If he could spot a suitable aircraft he might just have another emergency getaway plan.

He caught a metal splinter in the eye one afternoon and at the end of his shift he took it to his GP rather than get bogged down with injury reports at the yard. The GP removed the splinter; it would heal without further treatment. He chatted to the GP about this overseas holiday he was saving for and he had another entry on his patient card.

•

February 1997. A reliable witness claims to have seen Rose at Kippa-Ring Shopping Centre, north of Brisbane, with an older woman. The shopping centre is close to Redcliffe, where Rose's mother, Glenda Frances Rose (aged sixty-one), lives, so it seems feasible.

They make contact with the Queensland Homicide Squad, requesting assistance with surveillance of Rose's parents and the shopping centre for two weeks. They send two detectives up to Queensland. They come back with nothing.

•

Baker meets with Anton, the man who claimed to have been assaulted by Rose. He agrees to come in to Surry Hills and make a statement.

He'd been drinking with friends at the Coronation Club in Burwood. He drove home and parked his car in the underground car park and Rose warned him not to drive in so fast. Anton answered back and Rose laid into him with some object.

By the time he'd finished there was blood spattered across the stainless steel walls of the lift. His flatmate drove him to the medical centre, the one owned by Geoffrey Edelsten on Burwood Road. He was sent to Concord Hospital where he received forty stitches for three large head wounds.

He had a serious concussion, a partially closed eye, a week off work and suffered from blurry vision and flashing lights for months afterwards. He has photographs of the injuries at home.

More than a year later he'd healed and was drinking at the Burwood Hotel when he saw the man who'd assaulted him. 'He came over to me and introduced himself and said words to the effect, "In case you are wondering it was me!"'

He'd seen Rose at the Burwood Hotel on four or five other occasions and each time Rose bought him a drink, came over for a chat and each time Anton left the pub soon afterwards. He was fearful of upsetting Rose even though he began to show some remorse, even offered him a night at his massage parlour.

•

Lindsey drove home from work on a Friday, had a shower, checked the five o'clock news and was ordering his first beer by 6 p.m. The first always went down fast. He was ordering his second when the bar staff announced that the strip show was about to start in the back room. It wasn't really his thing and even if it had been he had a fair idea about the sort of scrubbers that would be on show for what the Gaslight could afford.

Sixty men ambled out the doors at each side of the bar. Only one other person remained, sitting at the bar, reading a newspaper. Lindsey glanced up at this other bloke and he was familiar, from Sydney.

Lindsey turned away and scratched the side of his head, trying to cover his face. Was it one of the ex-cops he'd worked with as an inquiry agent? There was nowhere really to hide and reflected in the mirror behind the bar was Gary, the agent who'd helped him see off those bikies at Campbelltown.

And Gary was looking back at him, frowning, and even with long hair and a beard it was only a matter of time before Gary worked it out. Lindsey called for the barman, asked for a beer for his friend.

He moved to Gary's side and reached inside his jacket.

'You won't be needing that, Rosie,' said Gary. 'I know the score, mate; you've got nothing to fear from me.'

Lindsey removed his hand slowly from his jacket and held up the wallet to Gary. 'Just paying for the drinks,' he said, and pulled out a banknote. 'They your girls in there?'

'Aha! Yep, can't get much past you, Rosie,' said Gary.

They drank and the conversation started local and he tried to assess Gary to see if he could be trusted.

When the strip show finished the strippers, clothed, but barely, filtered out into the bar area and Gary went to do business with the bar manager. The girls started to leave and a similar number of heavy breathing punters accompanied tattooed ankles out the door. So the strip show was a cover; Gary was still in the business.

'So, what are you going to do?' asked Gary.

'Need to get a passport and then I'm going to get out of the country.'

'Passport? I know someone. Might be able to help you out.'

Lindsey stroked his chin. It might help to have a back-up. And he might get it sooner. But on the other hand he'd then have his security invested in another person, something he'd been trying to avoid. As it was, now that Gary knew his local, he was compromised – it would take minutes to ask around the locals until one of them pointed out Cody or one of the other boarders who knew his address.

He'd used his original birth certificate to get a driver's licence in the name Lindsey Lehman. And he'd parlayed that into a Medicare card and opened a bank account. But he'd had to use the Taylor Street address on all of them; the doctor's surgery had it as well and he'd started to get edgy, waking at night, hearing things.

And now Gary, and that was the tipping point. He'd have to find a new place to put his head down at night and no-one would know about the new place so he'd take the risk on Gary's passport guy.

'I'm interested,' he said. 'Is he a pro?'

'Oh, yeah. One of my mates has been in and out on one of his. He's the real deal.'

'How much do you reckon?'

'Dunno. I can ask for you.'

They agreed that Gary would drop back in to the Gaslight to see him when he had an answer.

'Just ring the bar. They'll tell you if I'm in. Oh, and needless to say, you never saw me or there's going to be a problem. If you know what I mean.'

Gary was just fine with that.

•

He thought about asking one of Cody's mates if they had a spare couch but he knew he'd never sleep easy so it would have to be another boarding house. He'd have to keep the room on Taylor Street as his documented address, but paying two rents was going to break him – he needed more income.

In February he found a higher earn and quit both mechanic jobs to work as a fitter for the Patawalonga Creek Dredging Project, clearing more than $1000 a week.

He took another room in a boarding house on Eleventh Street – only one kilometre from Taylor Street. The Gaslight was halfway between them.

He made sure he was seen at Taylor Street from time to time – and went there to pay his rent, collect mail – but he always slept at Eleventh Street.

Cody agreed to provide an early warning system. If anyone came asking for him at Taylor Street – even if it was the cops – Cody was to tape a large cross on the left-hand side of the glass noticeboard at the front of the Gaslight Tavern. He was to do it immediately, not wait for morning. Lindsey left early for work and would go past and check for the warning sign on the way.

After a few weeks at Eleventh Street he recruited a lookout there too. If trouble came knocking he was to tape a cross on the other side of the noticeboard. That way he'd know which residence was compromised.

The punt to the dredge left at 5.30 a.m. Each morning he'd leave early enough to have fifteen minutes spare for surveillance. He'd park on the east side of the creek, opposite the boat ramp, and walk down to a partly concealed observation post. Walking, he'd check for an abnormal number of vehicles in the car park and from the observation post he'd use binoculars to check the surrounding streets for suspicious vehicles. If he got a whiff of cops he had his bag packed; he'd head north and they'd be wondering how the hell he knew not to turn up to work that day.

He stopped taking the Salvos' hot meals and as March came around a calendar began flipping over in his head. In three months the GP would sign his photo and he'd be applying for his passport. Unless Gary's mate came through sooner.

71

April 1997. The property at Wentworthville has been on Yandee's 'to do' list for months. Rose had run a motor repair workshop there but he'd also been friendly with Malcolm West, whose mother owned the property. More recently Alan Thomas had mentioned that there was a bunker underneath a nearby shed on the same property. 'You could hide anything down there, even a body,' Rose had apparently told him.

They have him pegged for four murders, but Thomas had told them that five was the number of murders that Rose had several times claimed. The detectives have recently learned that Rose's uncle, Maxwell O'Malley, has been a missing person since 1990. If O'Malley was the fifth victim, maybe the body was buried in an underground bunker in Wentworthville.

•

Detectives Williams and Perry visit the owner, Bev West, and ask to have a look. The shed with the alleged bunker under it is not the property that Rose was renting. 'This shed is always locked and Rose never had a key,' she says. But they have a look anyway and it appears to have a solid concrete floor. There used to be a hole there for storing diesel tanks, she says, but that had been covered with concrete years ago.

In any event, West has stated that Rose had rented the nearby workshop for only the last three years. O'Malley had been missing for more than six years, so it looked like a dead end.

•

Lindsey was driving from the car yard to the Gaslight and there was a blue Commodore behind him. When he turned off it was two cars back and it took the same turn and he knew it, he'd seen it before. They were on a secondary road and when he turned again it dropped off like any good tail would.

He pulled over and waited, watching, then he doubled back and parked again in a secluded street and checked over his car for tracking devices. Nothing.

He resumed his trip, no followers, and thought about the odds they were on to him. Wouldn't they just arrest him? Maybe he was jumping at shadows.

He thought about moving back to Sydney; he missed his home town, his old life and his daughter. Maybe he should just turn himself in, minimise the damage, face the music. Better to see Penny in a prison visits room than never again. But, no, he still had a chance to leave the country. *Hang in there until you can get your passport.* Once he was settled there'd be a way, he'd find a way, for Penny to come and visit – one day.

He'd heard back from Gary and the extra passport was going to cost him two grand. He could only pay five hundred dollars up front and he gave him the photograph.

He asked Gary if he was into the drug scene. Not really, but a couple of his girls were users. Yeah, sure, he'd be willing to introduce Lindsey with a recommendation, see if they'd take him to see their dealer.

The next day he visited the GP again. It wasn't just for another entry on his patient card – this time it was for hypertension and haemorrhoids.

•

They talk to Alan Thomas again and ask him again about the bunker at Wentworthville and he says, no, it was a recent conversation and there was no doubt that there was a subfloor space that Rose had been in. Baker determines to follow it up. He takes Matt Appleton to Wentworthville on 3 April and this time they talk to Malcolm West, the son. He contradicts Beverly, his mother. Rose *did* have access to that shed and Malcolm drops that he had often seen Rose on the premises with firearms.

Malcolm unlocks a padlock to a separate, smaller structure attached to the outside. Inside they find a dozen black plastic pots filled with small clay pebbles. There are electrical fittings hanging above the pots, some with the lights still attached. There is dusty cannabis residue on the floor. Oh yes, that must belong to Lindsey, says West. Baker makes some notes, says nothing, they move on.

The shed is square and set on a concrete slab about ten metres across. They look around carefully and in a corner they discover a metal ring set in the floor. It pulls up a concrete trapdoor covering a hole not much wider than a grown man can fit through. The damp smell is immediate and when Baker shines his Maglite it reflects back at him: the hole is full of water.

What's down there? he asks West, who shrugs. They find a length of timber and Baker pushes it down into the water. He has to reach his whole arm into the darkness before it hits bottom. The water is about as deep as Baker is tall. Six foot. They've found their bunker.

•

That night Baker writes up the application for a search warrant. He includes the reference to Rose having been seen on the premises with firearms in his argument for its granting. The dimensions of the subfloor area, as far as they can tell, match those given by Thomas so it ties back to the 'hide a body' comments and he is confident the warrant will be granted. The weapons used in two double murders have never been recovered, he adds, just to make sure the message is clear. The next day Baker goes before Justice O'Connell at the Central Local Court and the search warrant is granted. He spends the rest of the day preparing the team and the orders.

The briefing is at Wentworthville police station at 6 a.m., Saturday 5 April. Present are Baker and Appleton; two members from the Police Rescue Squad; two from the Crime Scene Unit; the commander and a detective from Wentworthville Patrol; one each from the Video Unit and Media Unit; and a detective from a different, but related, task force.

They arrive at the Wests' property at 6.40 a.m. and present the search warrant. Bev waves them through, she's not much interested in reading it.

Police Rescue have their mobile water pump and it takes all morning to drain the pit. One of the Rescue Squad lowers himself into the hole and looks around. He passes up a white plastic bag with something in it then asks to be pulled back up. The hole extends under the entire concrete slab. The dirt walls and floor are eroding and there appear to be limited foundations. Rescue Squad don't think the hole is safe.

The Wentworthville commander rings the local council, Holroyd, and arranges for an urgent inspection by one of their engineers.

While they wait, the Crime Scene members don rubber gloves and examine the plastic bag. Inside are a pair of worn thongs, size 8, and a hypodermic needle – the kind used by diabetics. Baker looks at Appleton. Maxwell O'Malley had been diabetic. He had small feet, apparently.

The council engineer arrives within an hour and it doesn't take long for him to establish that the structure is unsafe and no-one should enter, not even the shed on top of the slab.

'But we need to search that cellar for a body,' says Baker.

'You'll have to knock down the shed then dig it out,' says the engineer. 'I'll need to issue a demolition order for this, anyway. I can make it an emergency demolition order to speed things up.'

Detective Rod Baker agrees. He wants the site to be guarded over the remainder of the weekend to prevent any contamination of evidence – they are now treating it as a crime scene. The Wentworthville commander says he'll arrange it and before they leave a constable arrives for the first twelve-hour shift.

On Monday Baker checks the legals. First he speaks to an inspector at the Office of the Solicitor. He confirms that they are entitled to demolish a shed under the Search Warrant Act if it is the only way to execute the search warrant. Next he contacts the Justice who had issued the search warrant and she agrees and grants an extension of seventy-two hours to the warrant to allow time for the demolition and search. And, just to be sure, Baker speaks to the NSW coroner, Derrick Hand. The coroner concurs with the previous advice but has no additional powers that can assist.

Meanwhile, the demolition order has been signed, but Holroyd council doesn't have the ordnance to complete the work. They would normally subcontract that sort of job and a figure of $2500 is suggested as the potential cost. Police Rescue says they can handle it and Baker doesn't have to be asked twice.

The next morning Police Rescue pulls down the shed with their bulldozer.

Baker has Integral Energy check the wiring leading into the annex with the hydroponics. As expected, the connections are illegal and an order is made for them to be disconnected.

There is a lot of activity and the media are alerted. Baker talks to the media liaison officer and they prepare a draft media release and circulate it for review. The media is invited to attend the site at noon the next day for the briefing.

In the afternoon Police Rescue punch some holes through the concrete slab but they run out of light so again they leave their equipment and a guard overnight.

They recommence at first light and by midday they've cleared the slab and started digging up the dirt of the basement floor. 'We've got bones,' someone shouts up from the pit and it's just in time for the media briefing at noon.

Appleton fronts the scrum; there's a TV crew and he goes through the background and what they're looking for and tells them that bones have been found. The media kit includes the wanted poster and mug shots of Lindsey Rose and that's the focus: that he's wanted for questioning in relation to these two murders and that he is on the run.

Baker congratulates Appleton on his performance. Baker could have done it himself, but he'd done plenty of media before and wanted to give Appleton the experience.

'You realise those are some sort of animal bones dug out of the pit?' Appleton says to Baker.

'Couldn't say for sure,' says Baker. 'Best to wait for the forensic analysis before jumping to any conclusions. We wouldn't want to tell the media what sort of bones they are without proof, would we?' Baker winks and Appleton bursts out laughing.

They poke around in the pit for the rest of the day and don't turn up a thing. No weapons, no bodies and the bones are indeed quickly shown to be those of a mid-sized domestic animal. After all that effort, they've found nothing of substance.

'Anyway, looks like we'll get the media coverage we need,' says Baker to Appleton. 'And who knows what might turn up if Lindsey's mug shot goes out on the news tonight. Just hope he doesn't see it.'

•

Shed may yield clue to brothel murders

Detectives began demolishing a backyard shed at South Wentworthville yesterday afternoon, searching for clues to the brutal murder of two women in 1994.

... Lindsay [sic] Robert Rose, lived in the shed. He is wanted for the murders ... and it is believed that he might have been 'a contract killer.' ...

(Greg Bearup, *Sydney Morning Herald*, 9 April 1997)

•

Tom was the captain of the darts team and a week earlier he'd picked Lindsey, Pete, George, Angelo and Harry for the winter home and away competition.

The first game was Wednesday night so Lindsey got there early for a practice with the team. The visitors from the Commercial Hotel were no match and the Gaslight team did them over seven legs to three.

They continued on, celebrating, until closing time and on the walk home he calculated he'd only get about four hours' sleep so his head hit the pillow seconds after he walked in the door.

•

9 April 1997. Wednesday. Rod Baker, recently promoted to detective inspector, is at his home in Maroubra after wrapping up the operation at the site of the former shed at Wentworthville. Two hundred and seventy-nine days have passed since Rose lost the surveillance team at Parramatta. Rose is an experienced private investigator and he's smart. But not so smart that he'd learned to keep his mouth shut. The task force would never have got wind of his crimes were it not for the people he'd told. So even though Rose has eluded them for so long, Baker still thinks he'll turn up eventually. It was possible that Rose had fled the country, but Baker doesn't think he has. Doesn't think he'd have the connections.

At 8.30 p.m. Baker is washing dishes when the phone rings. It's the duty operations inspector from Police Radio Sydney. South Australian police had contacted them: a member of the public had seen the news report and knew something of Rose's recent whereabouts.

First he rings the task force head, Darryl Wilson, then he drives to the task force offices in Surry Hills. Appleton joins him.

Detective Sergeant Daws of Adelaide Detectives briefs them over the phone. The citizen had seen the reports on Foxtel Sky News about the shed at Wentworthville and he recognised the face and the first name, 'Lindsey'. He'd seen that man working as a truck mechanic near Parafield Airport.

Baker tells Detective Daws that Rose is extremely dangerous. All precautions should be taken in any arrest, including use of the siege-trained STAR (Special Task and Rescue) Force personnel.

Baker and Appleton fax documents down to Adelaide to prepare for an arrest. Baker rings Daws to check in every thirty minutes for the rest of the night.

By 9.30 p.m., Daws has tracked down the manager of the mechanic shop. They drive to the manager's house – he doesn't know of a Lindsey Rose but does recall that a Lindsey Lehman had worked for him. That's a known alias on the sheet that Appleton had faxed down so Daws knows it's the right man. But Lehman had stopped working there a couple of months before, the manager tells them. So the caller's information is correct, but out of date. It's 10.30 p.m. and the manager drives with Daws and the constable to the mechanic shop to review their personnel files. Lehman's folder is quickly located and now they have an address in Taylor Street, Brompton and his car registration: SCU-126.

Daws makes some more calls and then drives with a constable to Thebarton police barracks to meet members of STAR Force. One of the team has run the motor registry checks and found that SCU-126 belongs to a green 1977 Mazda 929 registered to Lindsey Lehman of Taylor Street, Brompton.

They commence surveillance of the address in Brompton. It's a weatherboard cottage with a corrugated iron roof. Peeling paint; rusting iron. There is no lock-up garage in evidence and no sign of the green Mazda. They wait. There is no activity.

After an hour – it's past midnight – Daws gives the order. It seems unlikely that Rose is home but they spare no caution. An officer is positioned outside each window and at the back entrance. They knock on the front door. It opens in seconds and the smells of unwashed bodies and cigarette smoke flow past a man wearing a cotton tracksuit and threadbare slippers. He is too old and thin to be Rose. Daws looks inside and it's a straight-run, narrow hall with closed doors on each side. It's a boarding house and this man is the caretaker.

He tells them that Lehman was indeed a guest but often stayed out all night and tonight was apparently such a case. Lehman had recently started work at Glenelg, he said, on the dredging project in the creek there. Daws asks if he can check Rose's room. No-one.

Daws sends a detective out to Glenelg to see if they can find the work site.

The detective rings them from Glenelg an hour later. They've found the site and the signage gives them a contact phone number for Hall Contracting, who are operating the project to dredge the Patawalonga Creek. Daws makes the call and it's a pen-pusher who answers but he has the contact details for a mechanical engineer who is most likely supervising Lehman. He can't be raised by telephone so again Daws finds himself doorknocking someone from sleep; this time it's West Beach at 4.30 a.m.

The engineer indeed supervises Lehman/Rose. He's due to start his shift at 6 a.m. at the Patawalonga boat ramp, Glenelg.

Daws calls Chief Inspector Peter Hoadley, head of STAR Force, who has been on standby. They have one hour to establish a surveillance operation and an arrest plan before Rose arrives for work.

72

I ask Lindsey about regret and he tells me about a time he was being escorted from the High Risk Management Unit to the main gaol for a medical check-up. One of the guards looked out at the yard full of prisoners and casually commented, 'I bet if you had your time again you'd do things differently, hey, Lindsey?'

'I'd do it all again in a heartbeat,' he replied and laughed when he saw the screw's jaw drop.

I ask: 'Surely . . . even after arguing that severe injustices in your life tipped you over the edge, if you had your time again, surely you'd prefer that you'd copped it on the chin, got on with your life and not ended up in here?'

'Nuh. Cavanagh flew guys up from Melbourne to bash my mate Russ. You should have seen him; he nearly died. I said I was going to kill Bill for that and so I went and killed him. And that fucking bitch in Gladesville who was trying to ruin my life had it coming as well. Fucken oath, I'd do them again if I had my time again,' he says. He is relaxed as he says it.

I talk to Lindsey about criminal psychology and how he may have come to be who he is. 'On top of the bullying, do you think the horrors of the Ambulance Service desensitised you to violence?'

'Oh. Well, yeah, I guess it played a part. "Desensitised" is a good word. But I think you need to look at everything in totality to see.'

73

He woke to his alarm at 5 a.m. No hangover but his bones were leaden from the heavy labour of the week and the abbreviated sleep. He snoozed the alarm once and that would cut it fine. He got up, had a one-minute shower and was on the road to Glenelg an hour before dawn.

He didn't have time for his surveillance routine so he drove straight in to the compound and parked. He was walking towards the office to sign in when the end came. He saw a shift in the shadows up ahead then he heard the voice call out from the side: 'Police, don't move. Police, don't move.' Lights shining in his eyes.

It wasn't a shock – he'd rehearsed this moment in his mind – and he deliberately let his carry bag slide from his hands and held his arms out to the side, away from his body. He looked slowly, slowly around, moving only his neck and eyeballs and there they were, at least half a dozen, and in full kit – must be Special Operations or whatever they called them in Adelaide. They were pointing automatic rifles and the strident voice was still barking out orders.

He'd been through it all before. He kept his body loose so when they came up to cuff him there'd be no resistance against which they could apply pressure.

They grabbed at him from both sides and dragged him face-first down to the road. Once the handcuffs were on they searched him, emptied his pockets and called over the detectives. One of them gave him the drill.

'My name is Detective Bob Daws. This is Detective Roberts. We are police officers from the Holden Hill CIB. What is your full and correct name?'

His cheek was pressing into the bitumen. 'You know who I am.'

'Are you Lindsey Rose?' asked Daws.

'My name is Lindsey Lehman. That's my proper birth name from my mother's side.'

'I am now detaining you under Section 78a of the Summary Offences Act, which relate to four first-instance interstate arrest warrants for murder which have occurred in New South Wales. Do you understand?'

'This is all bullshit, mate.'

'Lindsey, because you have been detained by police you are entitled to the following rights. You can make a telephone call to a relative or friend to advise them of your whereabouts. You can have a relative or friend present during any subsequent police interview. You can contact a solicitor about this matter and you are not required to answer any further questions about this matter unless you wish to do so but anything you do say may be given in evidence in a court of law at a later date. Do you understand these rights?'

'Yeah.'

'Do you wish to exercise any of these rights?'

'No,' and they began to lift him up off the road. 'What happens now?'

'You will be conveyed back to Holden Hill police station,' said Daws, 'where you will be held in custody pending extradition proceedings being sought by detectives from Sydney.'

'This is all a big mistake.'

One of the other cops picked up his bag and they started walking him back towards the car park where the paddy wagon was pulling in. A few of the other workers from the dredge were moving through the car park and he called out to them, 'Looks like I won't be in today, boys.' One of the cops joined in the laughter.

•

Baker gets the call at 6.45 a.m. Sydney time. It's Daws.

'We have Rose in custody.'

'Everyone safe?'

'Yep, without resistance and unarmed.'

'Great work, Bob, unbelievable news. You know he's been on the run for more than nine months?'

'It's good to have a win now and then,' says Daws.

Baker rings Chief Inspector Wilson with the news and he agrees they should fly down to Adelaide that afternoon. The flights are booked,

Baker and Appleton prepare their notes for the questioning and a search warrant application for Rose's residence is faxed to Adelaide.

Baker, Appleton and Wilson fly out of Mascot. The only suitable flight is via Melbourne so they'll be on the plane for four hours. Baker goes over the notes with Wilson. He nods his approval, warns Baker to be careful when talking about the possibility of reductions in sentence. It's advice that Baker scarcely needs. He hasn't come this far to lose a conviction through an improper inducement.

Baker has another thought in the back of his mind. If Rose starts talking he might *keep* talking. Baker wants to see what he'll tell them about Max O'Malley's disappearance.

74

At the Holden Hill police centre he was interviewed almost immediately. Daws explained that the arrest was in satisfaction of eight first-instance warrants that they'd received from New South Wales overnight.

Then they asked him what he knew about the death of a prostitute, Susan Borbridge. Nothing, he said. But they pressed him some more. She had been murdered in Adelaide only four months before, found with four bullets in her head on an Adelaide beach, only ten minutes' drive from the boarding house at Brompton. Knew nothing about it, he said again. He was cooperative and it was all very civil and then he was given a meal. He was taken to the Holden Hill Court and charged and they told him some detectives from Sydney would see him in the morning and then he was returned to the cells for the night.

•

The flight is delayed in Melbourne so the Sydney detectives don't get to Adelaide until evening. They catch a taxi in to Adelaide headquarters and are shown into the offices of the Major Crimes Task Force. Introductions, then Daws brings them up to date.

Rose's vehicle has been impounded at Holden Hill and they agree Appleton will accompany the South Australian police in searching the car. Baker will lead the search of Rose's premises on Taylor Street.

Three hours later they meet back at Adelaide HQ. They'd been hoping to find some conclusive evidence, perhaps the weapon used for the Gladesville murders, or others, but both searches have come up empty. It's after midnight when the detectives from Sydney check in to their motel rooms. Other than brief naps on the flight, it's their first sleep for more than forty-eight hours. Just another day on the job, thinks Rod Baker as his head hits the pillow.

•

The next morning Lindsey was taken to an interview room and there was Rod Baker with another detective.

'G'day, Lindsey, how are you?' asked Baker.

'I'm okay now. My shoulder is still a bit sore from when they got me, but I'm okay. Who's this?'

'As you know I am Detective Inspector Rod Baker. This is Detective Sergeant Matt Appleton – he's one of my sergeants from Task Force Yandee. I want to explain to you why you are here and what will be happening to you. Is that clear?'

'Yes, I've been expecting this to happen. I thought about coming back to Sydney. I suppose I really should have; you've got no idea what it's like on the run.'

'I can imagine. Now I want to explain a few things to you. Firstly, you are not obliged to say anything or answer any questions I may ask of you unless you wish, but anything you say will be recorded and may later be given in evidence at court. Is that clear?'

'Yes.'

'Secondly, you have been arrested on eight first-instance warrants issued in New South Wales. That means that a magistrate has examined a brief of evidence on each of those matters and is satisfied that you have a case to answer at court. Is that clear?'

'Yes.'

'The first two warrants relate to the murders of Kerrie Pang and Fatma Ozonal at Gladesville on the 14th of February 1994.'

'You know I didn't do them. I was there and I told you who did them.'

'Two other warrants relate to the murders of Edward Cavanagh and Carmelita Lee at Hoxton Park on the 20th of January 1984, is that clear?'

'Not me, I was in Melbourne at that time and I can prove it.'

'We have a warrant for conspiracy to pervert the course of justice by providing a false alibi. And one for corruptly receiving benefit on or around 3 February 1995.'

'What's that relate to?'

'That's in relation to accepting commission, with Alan Thomas, and promising to assist with the dropping of charges in relation to a cannabis seizure.'

'If you say so.'

'And the last two warrants are for failing to appear. Kogarah Local Court on 24th July last year as part of your bail conditions for drug possession and for unauthorised firearms. And 4th July you were due to report to us at Surry Hills.'

'Ah, yes. Did you like where I left the car?'

'At Adelaide airport?'

'Yes.'

'Do you realise that the car wasn't found for well over a month?'

'You're kidding.'

'No, it remained in the car park for about forty days before any enquiries were made about it.'

'Did anyone get into trouble about me taking off?'

'No.'

Then Rod Baker asked him about Maxie. Bit of a coincidence, isn't it, that you're facing murder charges and your uncle has disappeared?

Why would he? he said. His own uncle. And how could he? He'd been in prison in Queensland when Max disappeared and he'd only found out about it when he got back to Sydney.

But you threatened to kill him, Baker said. It took a few seconds then Lindsey remembered the day in Burwood when he'd exploded after finding that Max had been blowing his own mother's nursing home money on the pokies. Stanley was there when he said it, so the cops must have interviewed him.

For fuck's sake, he thought. Max was retarded and Lindsey had saved his life on at least two occasions so that made no sense whatsoever.

'We'd like to interview you on record in relation to Max's disappearance. Would you be agreeable?'

'Sure.'

'As I have explained to you earlier, you do not have to partake in any interviews or speak with me about those matters unless you wish, but any statements you do make, may later be produced in evidence at court. Is that clear?'

'Yes, but if I do speak to you what's in it for me? I'm looking at four life sentences.'

'In relation to that, you should be aware that in New South Wales, under truth-in-sentencing legislation, the court can sentence an offender to life imprisonment with no chance of parole. But there have also been recent changes relating to offenders telling the truth and cooperating with the police and the courts. When sentencing an offender, magistrates and judges must take into account the contrition of an offender, the fact that he admits his guilt and assists police and pleads guilty at court. Do you understand that?'

'Yes, I understand that. I'll think about it.'

'There is one other matter that I want to speak with you about – an assault you committed on an Anton [—] in a block of units which you were living in at Burwood in 1992.'

'Yes, he deserved a flogging; he nearly ran me over. I was carrying two bags of Betty's crystal when he came screaming into the driveway. He was half pissed and I gave him a flogging in the lift. But I will admit that he got a lot more than he probably deserved.

'We became good mates after that. He is really a good bloke. Whenever he came to the pub I'd buy him a drink and we'd have a talk.'

'What will happen next is that you will be shortly taken to court and I will be applying for your extradition back to New South Wales. Are you going to be opposing that extradition?'

'No. Even though I know I'm going to spend a long time inside I'm still looking forward to going home.'

'After court I wish to start some interviews with you. They must be voluntary on your behalf. Is that clear?'

'Yes, I'll give it some thought.'

'Is there anything else you need?'

His clothes, said Lindsey, from home. He'd been wearing the same clothes for a day and a half. And cigarettes. Rod Baker sent someone for the clothes and said he'd bring cigarettes. He already knew the brand: B&H Special Filter.

•

Baker and Appleton came for him at 4.30 p.m. and took him to an interview room back at Adelaide police headquarters. Baker handed him the packet of cigarettes. The clothes would be waiting for him when he was returned to his cell.

'Thank you.'

'Now, the first two matters, as we have previously discussed, are the murders of Kerrie Pang and Fatma Ozonal.'

'Yes.'

'We have a young man in custody who has been arrested and charged in relation to these murders. And he has already made admissions as to his involvement and agreed to repeat those in court.'

'Oh, yes.'

'The nose pad from a pair of spectacles was found at the scene and we have records from an optometrist on Burwood Road showing that you had your glasses repaired there two weeks after the murders. We also have statements from a detective sergeant of police detailing admissions you made to him in relation to those murders.'

Baker wrote on his ruled notepad as he spoke.

'You've been doing your homework, haven't you?' said Lindsey.

Baker had written on his notepad: Pang. Ozonal.

Now he wrote: Cavanagh. Lee.

'Another is the Cavanagh/Lee murders. Then we have the assault of Mr Anton [—] and the disappearance of Maxwell O'Malley.'

Baker listed them down the page.

'Have you decided if you are willing to be interviewed about any of these matters?'

'I'll tell you about the assault, that's fair enough. You can ask me what you like about Maxie, but I've got no idea what happened to him. About the others . . . Can I use this? It helps me to think.'

'Yes, sure.'

He picked up a pencil that Baker had been using. He drew an asterisk next to the names Pang and Ozonal.

'What's in it for me?'

'As I explained to you earlier today, magistrates and judges must take into account contrition, admissions of guilt and any assistance given to police and the courts when sentencing offenders.'

'So if I tell you the truth about these matters and help you I'll get a lighter sentence?'

'I'm not in a position to promise you anything,' said Rod Baker.

Lindsey drew another asterisk next to the words Cavanagh and Lee on Baker's ruled page.

'What have you got on me for these ones?'

'I'm not in a position to outline specific details, but I will reiterate that a magistrate has examined the brief and has issued a warrant for your arrest for each of these murders.'

He'd had enough. If Donnie and Choppie had both turned, then he was gone anyway. No point holding back. Let them have it, tell them everything, show them everything he'd done under their bent cop noses for years.

'What can you tell me about these two murders?'

75

It's a six-hour round trip for me to visit Goulburn for the one hour we get to spend together. In May 2014 I make my twenty-fifth trip, nine years after the first. Our meetings are becoming an ordeal for both of us. There are no big stories left that he'll tell me about, just me picking at details, trying to get them right.

I ask again about the PNG job. He'd mentioned it only three times. He'd worked in Bougainville contracting to an overseas firm specialising in infiltration, surveillance, etc. Somehow he'd spent time working for both sides in the secessionist war. There was a large cruiser full of surveillance equipment and posing as a tourist vessel. There was a conversation with a German engineer in an Indonesian bar and there were manoeuvres in the jungle near the Panguna copper mine. These are the only snippets that he's let slip, years apart.

He's often cantankerous now and says recalling many of these memories is painful. Yet he persists, answering most of my questions only because he said he would. I have sometimes sent short chapters for him to review. In the early days he was complimentary and provided detailed corrections. Now he is more inclined to just tell me it's wrong: 'You might as well be writing fiction.'

And now, late in the piece, things keep coming up that he doesn't want to be published. I will respect his wishes where there may be repercussions for the individuals concerned. In some cases I will fictionalise people to hide their identities. In other cases there is no way around it and I have to cut.

I visit, it's purely work – going through my list of memorised questions – and despite the angst we part amicably enough. He'll write next. When the letter comes it is short and direct. He castigates me for a small betrayal – I divulged a private comment to someone on the outside, a trivial matter (I thought) for which I'd already apologised – and if he can't trust me with that then he can't trust me with other stories like the PNG job.

I've expended hours, days, I don't know how long, obsessing about background details – which car were you in, what year was that, where were you living and which girlfriend were you with? – and I've maintained this timeline of his life in a spreadsheet, in chronological order. With each question answered I update the spreadsheet, yet I still have this spaghetti tangle of contradictory evidence where this can't have happened before that because he'd already moved to this address, and so on *ad infinitum*.

I print out and mail him the spreadsheet; it runs to six pages. At the very least tell me where events are in the wrong order, I write, and the 'addresses lived at' column is a mess.

The return letter arrives within a fortnight. He's reviewed every line and swapped a few things around, made some notes and says in the accompanying letter:

> Just to annoy you some more your timeline 'living at' section is all wrong. That's what I never told you. I always had driver's licence, vehicle registration, voting and PI licence address different so any search on my licence or registration would pull up an address where I did not live, plus if someone came knocking I would be notified.
>
> Example: Belmore Street address – did not live there. Second address, Kogarah, licence address Lucas Road, Burwood and I actually lived around the corner in Shaftesbury Road and had a mate collect mail at Lucas Road.
>
> Ha ha, I can imagine the look on your face, what a can of worms!
>
> At one time I had a Mini Cooper, a Commodore, a Mazda surveillance van, a BMW 325 and a Valiant – actually two Valiants. All were registered and garaged in different places, some in my name, some not. Even Lydia did not know all of my cars. See, you are trying to make sense of 25 years of black bag, shadow addresses, criminal activity, businesses some you don't know about.
>
> So you don't want to hear this but you only have half the story. Ha ha ha.

76

He'd admitted to four murders and Appleton kicked off the questions in the first recorded interview.

Q16   We're presently sitting here at the Adelaide Police Station. Do you agree that you were arrested by South Australian Police at approximately 6.40 a.m. yesterday morning being the 10th of April, 1997?

A   It was 5.40, but yes I was.

Q17   I beg your pardon, 5.40 a.m. Right, and as a result of that you've appeared at the Holden Hill Magistrates Court in relation to a number of first instance warrants from New South Wales?

A   Yes.

Identification questions. Have you been married, kids, employment, his business in Canberra, experience with firearms. And then:

Q70   Detective Inspector Baker and I are making inquiries into the murders of an Edward Cavanagh and Carmelita Lee at Hoxton Park on or about the 20th of January, 1984. Is there anything you can tell me about that?

A   Yes. I did it.

Appleton looked up quickly – even though he knew it was coming – and reverted to background questions for a minute.

Q74   Okay. Well your answer to me before was 'I did it.' What do you mean, can you tell me what you mean by that?

A   I went to the house there and shot him . . . and that girl was there, the Asian girl was there and I tied her up and gagged her so she wouldn't make any noise and waited for Bill to come home.

Q76   Okay. Well what happened once Bill came home.

A   Shot him.

Q77   Okay. And what happened then?

A   I shot her.

An hour went by and they asked about every possible detail about why he did it and what he did on the day of the shootings and where did the weapon end up and he thought it was Salt Pan Creek, he said. There were lots of details he couldn't remember but it was obviously a solid set of admissions because there were enough details that only he could know.

> Q347   Alright. What I'm going to do is take a short suspension of the interview at the moment. Would you like a cup of tea or coffee or anything?
>
> A   Yeah, I wouldn't mind if you're going to have one . . . [31]

Later they asked some of the original questions a different way and he knew they were cross-checking for inconsistencies, probing, but he wasn't hiding much so there was no fear for him there. And they kept asking for the details of the shootings – where did the bullets strike, what order, was there a struggle, how many shots – and he'd never known the answers to these; from the moment he walked out Bill Cavanagh's front door the whole thing had been a blur, like a video playing on fast forward.

They terminated the interview at 7.30 p.m. and he was already yawning on the walk back to the cells.

•

Baker and Appleton move out to a briefing room and Baker congratulates Appleton on the interview and the result.

'When did you realise he was going to confess?' asks Matt Appleton.

'The first time he said we've been doing our homework, I knew we had him,' says Baker.

They plan the next day. Takeaway Chinese is brought by one of the constables and then they borrow desk space to write up their notes.

•

The next day they collected him at 10 a.m. and after a short conversation they started the tapes. They asked about the Gladesville murders. Baker led the questions:

Q17   Do you agree that on the 29th of June, last year, you were arrested in possession of a .22 calibre pistol and a very small amount of cannabis in Brighton Le Sands in Sydney?

A   Yes.

Q18   As a result of that arrest, you were charged with those matters?

A   I was.

. . .

Q20   Do you agree that later that evening, you attended a hearing at the New South Wales Crime Commission in relation to [the murder of Kerrie Pang and Fatma Ozonal]?

A   Yes.

Q21   Do you agree that in the interview at the New South Wales Crime Commission you stated that you were responsible for the murder of Kerrie Pang and Fatma Ozonal on 14th February, 1994?

A   I stated that I was present.

Q22   In that interview you also stated that a male person, a former Detective Sergeant Alan Thomas was present with you during the time of those murders, is that correct?

A   I did state that, yes.

Q23   Is that true?

A   No.

Q24   Can you tell me why you made that statement at the New South Wales Crime Commission?

A   I made that statement for the . . . for the purposes of retaliation or spite towards Alan Thomas as he was the one that initially put me in for the murders and other . . . other reasons. He owed money to friends and . . . and never intended to pay them . . . so I put him in maliciously and there was no truth to that statement.

. . .

Q26 What can you now tell me about the murders of Kerrie Pang and Fatma Ozonal at Gladesville on 14th February, 1994?

A I was the person involved . . . and I committed the murders.[32]

When they stopped the tapes it was 1.24 p.m., three hours since they'd begun. He was given a meal and a shower. There would be more interviews.

•

In the afternoon he answered questions on tape about the bashing of Anton and the next morning there were some follow-up questions about the Cavanagh/Lee murders and in the afternoon they got to Uncle Max.

'Mr Rose, do you agree that the time on the monitor is 13.09 hours?'

'Yes. It'd be his birthday tomorrow.'

'That'd be Maxwell O'Malley's.'

'14th of April.'

They asked all the background questions and the last time he'd seen Max was when he helped Max and Stanley move out of the unit on Belmore Street when they fell too far behind on rent.

'Max just couldn't handle money and moved into a boarding house. He was slightly backward. He'd do a crossword quicker than you could do it and if you were playing darts he'd add up the numbers before you could. But then give him another task and he wouldn't be able to do it. Just depended, you know. He was a good darts scorer, though,' he laughed.

He told them about calling the paramedics when Max was in a diabetic coma; about taking him to the chemist to fill his prescriptions.

Baker told him that records showed no prescriptions had been issued for Max since he disappeared.

'What would that indicate to you?'

'That he's dead.'

Then they tried to establish a motive.

'How often did you have harsh words with Max O'Malley?'

'I can recall probably twice in the last . . . Oh, when we were kids we used to fight all the time; we were like brothers.'

'There's been an allegation that you and Max had a fist fight in the Burwood Hotel. What can you tell me about that?'

'Well, I'll say this to you – whoever gave you that information is talking through their hat. He was a very placid person. One time I was in a fight at Burwood and Max was in the middle of it. He'd stopped me from fighting and he often stopped me from getting into scraps with people.'

'I've also been told that when this incident happened with Max O'Malley that you threatened to kill him. Could that have been possible?'

'Quite possible. Because I'm the sort of bloke when I get angry I say I'll kill you, you little bastard, or something like that. But whatever I said, if I said it, it's just a figure of speech.'

'If I was to say that words similar to "I'm going to put a bullet in your fucking head" were said, would you say something like that?'

'I doubt whether I'd say that to my uncle. That's a bit harsh.'

'Did you kill Max O'Malley?'

'No.'

'Do you know what became of him?'

'Absolutely not.'

'Do you know where his body is?'

'No, I don't.'

'Anything else you would like to say in relation to this inquiry?'

'I sincerely hope that you guys are successful in finding him or his remains . . . clear the matter up because it . . . it, um, leaves a bad taste in my mouth that I could be a suspect in his disappearance.'[33]

•

The next afternoon he was on Ansett flight AN108 back to Sydney. He was locked up tight and there were armed cops on all sides of him. There were a few funny looks because it was a commercial flight and the other passengers weren't told what was going on. At Sydney Airport they took him out the back way to avoid the waiting TV crew.

He spent the night in the lock-up at the Sydney Police Centre in Surry Hills. It didn't much feel like being back home.

77

Rose's arrest has received considerable press so Rod Baker and the head of Yandee, Darryl Wilson, feel that Mark Lewis would see his own position as precarious. They think an early arrest is wise. He's a desperate man with sole custody of a small child and a history with weapons. It's possible he might abscond or seek to harm Rose, or Donnie, who was now out on bail.

Two days after returning from Adelaide, Baker and Wilson clear it with Commissioner Bradley of the Crime Commission, and the Director of Public Prosecutions, Nicholas Cowdery QC. Baker prepares the plan for the arrest of Mark Lewis.

That afternoon, Rod Baker knocks on Mark Lewis's front door with four other detectives. He's arrested without incident and they find a gun rack with two rifles in his bedroom.

'They're both loaded,' Mark Lewis tells Baker. 'I know they shouldn't be but they're there for protection. I thought I might need them. When you told me Lindsey Rose was on the loose. You told me he was going to kill me.'

Detective Rod Baker takes a deep breath.

'We never said he was going to kill you, Mark. We did a threat assessment and decided we should inform you that Lindsey Rose was on the loose. That's all.'

Mark Lewis is charged with the murders of Kerrie Pang and Fatma Ozonal, soliciting Lindsey Rose to murder Kerrie Pang and for making a false statement to the Victims Compensation Tribunal. He's also charged for not keeping his firearms secure.

•

Alan Thomas is next. He's easy to find as he's still in Long Bay on the conspiracy charges. Baker pays him a visit to explain there will be additional charges. On advice from his lawyer Thomas declines to be interviewed so the next day he's taken to the Sydney Police Centre and charged with two counts of concealing a serious offence.

78

After the arrest of Mark Lewis, Baker does the ring-around to inform members of Kerrie Pang's family that Lewis is in custody. Old witnesses are reinterviewed and some are phoned as a courtesy to let them know they may be called upon to give evidence at court and to keep their contact details up to date.

•

In June 1997 Lindsey fronted Sydney Central Court with his solicitor, John Bettens, and the charges were heard for the four murders, the false alibi and for two instances of failing to abide by bail conditions.

In August he made a deal with the Crime Commission. Legal aid wouldn't pay for silk and he couldn't afford it. The Crime Commission agreed to pay for a barrister in exchange for further confessions and another hearing before the commissioner was arranged.

•

So then, for the first time, he talked about the woman at Bill Graf's place and he couldn't remember her name or even for sure the year but he told them how Graf had been the main suspect, even though he was now dead – natural causes – but that it was actually Lindsey who'd killed the woman when she'd come at him with those scissors.

The commissioner told him that should be enough information to identify the unsolved murder and now he is up for five.

Q   All right, now that was the murder at Top Ryde?

A   Yeah, there's no other murders.

Q   No other murders?

A   No, absolutely not.

Q   What about interstate?

A   No.[34]

•

358

Another task force detective will run with the fifth murder. He calls Eastwood detectives and the case file is quickly located. The victim was Reynette Holford, the 45-year-old de facto of 77-year-old Bill Graf.

The Eastwood files contain statements from members of her family as well as the police interview with Bill Graf, who was apparently their only viable suspect. The statements paint a picture of a quiet, naïve woman who had moved out of the family home as a teenager to live with Bill Graf, who was a friend of her parents. Bill had promised to eventually marry her. Reynette's parents had disapproved and her three siblings had few kind words for Graf. Eventually they came to accept that no marriage would eventuate, but Reynette was still fond of Bill and stayed on. She supported herself with a job at a department store in the city and in recent years had cared for Graf as his health declined.

The initial investigation had found a weak motive for Graf to wish her harm, but no evidence. No evidence against Graf or any other person.

•

19 August. Detective Inspector Rod Baker is back at Central Local Court to see Rose formally charged with Reynette Holford's murder. The court is open and there is an unexpected visitor in the gallery. He's known to police and Rod Baker recognises him – he's a former close associate of Bill Cavanagh.

A few days later Baker gets a phone call from Crime Agencies. The man Baker had seen in court has been overheard threatening to take revenge for Cavanagh's murder by raping and murdering Rose's fourteen-year-old daughter.

Maybe it's just pub talk. Maybe the witness to this supposed threat is unreliable. But they don't want to take any chances with this particular gentleman: he'd previously served time for armed robbery, abduction, rape and murder.

Baker puts himself and Appleton on a plane to Perth. They don't want to alarm Lindsey's ex-wife Lydia or their daughter so they frame it as another interview. Lydia's husband comes too and the girl stays with one of his relatives.

A Perth detective drives Lydia and her husband to a unit in Victoria Park. Fourth floor. The living area is open-plan: kitchen and living room separated by a benchtop, more like a serviced apartment.

'You know he's confessed to a fifth murder,' Appleton says.

'I've told you before, I don't know anything about that stuff,' she says. She can't sit, keeps pacing.

'We suspect him for others, including his uncle, Max O'Malley. Do you know anything about them?'

'Maxie? Sounds like bullshit. How long's this going to take?' She wanders through the kitchen.

'Think about the families of the murder victims. You'd be well looked after by the witness protection program if you tell us what you know about any other crimes.'

'Why do you keep asking me?' she says.

The living room of the unit has floor-to-ceiling glass doors out to the balcony and looks north-west, where the city high rise is visible across the Swan River. Lydia looks out and beckons to her husband. 'Is that your office just down there?' she asks. He stands up and looks with her.

Then Baker speaks: 'Here's a card with the address of this unit and a phone number. If you ever feel threatened, call the number and come to this address and someone will let you in. You'll be safe here.'

'Why on earth would I feel threatened?' she says.

Baker tells her. Lydia sits down, quickly.

79

A few months in, while he was still on remand pending trial, the hatch in his cell door opened and one of the screws handed him a piece of paper. Lydia and Penny were here and would he accept a visit?

Oh shit. Lydia. What must she be thinking?

'I'll see Penny – she's my daughter. But I don't want to see Lydia. I'd rather spend a day locked up with the most violent crims in here than cop it from her.'

He's taken to the visits room and they have the room to themselves. There'd been letters but he hadn't seen Penny since her mother had taken her to Perth more than four years prior and here she was, now a pensive teenager, stocky like him and with her mother's fleshy cheeks, edging towards him.

'Hey, Dad.'

'Hi, sweetheart. How are you? Who brought you?'

'Rod arranged it. Rod Baker. He drove us down from the Central Coast where we're staying. Why couldn't Mum come in with me?'

'You know I've done some bad things, yes?' She nodded. 'Well, I'll be going to gaol for those things. That's punishment enough. I don't need your mother in here tearing strips off me as well.'

Penny took it in. He read her.

'Your mother. Is she alright?'

'Well . . . not so good. Since . . . Well, you know, the police told us that someone wanted to hurt us, to get revenge against you? Mum's been . . . you know, crying a lot and then she gets angry and then she gets scared and thinks someone's following us. All the time. The police offered us witness protection but Mum said no.'

'Oh, f—. Jeez. Yeah, Baker told me about that. I'm sorry, sweetie. Tell your mum I'm sorry she went through that. Okay?'

'Okay, Dad.'

They talked for half an hour and she told him about her school, life in Perth, her stepfather and what she wanted to do after school.

When their time was up they hugged goodbye and he looked back once at his daughter.

It would be another five years before she visited again – the fateful visit to Goulburn after she'd castigated him for the Darth Vader joke – and after that even the letters stopped. In 2006 she sent him a letter with a photo of herself in her graduation gown – she had her law degree. She invited a reply, but he did nothing. *That'll show her.*

•

It had been nine months of prison life and meetings with his solicitor, John Bettens, who told him a forensic psychiatrist would prepare a report in case it could help his defence.

He told the psychiatrist, Canaris, about Russell's bashing: 'and I sit there and I look at my mate's wife and kids around the hospital bed. The police aren't going to do anything about it, Cavanagh is involved with the police. He was a hated man.'

> Mr Rose became visibly angry as he told me this.
> He did not relish killing them in any way and he reiterated . . .
> on a number of occasions that these were things that 'simply had
> to be done'.

He told Canaris about the horrors of his childhood and Granville and of a small boy who'd been dragged through the wheel well of a school bus and died in the gutter as he and his ambulance partner looked on, helpless.

> He is almost completely dependent on external structures for
> his sense of morality. In his earlier days he sought this in highly
> structured, indeed paramilitary and military, settings such as the
> Scouts, St John's Ambulance Brigade, Ambulance Service, Army
> Reserve. His departure into the less structured world of the private
> investigator . . . left him with no basis for the moral decision making
> expected of the average citizen . . . The killings were congruent
> within the framework of his primitive morality which was well

adapted to the world of corrupt police and criminals. He took on the ethos of this world in much the same way that he took on the ethos of the Boy Scouts, the Ambulance Brigade and the like. He suffers from what in the older literature on antisocial personality is referred to as 'moral insanity.' This finds its sources in the brutalisation of his childhood and was reinforced by the criminal milieu to which he gravitated in adult life.[35]

80

The trial concludes on 3 September 1998 and the courtroom is full to hear Justice Levine read out the sentence. Rose has pleaded guilty to five murders so the only mystery is whether he'll get a long sentence or life. The Crime Commission has come good with the silk and Stuart Littlemore QC has argued against a life sentence on the grounds of his confessions, guilty pleas and his exemplary service as an ambulance officer despite his dysfunctional upbringing.

Detective Inspector Rod Baker is there and so are all of the Yandee investigators who'd worked on the Rose cases.

Justice Levine takes more than ninety minutes to read through the judgment. He starts by outlining the circumstances of each of the murders and quotes from the police interviews to demonstrate the brutality of the crimes and Lindsey Rose's attitude to them.

Rod Baker can only see the back of Lindsey's head. It doesn't move. He looks across the gallery. All eyes are on the judge. Baker sees Martha Jabour from the Homicide Victims' Support Group sitting with Reynette Holford's sister. Other victims' family members surround them. They are all perched on the edges of their seats.

'A submission was made for him that he should be entitled to see the light at the end of the tunnel,' says Justice Levine. 'A light, I suppose, that to some extent can be compared to that which he extinguished so brutally in each of his victims. I am not prepared to accede to that submission. There is simply no warrant for leniency in this case . . .

'Lindsey Robert Rose, stand up. In respect of each of the five counts of murder to which you have pleaded guilty, you are convicted and in respect of each of them you are sentenced to penal servitude for life, each sentence being deemed to commence on 10 April 1997. The prisoner may be removed.'[36]

All the air has been sucked from the room. *Show nothing.* Then there is a collective exhalation and he's led out of the silent chamber.

•

Bettens lodged an appeal six days later, but it took more than a year to be heard. In October 1999 the appeal against the severity of the sentence was dismissed by the NSW Court of Criminal Appeal, but only after anxious consideration by one of the three Justices, who wrote:

> Life imprisonment under s.19A of the Crimes Act is an extremely blunt instrument. There is much to be said for the power of the court to specify a minimum term in association with a life sentence under that section but the legislature has chosen not to confer that power.[37]

81

In December 1998, three months after the five life sentences were handed down, Lindsey Rose again fronted the Sydney District Court. He pleaded guilty to the rest. Eight years for conspiracy to pervert the course of justice; six years for robbery and six years for kidnapping (hijacking the semi-trailer of Rothmans cigarettes); five years for robbery whilst armed; four years for robbery; three years for maliciously destroying property by fire (torching Mark Lewis's property at West Ryde); three years for malicious wounding (the assault in the elevator); three years for larceny; one year for supplying a prohibited drug. All to run concurrently. And all quite redundant on the back of five life sentences.

•

Peter [...], the signwriter, was tried for murder. He admitted being present at the murders of Bill Cavanagh and Carmelita Lee but said he had been told it would be a robbery. Rose refused to give evidence and Peter's blood was of a different type to that found under Cavanagh's fingernails so there was nothing to indicate that he'd participated in the murders in any way. The trial only lasted five days before the judge ordered the jury to find him not guilty.

•

Donnie R. was tried in August 1999. He pleaded guilty to two counts of accessory after the fact of murder. The judge indicated that a full-time custodial sentence would normally be called for in such a serious case, but Donnie's case was mitigated by his early plea, willingness to assist, his youth at the time, his demonstrated rehabilitation (he had started a family) and remorse (he was suffering from post-traumatic stress disorder) and the fact that he'd already spent three months in custody.

He received eighteen months periodic detention.

•

Alan 'Choppie' Thomas pleaded guilty to a long list of offences including two counts of conspiracy to pervert the course of justice; three counts of perjury; corruptly receiving commission; unlawfully accessing the police computer system; and two counts of concealing a serious offence (the murders of Pang and Ozonal).

He tried to argue 'noble cause' corruption (that he'd only broken the rules in the interests of justice), that he had an otherwise unblemished record and was a family man. In June 1998 he was sentenced to eight years in prison (reduced to seven on appeal), with a minimum of three years. He was eligible for parole in January 2000 after taking into account time served. The trial judge remarked that were it not for his guilty pleas and the assistance provided, the non-parole period would have been six years rather than three.[38]

Alan Thomas did his time and, needless to say, did not return to the police force.

One of the people I interviewed for this book rang me late in 2013 after spotting Alan Thomas in a Western Sydney pub. Apparently he has not aged well.

•

In the face of all evidence to the contrary, Mark Lewis maintained the story that he had left Kerrie's Oasis before 6.30 p.m. on the night of the Gladesville murders and was therefore innocent. On 14 November 1999 – more than two years after his arrest – a jury found him guilty after a two-week trial. He was sentenced to life imprisonment for the murder of his de facto partner Kerrie Pang, the judge placing the crime in the worst category, finding that it was a contract killing planned by Lewis, who had delivered the victim to her death. The judge found Lewis had not intended the death of Ozonal but he received eighteen years for her death under the felony murder principle.[39]

The task force members had been certain Lewis was culpable, but far less certain that the prosecution would be successful – Rose had refused to give evidence. For Rod Baker, and the rest of the Yandee team, the conviction of Lewis was the sweetest victory of all. 'Mark Lewis is as calculated, as cold-blooded, as Lindsey, but more of a coward. Not willing to do it himself, but quite willing for someone else to do his dirty work,' Rod Baker said.[40]

Mark Lewis appealed his convictions and sentences. Unsuccessfully. At the time of writing he is living out his fading days in Lithgow prison.

•

Max O'Malley was never found. In 2010 the police reopened the investigation. Donna and her father had been close to Max from all those family get-togethers at the Boulevard Hotel and the Enfield RSL every Anzac Day, so the cold case investigator asked them into a police station to make a statement. The detective sergeant told them they were convinced that Lindsey had done away with Max and there were eleven other murders they were examining. After two hours of questioning, Donna left the police station confused and upset.

Donna gave me the detective sergeant's phone number but he stopped returning my calls shortly after and it seems he dropped the investigation.

But in 2014 two detectives from Burwood knocked on my door unannounced. They were compiling a brief for the coroner; there was to be an inquest into Max O'Malley's disappearance and I had been named. The coroner might wish to call me to give evidence, or subpoena my almost-complete manuscript, or both. The story I was writing had caught up with me.

I showed the two detectives through to my dining room. The detective sergeant was six foot two, wore a calf-length leather coat, had black slicked-back hair, a hawk nose and an American accent. The partner (detective senior constable) couldn't have been more of a contrast: five nine, grey suit, bulbous green eyes. After we'd sat down the detective sergeant explained the investigation they'd been conducting. They'd already been to see Lindsey and they'd saved me till last.

'You've obviously been conducting an investigation of your own,' he said. 'We'd like to ask you a few questions to see if you uncovered anything we missed.'

It took less than an hour to discover that I hadn't.

The detectives stayed in touch and there were a couple of follow-ups and they let me know when the hearing was scheduled. So, on 21 January 2015, I attended the hearing at the NSW Coroner's Court in Glebe for the Max O'Malley inquest. I hadn't been subpoenaed and I wasn't called to give evidence, though I was introduced to the court along with the only two other people in the gallery (Lindsey's Aunt Marjorie and a university student walk-in).

The presiding coroner found that Max O'Malley died in Sydney in October 1990 – the month he stopped filling his insulin prescription. The cause could not be established but was most likely to be suicide or natural causes through failure to take insulin. There was no evidence to suggest homicide and the detectives were complimented on the excellent quality of their investigation.

82

There can be no pat answer for how Lindsey Rose became a violent criminal, but I've read another book that provides a useful frame of reference: *The Creation of Dangerous Violent Criminals* by Lonnie Athens. Athens was described as a maverick criminologist because, rather than gathering and analysing reams of statistical data – the prevailing approach to criminology – he spent years conducting in-depth, standardised interviews with fifty violent criminals.[41]

Athens found that every one of those fifty brutal men had shared the same broad experiences, which he termed 'the process of violentisation'. All fifty experienced the same four phases: they were brutalised by violence; were taught to seek revenge for their traumatised selves; they carried out violent retribution; and they found acclaim or solace in those violent acts.

Not all violent criminals have a genetic disadvantage or a problematic upbringing and this is a great challenge of criminology – to tweak the data, improve the measurement of risk. Athens's theory puts all that to the side by asking the more modest question: what subset of experiences do violent criminals all have in common? It is helpful to know the answer – look after those who have been brutalised, for example, for they are the ones at risk of themselves becoming violent. 'Break the cycle' rings true.

I can identify the four stages of violentisation in the stories Lindsey has told me about his life. Brutalised by his upbringing, which exacerbated an inherited risk factor, and encouraged by the shadowy world to which he gravitated. It is a revelation, but also a kind of disappointment. When I began my research into his life and this dilemma – that I knew a man and didn't know him at all – I imagined that he was somehow a special case; that he was some form of unique outlier. But in everything I've read he fits this well-worn profile: the cold-blooded professional criminal, so detached as to be able to operate a 'normal' life in parallel.

I describe Athens's stages of violentisation to Lindsey. Do they sound familiar? His lips thin and he holds my gaze with his small eyes and the pale blue irises, painted on, depthless.

'Think about how monkeys behave,' he says. 'They first have a show of force: pump up their chests, wave their arms over their heads. Then they might pound the ground or thrash with a branch. Only if those measures fail do they resort to actual violence.

'Was I taught to be violent? Yeah, maybe I was. If I'd grown up being taught conciliation skills maybe I'd have used them instead.'

•

So people who commit criminal acts are people first: capable of charisma, loving relationships and friendships, intelligence and a strong work ethic. That they may acquire a mindset that internally justifies antisocial, even murderous, behaviour does not negate other facets of their humanity.

I posed a question earlier: is Lindsey Rose a good person who performed evil deeds or an evil person who also did good? Here's the answer: they are the same thing.

EPILOGUE

The procedure for making a phone call is painful and he only bothers once a year.

He has to give twenty-four hours' notice of his desire to make a call. He has to provide the phone number to be called and he will have only six minutes to speak. The call is monitored and will be immediately terminated if anything untoward is uttered. So he's taken from his cell in shackles with the mandatory three guards and is locked into the small cage with the phone. He checks to make sure he remembers the correct buttons to press to operate the phone and then he uses the little LCD window to check the balance in his phone account. But this is just the dry run; he hasn't dialled a number and he waves to the screws that he's finished and is led back to his cell.

The next day he tells the screws that he wants to book the call and so the day after that the whole process is repeated, but this time he punches in the number and it's a Saturday morning and she is home and expecting his call.

'Happy birthday, Donna.'

'Hi, Lindsey, how are you?' He can hear the emotion catch in her throat.

'Fine. How's your day going?'

'Oh, it's fine. I do worry about you in there.'

'Never mind about that. What are you up to for your birthday?'

'Oh, the kids brought me breakfast in bed and they were beaming. The bacon was *almost* cooked through and the toast was only a bit burnt. They worked so hard on it.'

He rumbled a gentle laugh. 'Enjoy them, Donna. They grow up fast and then they won't want to know you.'

'How is Penny?'

'Oh, she's okay. She went swanning around the world for a couple of years, working for this rich Italian. She sent me a postcard from Paris, the cheeky bugger. But I've got to give her credit: she came back, settled down and now she has a law degree.'

'Do you hear from her much?'

'We had a bit of a falling out – fair to say she isn't real happy about what I've done. She visited a couple more times after that – it's been a few years now. Enough about that. What are you doing for the rest of the day?'

'Paul's taking us to the club for lunch and tonight he's cooking a roast and some family are coming over.'

Then it was talk of the dinner plans and there'd be a glass or two of bubbles and the three kids are growing up fine, thanks. The second beep sounds in their ears – the six minutes are nearly up – and she says goodbye first and he says, 'Bye, Donna, take care,' and hangs up the phone.

ACKNOWLEDGEMENTS

I have privately thanked, of course, the many people who have helped with this endeavour. I publicly acknowledge the following people, some pseudonymously.

The people who aided my research or shared their stories with me: Denis, Donna, Dr Mitch Byrne (University of Wollongong), Damien, Eric, 'Lydia', Martha Jabour (HVSG), 'Oscar', 'Penny', Rod Baker, Stuart Littlemore QC and Lindsey. The people who helped bring this book to print: Benython Oldfield, Claire de Medici, Doug Wagner (The Editorial Department), Mary Cunnane, and the wonderful team at Hachette. Family and friends for forbearance and support.

1   Athens, Lonnie H., *The Creation of Dangerous Violent Criminals*. University of Illinois Press, 1992, p 6.

2   The HRMU has since become a separately managed facility rebadged as the High Risk Management Correctional Centre (HRMCC).

3   Doherty, Linda. 'High-security Prison to House the Very Worst', *Sydney Morning Herald*. 2 June 2001.

4   Mailer, Norman. *The Executioner's Song*. Vintage, 1994, p 296.

5   New South Wales. Parliament. Legislative Council. General Purpose Standing Committee No. 2. The management and operations of the Ambulance Service of NSW [report], October 2008. http://www.ambulance.nsw.gov.au/Media/docs/081020councilreport-83758ed3-d308-46ff-8a4d-0882822581fa-0.pdf. Accessed 6 December 2016.

6   Eagleton, Terry. *On Evil*. Yale University Press, 2010, p 117.

7   Transcript of evidence, NSW Crime Commission, 18 June 1997. Listed as Exhibit A in the sentencing brief from *R v Lindsey Robert Rose*, Supreme Court, Case No. 70094 (1997), henceforth *R v Rose* (1997).

8   Transcript of electronic recording of interview with suspected person (ERISP), 11 April 1997, Adelaide. Exhibit 5, *R v Rose* (1997).

9   Bottom, Bob. *Shadow of Shame*, Sun Books, 1988, pp 62–64.

10 Transcript excerpts in chapters 26 and 28 from ERISP, 11 April 1997.

11 Moir, Anne and David Jessel. *A Mind to Crime*. Michael Joseph Ltd, 1995.

12 Transcript of ERISP, 11 April 1997, Adelaide. Exhibit 5, *R v Rose* (1997).

13 Note that the 'International Statistical Classification of Diseases and Related Health Problems' (ICD) performs the same role as the DSM, but I have referenced the DSM as it appears to be more widely mentioned/recognised.

14 Perkins, Kevin. *Bristow: Last of the Hard Men*. Bonmoat, 2003, p 315.

15 Transcript excerpts in this chapter from ERISP, 13 August 1997, Sydney. Exhibit 4, *R v Rose* (1997).

16 Based on police files viewed by the author.

17 Hare, Robert D. *Without Conscience: The Disturbing World of the Psychopaths Among Us*. Guildford Press, 1993.

18 Based on police files viewed by the author.

19 Excerpts in chapters 48 and 50 showing Q numbers are from ERISP, 12 April 1997, Adelaide. Exhibit 2, *R v Rose* (1997).

20 NSW Institute of Forensic Medicine. *Medical report upon the examination of the dead body of Fatma Ozonal*. 28 March 1994. Exhibit 11, *R v Rose* (1997).

21 Hare, *Without Conscience*, 1993, p xi.

22 Hare, *Without Conscience*, 1993, p 24.

23 'The Valentine's Day Murders'. *Forensic Investigators*, Southern Star, Channel Seven, 9 August 2006.

24 Quoted in New South Wales, *Royal Commission into the New South Wales Police Service,* Final Report (1997), vol 1, p 2.

25 State Technical Investigation Branch.

26 The allegation of corrupt police dumping unregistered weapons in the Hawkesbury River is supported in Committee on the Office of the Ombudsman and the Police Integrity Commission, *Research Report on Trends in Police Corruption.* December 2002, p 60. www.parliament.nsw.gov.au/committees/DBAssets/InquiryReport/ReportAcrobat/5338/Research%20Report%20on%20Trends%20in%20Police%20Corruption.PDF. Accessed 6 October 2016.

27 *The Mask of Sanity* by Hervey Cleckley was originally published in 1941 (many editions followed).

28 Based on police files viewed by the author.

29 Based on police files viewed by the author.

30 In fact, Pang was aged 36 and Ozonal 25 at the time of their murders.

31 Transcript of ERISP, 11 April 1997, Adelaide. Exhibit 5, *R v Rose* (1997)

32 Transcript of ERISP, 12 April 1997, Adelaide. Exhibit 2, *R v Rose* (1997)

33 Based on police files viewed by the author.

34 Transcript of evidence, NSW Crime Commission, 18 June 1997. Exhibit A, *R v Rose* (1997).

35 Canaris, Christopher, Assessment of Lindsey Rose, letter dated 17 June 1998. Exhibit B, *R v Rose* (1997).

36 Levine, Justice J. Remarks on Sentence, *R v Rose* (1997).

37 Sully, Justice J et al, Judgment, *R v Rose* [1999] NSWCCA 327 (11 October 1999). www.austlii.edu.au/cgi-bin/sinodisp/au/cases/nsw/NSWCCA/1999/327.html. Accessed 6 October 2016.

38 *R v Thomas,* Judgment, NSWCCA 34, 60466/98 (11 March 1999).

39 *R v Lewis,* Judgment, NSWCCA 448, 60724/99 (9 November 2001).

40 Rod Baker quote from 'The Valentine's Day Murders'. *Forensic Investigators,* Southern Star, Channel Seven, 9 August 2006.

41 Athens, *The Creation of Dangerous Violent Criminals,* 1992.